Being Realistic Isn't Realistic

Collected essays on disability, identity, inclusion and innovation

Emma Van Der Klift
and
Norman Kunc

Tellwell Talent
www.tellwell.ca

ISBN
978-1-7737-0837-9 (Paperback)

TABLE OF CONTENTS

INTRODUCTION AND ACKNOWLEDGEMENTS..................ix

PART 1: IDENTITY

CHAPTER 1: THE RIGHT TO BE DISABLED.....................3

Norm's Story 3
Pacemaker...3
Physiotherapy 5
Fred 7
Relocating the Problem of Disability 9
Accommodations 10
Heavy Doors and the Blunder in the Biffy.............11
Rehabilitation 13
The Question of Cure 15
Pride 19
Silent Calm...19

CHAPTER 2: THE RIGHT TO BE DISABLED 21

Emma's Story 21
Passing in the Outsider Lane....................................23
Everything Worth Knowing about Advocacy I
    Learned from Belly Dancing 27
Finding My Place 29
Postscript..33

CHAPTER 3: NORMALCY/ABNORMALITY: THE
BIRTH OF A FALSE BINARY................................37

Norm 37
Norm and Emma..39
Normal as Ideal 39
Normal as the Majority 40

Normal as Functional Ability..41
Abnormality as a Measurable and Observable Difference...42
A Categorically Different "Kind" Of Person 43
Origins, Meaning, and History 44
Traits, Subjectivity, and a Few Examples.........................46
Social Constructionism (It's Not That Complicated...)......49
What's a Narrative, and Why Is Understanding the
    Way Narratives Operate Important? 50
Changing the Narrative 55

CHAPTER 4: LANGUAGE AND IDENTITY....................57

Emma...57
Five Problematic Descriptions 60
The Problem with all of these Labels 69
Language and Identity...71

CHAPTER 5: DO YOU KNOW WHERE OREGON IS? 76

Norm 76
Norm and Emma: Is it Just Ignorance? 79
Being Polite 81

CHAPTER 6: IN SPITE OF MY DISABILITY 86

Postscript..95

CHAPTER 7: WE DON'T KNOW WHAT WE'RE
HANDING YOU 96

Emma..97

PART 2: INCLUSION

CHAPTER 8: THE NEED TO BELONG:
REDISCOVERING MASLOW'S HIERARCHY
OF NEEDS..105

The Special Education Paradigm: Skills as
    Prerequisite to Inclusion...106
Anomalies in the Segregation Paradigm: Lack of
    Progress...107
Maslow's Hierarchy of Needs: A Paradigm for
    Motivating Learning 109
It isn't just the Disabled Kids: Inverting Maslow's
    Hierarchy: the problem with having to earn the
    right to belong 115
Casualties of the Inversion of Maslow's Hierarchy 116
The Problem with Gifted Programs 117
School Dropouts...118
Gangs 118
Perfectionism and Suicide..120
Segregation: forcing people to earn the right to belong....121
Belonging Without Valuing Diversity: The
    Inappropriate use of Maslow's Hierarchy to
    Support Inclusive Education and So-called
    Inclusive Community-based Programs 123
Inclusive Education: An Opportunity to Rediscover
    our right to Belong 124

CHAPTER 9: ABILITY & OPPORTUNITY IN THE
    REARVIEW MIRROR..129

Ability and Opportunity...130
Norm - When Ability is Seen to Precede Opportunity 131
Emma - Opportunity is Not Enough 133
Ability and Opportunity in the Rear-view Mirror...........135
Swimming Lessons...136
Conclusion...137

CHAPTER 10: SEGREGATION VERSUS
SOLIDARITY: RETHINKING THE UNCRITICAL
COMMITMENT TO INCLUSION 138

Segregation versus Solidarity..139
Enforced versus Voluntary...140

Imposed Agenda versus Common Purpose 140
Remediation versus Acceptance...................................... 141
Damaged Identities versus Positive Identities 142
Shame versus Pride 142
Low Expectations versus High Expectations.................. 143
Benevolence versus Respect 143
Non-Disabled Professionals versus Relatable Role
    Models.. 144
A Final Distinction: Social Justice 145
Find Relatable Role Models and Teach Disability
    History 146
Find Places for Students with Disabilities to Gather 147

CHAPTER 11: HELL-BENT ON HELPING:
Benevolence, Friendship, and the Politics of Help 149

Benevolence and the Politics of Help 151
Friendship and Help 153
What's Getting in the Way? 156
The Politics of Help... 158
Responses to Diversity: From Marginalization to
    Valuing 161
Tolerance and Benevolence 162
From Tolerance to Valuing... 165
Don't Make Friendship a Big Deal.................................. 165
Respect Personal Boundaries 166
Modelling Behaviour 169
Reciprocity and Contribution.. 174
Merging Respect and Help.. 179
Empathy and Social Justice... 183

PART 3: INTERSECTIONS, IDEAS,
AND INNOVATION

CHAPTER 12: CHESS, ARTIFICIAL
INTELLIGENCE, DISABILITY, AND INNOVATION...189

Norm: How Chess Got Me Included in a Regular School... 191

Norm: Life Hacks and Lessons Learned..........................194
Emma: Chess and Disability and Rehabilitation.............195
Extending the Chess Metaphor: Enter Alpha Zero..........200
What Do Disabled People and Alpha Zero Have In
    Common?..202

CHAPTER 13: MY YEAR WITH "FRANKENKNEE"
(AND WHY SIMULATION EXERCISES DON'T
WORK)...205

Emma..205

CHAPTER 14: COUNSELLING, SUPPORT
GROUPS, CHRONIC SORROW, AND THE
MYTH OF CATHARSIS...213

Chronic Sorrow..214
Counselling..215
Support Groups..216
A Brief History of Catharsis..218
Does Catharsis Deliver on its Promise?..............................219
Counselling and Self-Help in an Ableist and
    Individualistic Society..220
The Consequences of a Belief..222
Grieving the "Death" of the Perfect Child..........................223
What Can We Do Differently?...227
The Washington Father's Group...228
Parenting Autistic Children with Love and
    Acceptance (PACLA)..230
Respectfully Connected...230

CHAPTER 15: THE I AM AUTISM COMMERCIAL
AND THE COMPONENTS OF A GOOD MAGIC
TRICK...231

Misdirection; Expectation, Intention, Repetition,
    and Force..232
Misdirection..233

Expectation 233

Intention 234

Repetition..235

Force...237

Misdirection, Expectation, Intention, Repetition,
    Force… and Disability Fund-Raising........................238

A Horror-Able Commercial..239

I Am Autism...240

Fund-Raising, Misdirection, and the Consequences
    of Falling for the Trick 242

The Best Person to Decode a Magician's Trick is
    Another Magician 246

CHAPTER 16: BEING REALISTIC ISN'T REALISTIC...250

Norm 250

Herman Moll 252

Think Like Houdini 254

We Live in a Qwerty World...255

Autocorrect 256

Coffee and Kraft Dinner 257

Innovation Delivers What Rehabilitation Promises 259

Emma: The Problem with Innovation 259

Dangerous Assumptions 263

Evelyn Glennie 264

Danny Delcambre 264

Think Like Socrates 267

Two Dogs 269

A CREDO FOR SUPPORT 271

REFERENCES 275

INTRODUCTION AND ACKNOWLEDGEMENTS

Just a boy and a little girl, trying to change the world.

—John Lennon

This book is about synergy. It is, at its heart, a love story. While it is absolutely a love story between the two of us, Norm and Emma, it is also a love story that acknowledges the deep debt of gratitude—and the love—we have for those who have shaped our thoughts and pushed us to think harder than we ever thought we could. We stand, as is often said, on the shoulders of giants. These giants are not always the ones that are well known, and although we want to pay tribute to them too, many of the giants we are most indebted to are the quiet people who show us through the way they live their lives just what's important and why. These are the people who have often sustained us through their ethics, their humour and through story and insight (and sometimes a cup of coffee or tea or a glass of beer or wine).

Anything useful we have to offer in this book is only one small part of a much larger, deeper, and important conversation that includes so many people, both past and present.

Our aim in writing this book was to bring some of the ideas and what we've learned through Critical Disability Studies to a wider readership. Our joke is that we wanted to make disability studies accessible; to take what is often a highly academic (and as a result, somewhat jargonized and esoteric) field more available to those readers who don't (or can't) spend time in academia.

We worry that we may have forgotten important people who have contributed much to our thinking, and unintentionally overlooked them. Remember the lawsuit against George Harrison by the Chiffons in the 1970s? They claimed he'd morphed "He's so Fine" into "My Sweet Lord." It was later called "subconscious plagiarism." We hope we have not done this, but as has often been noted, we live in a "corridor of echoes," and those echoes reverberate through the essays that follow. We hope that what we've written will provide insights that might prove useful and that will do the original speakers, writers, and colleagues who so profoundly influenced our thinking proud.

Arthur Frank (2010) reminds us that

> as the gateway to Dante's inferno warns those who pass through it to abandon all hope, so the gateway to narrative analysis should caution scholars to abandon all pretense of saying anything original. That does not mean abandoning the hope of saying something useful and interesting that leads people to imagine different possibilities for how their lives are formed and informed – much as a story leads people to imagine different possible lives. (17–18)

Useful and interesting. This is what we hope we've accomplished, but you, the reader, will be the judge of that.

This is a book about chess, magic, belly dance, and other things that interest us. It is also a book about social justice, discrimination, and disability rights. These things may seem confusingly disparate, but we believe they are not. Life, as we all know, is full of moments and interactions that provide us with unexpected insights, connections, and learning. Both of us take particular delight in finding those connections and in seeing those patterns. Playful approaches to serious issues.

We began this project a long time ago. Both of us are writers, and although we were able to publish a number of chapters in other people's books over the years, the bulk of our writing remained firmly ensconced in our respective computers and in binders that took up a lot of office space. Although we often thought we should bring these writings together in book form, somehow we never got to it. It seemed a daunting task in the midst of trying to make a living and just living itself. It was our dear friend Catherine Frazee who was the impetus for dredging all of this up when she said, "Have you ever thought of putting a curator for your written work into your will?" We truly never had, but as sobering as that thought and the mortality issues it raised was, it made us think about all the half-written, the barely conceptualized, and even the finished pieces still lurking about in our apartment and in our computers.

When we finally decided to sit down and write this book, we were appalled to find that it was actually a more arduous task than we'd thought. It involved going through an awful lot of stuff! Some of it was useful, but much of it was more repetitive than we'd thought. Essentially, we had to write new stuff and get rid of old stuff. It was then that we realized that maybe, just maybe, it could be a little easier to accomplish our goal than we'd thought. Perhaps what we wanted was not so much a book that begins at the beginning and ends at the end but a series of essays. This was a revelation and a relief. Any of you who are writers will recognize that it's a lot easier to compile a bunch of essays than it is to make a book that flows from one chapter to the next and has to have a coherent trajectory.

What follows is a variation on what might facetiously be called a "greatest hits" collection. We've included some previously published pieces, but because several of them are more than a few years old, we've edited and even added to them. Hopefully this has made them more relevant. We've also added illustrative stories that we think make them more lively, readable, and relatable.

In addition, we've included unpublished pieces that reflect our current thinking (those are the ones about chess, magic, and belly dance, just so you know).

Our hope is that this collection will be of use to someone somewhere as they try to make sense of experiencing disability first hand or loving and supporting a disabled person.

It is impossible to include everyone we should thank here, but we'd like to try.

Catherine Frazee: it's like you're always on our shoulder (in a noncreepy way). We often ask ourselves, "What would Catherine say?" and we try to listen for your voice. Given the distance between us, luckily there is Skype and Zoom! Dave Hingsburger: when we despair over what's happening for disabled people, your unequivocal, practical, and powerful voice keeps us firmly rooted in pride and social justice. Samantha Connor, diva and unrelenting activist: you inspire (and you will understand the humour inherent in that word). Cal Montgomery: your questions, your searing critiques, your musing, and your straight-to-the-heart writing gives us something to live up to.

Thank you to Rich Villa and Jacque Thousand, long-time friends and colleagues. It was both of you who encouraged us to begin writing many years ago, and much of the earlier work we've republished here began life in your wonderful edited books. Over the years you have both challenged and supported us. In particular, we recall a moment driving home from a summer institute in Vermont where we expressed our concern about the issue of help and friendship and paternalism in schools, and you both said "Well, stop complaining and write about it. We'll publish it." That is the genesis of the chapter now revised and re-named "Hell-bent on Helping." (Much to our amusement, even though we wanted to, we couldn't give the original chapter that title due to the publisher's concern about the 'H' word. We also weren't allowed to use Canadian spelling back then. I guess we finally get to now).

Thank you also to Dick Sobsey and Kate Scorgie, who recently asked us to write chapters for Emerald publications that proved surprisingly challenging to conceptualize and write. We re-print them here with gratitude. If you hadn't asked, we'd likely have continued to muse about the ideas but never really brought them to fruition. In addition, we want to thank Dick Sobsey for his tireless and groundbreaking work on disability and abuse. Dick, your work has been a cornerstone of our understanding of disability as a social justice issue. Outrage has its uses, and you have helped us to understand that.

To all of those in narrative therapy and mediation communities we owe a huge debt of gratitude. You have changed our understanding of postmodernism by "putting Foucault on the ground" in practical ways that have not only challenged our views, but have offered a clear path forward. David Denborough, Cheryl White, David Epston, Stephen Madigan, John Winslade, Lorraine Hedtke and most of all, the late Michael White who we never had the privilege of meeting, but who's thinking and analysis has had enormous influence on both of us.

I (Emma) am incredibly grateful to my writing buddy, dear friend and co-conspirator Leah Kelley – I truly don't think this book and the other two underway would ever have been written without you. Almost every morning for more than a year we have synchronized our writing practice – sometimes in person for the odd writing retreat (which should really be renamed 'writing treat') but mostly online in timed pomodoro style. I can't tell you how much I appreciate your support and encouragement. Hopefully I've been able to reciprocate as you work to finish your dissertation. I think Norm is just as grateful, since the majority of the task of putting all of this to paper and editing our work has been mine while he has been busily working on video edits (and chess problems). He knows I might never have done this without you!

What I (Norm) want you to know, above all, is that this book has been a collaborative effort. I often get frustrated when the work that Emma and I do together gets attributed solely to me. This happens more often than you might expect, and when it happens, it reminds me of the story of Einstein's first wife Mileva Maric. Although Mileva did many of the calculations that proved the theory of relativity, and also co-wrote many of the articles that were attributed solely to Albert Einstein, she was never given credit for her ideas and work. I know I'm no Einstein, but at least I have never claimed to be the sole author of the work Emma and I have done together. So, as you read this book, know that as was said in the beginning, this is a book of love, synergy and collaboration. Neither one of us has any idea who originated the ideas presented here. In the final analysis, we don't think it matters.

Last but absolutely not least, we thank our families – staunch supporters and the inspiration for much of what we do.

* Note on the use of language. You may notice that throughout this book we use the words "disabled person" rather than "person with a disability." Some may think that that this is an oversight or a politically incorrect gaffe. It is not. We have intentionally chosen to use Identity First Language (IFL) rather than the more commonly accepted Person First Language (PFL). PFL is often seen as a statement that highlights the person above the disability. We respect and honour this use of language and its tradition, since we know that many individuals with intellectual disabilities and their families have fought hard against stigmatizing labels and therefore, prefer PFL.

Within the larger Disability Rights community, the Neurodiversity movement, the Deaf community and in Critical Disability Studies, IFL is preferred. We use identity language because we believe that our disabilities are not separate from us or something to be hidden or ashamed of. This represents a move away from the commonly held perception of disability as a negative attribute and towards the idea of disability as a something that can be openly acknowledged and claimed with pride.

You may also notice that we use capitals in some instances when we talk about Deaf or Autistic people. Deaf people who identify with Deaf culture and the Deaf community prefer the capital letter, as do Autistics who identify with the Autistic or the Neurodiversity Paradigm.

PART 1

IDENTITY

CHAPTER 1

THE RIGHT TO BE DISABLED

Norm's Story

I was seventeen years old when I discovered that I did not want to be cured of cerebral palsy. This bewildered me. For years I had dreamed of playing hockey, waterskiing, and playing the drums, but when the possibility of becoming nondisabled actually presented itself, to my utter astonishment I realized that I wanted to stay exactly as I was. This confusing insight turned out to be the first step in a long and fascinating journey that led me to explore concepts of disability and social bias, to question the notion of normalcy and professionalism, and ultimately to even rethink my presumptions about what it means to be fully human. What I learned along the way became the compass and map I have used to navigate life with a disability. What follows is a travelogue of that journey.

Pacemaker

The journey began the year I attended a conference sponsored by the Ontario Federation for Cerebral Palsy. I was seventeen years old when I saw a film showcasing experimental research on a device called a brain pacemaker. The pacemaker consisted of a receiver that was surgically implanted under the rib cage, connected to a wire running up to the cerebellum, and then to a transmitter worn over the chest. The receiver fired electrodes through the wire into the cerebellum. The researchers claimed that this device would dramatically reduce the spasticity caused by cerebral palsy.

The film was shown in a format much like a late-night diet infomercial, using typical before-and-after footage, and it featured a woman with cerebral palsy who was far more spastic than I was. The "before" shot showed her struggling, barely able to make herself understood. The "after" shot was a dramatic counterpoint. The same woman, postsurgery, was now able to pick up a glass with one hand and drink without drenching herself. I was ecstatic. If this device could help her to do this, then surely I'd be able to play hockey and play the drums—maybe even do a decent rendition of Gene Krupa's "Sing, Sing, Sing"!

I returned home and told my parents that I wanted to have wires implanted in my brain, and surprisingly, they agreed to look into it. We met with a local neurologist, who agreed to consult with the neurologist in New York doing the procedure. If I met the screening criteria, I would fly there for the operation.

I awoke one Saturday morning about two weeks after my meeting with the neurologist and, much to my amazement, realized that I didn't want to be cured of my cerebral palsy. *My* cerebral palsy. That was precisely it. If the operation was successful, I felt like I would lose an essential part of myself. It felt strangely analogous to contemplating a gender reassignment operation. In some respects I would still be the same person, but in others I would have to start over, reinventing myself. I realized I didn't want to do that.

There were people who were unconvinced by my explanation for refusing the operation. They felt sure that there were other, less apparent and probably dysfunctional reasons for my decision. Some claimed I was afraid of change; others said I was afraid of competing on an equal level. Some were sure I was romanticizing the disability. It always came down to me being either a coward or neurotic.

It wasn't until ten years later when I read Oliver Sacks's book *A Leg to Stand On* (1984) that I began to understand the intimate relationship between identity and body. I began to entertain the possibility that what I was feeling might actually be healthy. This new idea represented a radical departure from what I'd always assumed and the course that my life, up to then, had followed. Let me explain.

Physiotherapy

From kindergarten to grade seven I attended a segregated school for physically disabled children. In this school it seemed that rehabilitation was equally, if not more, important than education; students were always leaving class to go to therapy. In my case a typical week included approximately three hours of physiotherapy, two hours of occupational therapy, and two hours of speech therapy.

As a small child, I found the physiotherapy room a strange place. For example, amid the mirrors, balls, weights, bars, and beanbags, there was a particularly absurd piece of equipment: a four-step staircase with handrails on each side that went straight into the wall. The therapists would ask me to walk up the stairs. Puzzled by this odd request, I asked why and pointed out that the stairs didn't go anywhere.

Their response didn't actually answer my question. "Oh, don't be so silly. Just walk up the stairs."

Far from being silly, I thought my objection to their request was not only reasonable and logical but also had significant merit. Just the same, I succumbed to the white-coated representatives of authority, took a deep breath, focused on the top step, and forced my body to execute the perilous ascent. After a series of thoughtfully planted steps, a few panic-stricken grabs at handrails, and a huge amount of concentration focused primarily on my ever-elusive centre of balance, I victoriously reached my goal.

"OK," I said, "now what?"

"Walk back down the stairs."

"Wait a minute!" I said, incredulous. "If you didn't want me up here in the first place, why did you ask me to walk up here?"

"Because you want to walk better, don't you?"

I didn't know any better, so I said, "Yeah," and in that moment I learned something. I learned that it was not a good thing to be disabled. The implication was that the more I minimized my disability and worked hard to eliminate it, the better my life would be and the more people would like me. Apparently acceptance, belonging, and self-worth could all be mine if I could just accomplish this one important task: to overcome my disability.

With this new understanding and this end in mind, I declared outright war on my body. It seemed clear that if I wanted a full and enjoyable life; if I wanted to become a valued and respected member of society, get a good education, find a relationship, and perhaps even have children, the only thing standing in my way was my disability. Therefore, it obviously had to be conquered.

From that time forward I focused every part of my waking life on attaining this goal. In the therapy room, I turned into the kid physiotherapists see only in their dreams. If they wanted ten repetitions of a certain exercise, I did fifteen. If I was required to hold a precarious balancing position for thirty seconds, I held it for a minute. War had been declared. Cerebral palsy was my enemy, and I was determined to defeat it.

By grade seven, I saw that the next logical step in the process of conquering my disability was to leave the segregated school. If being disabled was a bad thing, I reasoned, it was clear that the more distance I could put between myself and those other devalued students, the more valued I would become. With this goal in mind, I managed to argue my way into a regular neighbourhood school. However, I soon discovered that far from winning the war against my disability, I had merely changed battlefields. The struggle in the physiotherapy room was now replaced by other challenges.

In the regular school, I faced a host of physical and attitudinal barriers on a daily basis. My daily challenges included making myself understood, navigating social situations with the other students, finding adaptations that allowed me to take notes and do math in the absence of fine motor control, and make still more improvised modifications so I could take part in physical education and industrial arts classes.

Yet despite my determination to fully participate in school and other aspects of community life, I continued to view my disability as something I needed to hide or minimize as much as possible. Although I knew I didn't want to be cured of cerebral palsy, paradoxically I still saw it as a negative attribute that detracted from who I really was as a person.

I carried this view of my disability with me into my first three years of university. And then everything changed abruptly.

Fred

The war against my disability came to an immediate and enduring halt one night in a university pub. I was sitting with a group of students when a friend began telling a story that involved me. When he came to my part of the story, he imitated my voice. Later that night I called him on it.

"Fred, why did you imitate my voice?" I asked.

He shrugged. "Because you talk like that."

"Yeah, I know, Fred, but look, I'm picking up a glass with one hand, I'm articulating my words clearly, and I'm not drooling. I've got an Academy Award performance going on. You imitate my voice, and my whole show goes out the window!"

Honestly perplexed, Fred looked at me and asked, "Norman, why are you trying to be nondisabled?"

No one had ever asked me that question before. I sat open-mouthed and speechless for a few moments, struggling to understand the implications of his question.

Fred and I drank a lot of beer that night. Somewhere in between the second and third jugs of draft, I remember saying that I had "the right to be disabled." I heard myself speak those words as if someone else had said them. I sat back, stunned. For the first time in my life, I questioned my own commitment to becoming as nondisabled as possible. Until that night I had divided the human population into two groups: normal and abnormal. Most people, I thought, didn't have disabilities, so they were the normal ones. By default, that meant that people like me – disabled people - were abnormal. Although from early childhood on I had aspired to be as normal and nondisabled as possible, and worked hard at it, I had slowly become resigned to the idea that I would probably live out my life as an abnormal person.

That night, for the first time, it occurred to me that *it was normal to have a disability.* Before, I had always seen my disability as a deficit located in my body. It was as if I had been viewing disability through a microscope that focused exclusively on my physical condition. Suddenly, with this newfound revelation, it was as if I'd turned the microscope's coarse adjustment dial and widened my view. I now saw something that should have been obvious, namely that there were millions of other disabled people currently living in the world, and there always had been. I began to consider disability in the context of history. I realized that my personal experience was simply a part of a larger epic history of the lived lives of disabled people throughout time and in various societies. It was a significant moment. I realized I wasn't alone and that I had, and always have had, a "people."

Recognizing the prevalence of disability throughout the world and in human history fundamentally changed how I viewed myself. I no longer saw myself as an aberration of what a person should be. Instead, I saw myself as being part of the inherent diversity of human beings.

It is fascinating how a simple insight can be life-changing. Like tipping the first of a series of dominoes, the recognition that I had the right to be disabled triggered more and more insights. Even though I had attended public middle school and high school and was now in my third year of university, I had never really felt like I fully belonged. Instead, I often felt like a foreigner who had infiltrated the nondisabled world. Suddenly, for the first time, I felt a sense of membership in society, and I actually started to develop a sense of pride about being disabled. This made a difference in pretty well every aspect of my life. For example, when I went on dates, rather than attempting to demonstrate my attractiveness by minimizing my disability as I had done in the past, I now expected the other person to accept my disability. This was radically different from merely hoping they would recognize "the wonderful person behind the disability." If a woman seemed uncomfortable, I figured she was the one who needed therapy, not me.

Relocating the Problem of Disability

One of our colleagues and friends is John McKnight, a professor emeritus and community organizer from Chicago who worked alongside African Americans to get the auto industry integrated during the civil rights movement during the 1950s and 1960s. John once said,

> Revolutions begin when people who are defined as problems achieve the power to redefine the problem. A critical point in the development of the civil rights struggle was the black movement's capacity to declare the central issue the "white problem." A people declared deficient and in need unshackled their labels and attempted to lock them on their oppressors. (McKnight, 1995, p.16)

This quote perfectly encapsulates the shift I'd begun to make. Rather than seeing the "problem of disability" as located within me, I began to understand that the real problem was a deficiency within society. This crucial shift in thinking not only changed how I perceived my disability but also the meaning I ascribed to the accommodations

I needed and the rehabilitation I experienced. Let's look at these separately.

Accommodations

To illustrate this shift in my understanding of accommodations, consider the following. There is a pervasive assumption in our society that disabled people shouldn't be disabled. No one ever says it out loud, but the reasoning goes that people are *supposed* to be normal, and a disability is an aberration of what should have been. In my case most people believe that an accident at birth resulted in me being different from the way I was meant to be. These people may be fully supportive of disability rights and inclusive education and in favour of ramps and other adaptations, but this does not necessarily alter the deeper presumption that disabled people shouldn't be disabled.

Adhering to the seemingly common-sense presumption that people should not be disabled may seem benign, but I would argue that it is not. Locating the "problem" of disability within the person and not within the society in which the disabled person lives has serious ramifications that may not immediately be apparent. For example, in a society that does not view disability as a normal variation of the human condition, accommodations like ramps, accessible parking spaces and washrooms, elevators, screen-readers, and TTY telephones are seen as favours granted by nondisabled people to accommodate those of us who have mobility or other impairments. When adaptations are seen as "gifts" and not as rights, a subtle (and sometimes not so subtle) power imbalance is maintained.

But what happens if we begin with the presumption that disability is an inherent part of human life? After all, bodies break down. Accidents happen. The idea that we should be non-disabled and be fully functional from birth to death is ludicrous. Beginning with this premise radically changes the location of the problem from something inside the disabled person to something within society itself. It also fundamentally changes our view of accommodations. Almost immediately, it becomes apparent that a building without a ramp was designed upon a false presumption: that no one should be disabled. In this context, adding a ramp to a building is not a benevolent gesture done to assist disabled people, but rather is the correction of an architectural error, ensuring that all citizens will now have access to the entire community. Once we recognize that ramps and other accommodations are not favours, but are architectural corrections, we begin to shift the problem of disability from being a deficiency in a person to a deficiency in society.

Heavy Doors and the Blunder in the Biffy

Susan Wendell, a disabled woman who is a scholar in disability and women's studies, described her slow realization of the same issue using the example of a heavy door. In her book *The Rejected Body* (1996), Wendell writes:

> The cultural habit of regarding the condition of the person, not the built environment or the social organization of activities, as the source of the problem, runs deep. For example, it took me several years of struggling with the heavy door to my building, sometimes having to wait until someone stronger came along, to realize that the door was an accessibility problem, not only for me, but for others as well…poor architectural planning creates physical obstacles for people who use wheelchairs, but also for people who can walk but cannot walk far or cannot climb stairs, for people who cannot open doors, and for people who can do all of these things but only at the cost of pain or an expenditure of energy they can ill afford. Some of the same architectural flaws cause problems for pregnant women, parents with strollers, and young children. This is no coincidence. Much architecture has been planned with a young adult, non-disabled male paradigm of humanity in mind (p. 46).

When I read Wendell's words, I was reminded of an incident that took place at my family's cottage. When I was about five, my parents purchased a piece of property in Muskoka, a summer vacation area in Ontario. Over a series of consecutive weekends, my father, brother, and several of my uncles travelled to the property to clear the trees and build the basic structure of a modest yet comfortable cottage. In many ways it was similar to an Amish barn-raising, except that in this instance, the consumption of beer was an integral part of the building process.

One uncle who was, shall we say, somewhat less than a skilled carpenter was given the task of building an outhouse. When it came to deciding the height of the toilet seat, he instinctively put it at what he thought was a comfortable height. However, somehow he'd managed to forget that he was six feet four inches tall. This oversight remained unnoticed since my father, brother, and uncles were all over six feet as well. The "blunder in the biffy," as we came to call it, became immediately apparent when my mother, sister, and aunts arrived a few weekends later. Anyone under five ten found it completely impossible to ascend the outhouse seat. My father had to build a step in order to make it accessible for everyone. Although this story quickly became part of our cottage mythology, endlessly told and retold at summer gatherings, it also became a powerful story that helped me clarify the issue of accessibility. Let me explain.

In the mid '80s, national and municipal legislation began to require public agencies and large corporations to make their facilities accessible to people who use wheelchairs. Despite the howls of undue hardship that echoed through government offices and corporate boardrooms, eventually curbcuts, ramps, accessible washrooms, parking spaces, and elevators started to become the expected community standard. Though I appreciated the changes, my habitual sense of being an outsider made me feel like I should be grateful and that these institutions and corporations had done disabled people a considerable favour in making these alterations. It was the memory of our outhouse that changed my perspective. In building the step, my father hadn't been magnanimous; he had simply corrected an architectural mistake. If my mother, sister, and aunts had thanked him for the step, he would likely have been confused. It was obvious to everyone that the problem was not that people were too short but that the seat was too high.

As obvious as this example may be, in our society we don't typically consider accommodations like ramps and automatic doors to be architectural corrections. Instead, they are often still seen as benevolent or grudging gestures for the sole benefit of disabled people. As mentioned above, this view exposes a widespread and unexamined belief that people should not be disabled; that all people can and should walk, talk, move, and think like the majority group. And lurking beneath this idea is an even deeper and disturbing presumption: that disabled people are not an equal or important part of society. We are seen as a different and sometimes inconvenient group of people who just happen to be uncomfortably coexisting with a nondisabled society. This causes disabled people to often feel like perpetual and unexpected guests who are tolerated but not valued. It became clear to me that the problem of accessibility goes far beyond the problem of missing supports for disabled people; it is about the status we have been afforded in society. Stating that we have the right to be disabled is a direct challenge to the idea that we are somehow second-class citizens. In short, understanding that disability is an inherent part of the human condition fundamentally changes the meaning we attribute to accommodations. Suddenly, my inability to get up stairs isn't seen a result of a mobility impairment in me; it's a shortcoming in the attitudes and practices of a society that has not questioned its view of disability. However, the idea that we have an equal right to access and are under no obligation to minimize our disabilities is not always well received by non-disabled people.

Rehabilitation

For years I had presumed that the goals of physiotherapy, occupational therapy, and speech therapy were beyond reproach. I believed that all these therapists were simply helping me move closer to becoming what I was capable of becoming. But I now began to see rehabilitation differently; in the context of a society that views disability as an aberration. I began to wonder if, beneath the stated commitment to help me improve, was the unstated goal of making me more normal, more acceptable, and more akin to what others thought I should be. I also wondered if, in becoming so focused on appearing as nondisabled as possible, I had been indirectly condoning the devaluation and prejudice against me and other disabled people. Were my actions somehow similar to the skin bleaching that some people of colour have done to appear more white?

Sometimes when I give presentations on these ideas and their implications, people raise objections. They say that I am encouraging disabled people to abdicate responsibility for improving their physical condition. The unspoken insinuation seems to be that claiming the right to be disabled is simply a sophisticated justification for laziness.

When I first heard this objection, I was both taken aback and puzzled. I was taken aback because, as my friends and family will attest, laziness is not one of my faults. In fact, I probably err on the other side of the spectrum: the realm of relentless productivity. And in this I am no exception. There are countless disabled people like me who hold down full-time jobs, pay taxes, and are fully contributing members of their communities. Presuming that a person becomes irresponsible when they say they have the right to be disabled is not only completely unwarranted, it also misses the point.

The point I want to make is that asserting my right to be disabled is a declaration of identity and as such is in no way related to personal responsibility or motivation. In other words who you *are* and what you *do* are not necessarily the same thing. By conflating identity with activity, objectors imply that I and other disabled people are simply trying to avoid our obligations—and primarily the obligation to improve ourselves. This plays out in a variety of ways. For example, if a disabled person is capable of walking but chooses to use a wheelchair, this is often seen as laziness. "Use it or lose it," we're told. It is disturbing and telling to see just how angry people can get when they become aware that someone using a mobility device can actually stand or even walk without it.

A recent example was covertly taped on someone's cell phone and then posted on social media. It showed a woman standing up out of her wheelchair to reach an item on a high store shelf. Accusations that she was "faking it" and "using her disability" prompted an outpouring of vitriol in the comments section of the post. Disabled people protested that not all wheelchair users use them all the time, but that didn't seem to make a difference. Clearly many people believed that a person who could walk but chose to use a wheelchair was nothing more than a fraudulent malingerer.

As someone who has always struggled with walking and began using a wheelchair only in my forties, I feel some resentment when I see examples like this. The amount of torque and the relentless exertion of energy that walking put on my body, not to mention the falls and chronic back problems that resulted, are largely absent now. Rather than an admission of defeat, failure, and laziness, it has been a huge relief to use a wheelchair. And it remains true that I can still stand and transfer relatively independently.

The expectation that disabled people should walk as much as possible exposes a double standard in our society around the issue of physical improvement. If a non-disabled person chooses not to jog, work out, or do other activities to improve their physical condition, they are generally not seen as lazy or irresponsible. Improving physical ability is usually seen as a choice, not an obligation. I say *usually* because this is changing even for non-disabled people as many workplaces have begun to demand that employees take part in mandatory wellness and gym programs. I wonder if this will result in non-disabled people gaining a better understanding of the scrutiny and expectation placed on disabled people. However, when I or others assert that we have the right to be disabled and possibly do not want to rehabilitate ourselves, we are seen as abdicating responsibility. Why is maximizing physical ability a *choice* for non-disabled people but an *obligation* for disabled people? Why isn't the decision not to walk given the same legitimacy as the decision not to jog or go to the gym?

The Question of Cure

Although I didn't immediately understand why, already at the age of seventeen I knew I did not want to be cured of cerebral palsy. As mentioned, my concerns about rehabilitation are often received with skepticism and concern. The claim that I do not want to be cured of cerebral palsy often generates a similar kind of controversy. Because it is difficult to argue with a personal assertion, some people agree that although this may possibly be true for me, it wouldn't likely be applicable for people with more severe disabilities. They point out (as if I didn't know) that I am fairly independent. I can talk, type, take care of daily activities, and even drive a car. Cerebral palsy imposes relatively few limitations on my life. They argue that it seems presumptuous of me to speak for people with far more severe disabilities.

To be honest, when I began giving presentations on this topic, I was apprehensive when people with more severe disabilities than mine were in the audience. As I talked about not wanting to be cured, I worried that they were thinking, "Nice problem to have!" However, over the years, many severely disabled people have approached me after such a presentation and said that they too would refuse a cure.

This said, I'm pretty sure that my school friends who had life-threatening illnesses like muscular dystrophy or cystic fibrosis would have welcomed a cure. And some of my Autistic friends who have epilepsy, acute anxiety, IBS or other co-occurring issues have told me they'd also appreciate a cure for these things. (However, it is important to note that most of them are adamant that this does not mean they'd want a cure for autism). So, although it would indeed be presumptuous to assume that all disabled people want to stay disabled, it would be equally presumptuous to assume that all disabled people want to be cured. Think about it this way: the idea that all disabled people want to be cured could in some ways be seen as a variation on the Freudian concept of "penis envy." In the early twentieth century, Freudian analysts believed that all women secretly wanted to be men. Today, most women are derisive when they hear this and heartily reject the idea. As surprising as it may sound to non-disabled people, many disabled people feel the same way and do not aspire to being nondisabled. For many of us, disability is an integral part of identity.

The importance of seeing disability as an inseparable dimension of a person's life was emphasized by Arthur Frank (1995, 2013), a professor of medical sociology who personally dealt with the life-threatening conditions of a heart attack and prostate cancer. Writing from both academic perspective and personal experience, Frank pointed out that the medical profession often mistakes *illness* for *disease* and that there is an important distinction between the two. Using cancer as an example, he maintained that cancer isn't a separate, distinct disease that somehow resides in the person's body. It is an illness that pervades and changes every aspect of the person's life. It is myopic and insensitive, he argued, to reduce and thereby overlook the life-changing implications of an illness and view it as a physical condition that must simply be diagnosed, treated, and overcome.

In the same way, a disability cannot be seen as a separate, distinct "thing" that a person has. I do not have cerebral palsy in the same way that I have a computer or a sailboat. Cerebral palsy has significantly shaped, if not defined, my life. In some ways, it's more accurate to say *I am cerebral palsy* rather than *I have cerebral palsy*. This is why I find it inconceivable to think of myself without my disability. It is like trying to imagine who you might be if you were not yourself.

The presumption that a cure would always be preferred likely arises out of the idea that a disability affects only a person's body. While disability does indeed affect bodies and brains, this is not all it affects. Having a disability influences perception, perspective, and, indeed, life itself in profound ways. Disability can be challenging but can also yield unexpected and important insights. Let me offer a few examples.

At twenty-four, Arnold Bessier had graduated from medical school and was a nationally ranked tennis player. Overnight, a bout of spinal meningitis left him permanently paralyzed and dependent on a ventilator to breathe. In his book *Flying Without Wings* (1988), Bessier recounts how not being able to move taught him how to be still.

> One evening, lying there alone, feeling particularly hopeless and bored, I looked down the corridor wishing for, perhaps expecting, someone or something. But I saw only the darkened hallway with a few doors opening onto it. There was no activity, and there were no people to be seen. My despair mounted, and I felt as though I could no longer stand

it. Then, slowly, I began to look at the corridor differently, and I began to see variations, shades of` gray and darkness, shadows and light. The doorways opening onto the corridor formed subtle geometric patterns according to the different ways the doors were ajar. I began to look carefully and wonder at this scene that only a few moments before had depressed me so. It now seemed startlingly beautiful. My perception had shifted, my eyes miraculously refreshed. This experience was full and whole. I looked down the hallway for a very long time. I think that at last I probably fell asleep, but I am not sure.

I do not know how that perception arrived, or why it left, but from then on I understood that what I sought was possible. My task now was to discover how to change from the one state to the other.

I had to look for that magic element. I knew now that it did not reveal itself in the hands of the clock, but its secret was somewhere between the ticks of the clock. It is a place far more immediate than the past, and far more certain than the future (pp. 7–8).

Later in the book, Bessier says that if he was asked if he would like to return to being able-bodied, his first question would be: "What would I have to give up?"

Let me emphasize that this is not to say that being disabled is a blissful state of heightened awareness and ever-deepening enlightenment. There is frustration, there is envy, there is exhaustion, and, often, there is pain. My contentment at having cerebral palsy vanishes, and jealousy takes over when I watch a skilled drummer infuse energy into a drum solo. I've also thrown the odd tool across the room when my hands refuse to carry out some fine motor task.

It is likely true that if I had been non-disabled, my life would have been less frustrating and maybe even more fun. But almost certainly it would have been less fascinating. However, speculating on what my nondisabled life would've been like is fruitless, and judgments about whether I should want to be cured or not are equally pointless. With Bessier, I believe that the far more interesting question is: "If I were to suddenly become nondisabled, what would be gained, and what would be lost?"

Pride

Some people find the notion of disability pride a strange idea. However, that is exactly where my journey has ended. Finding a people and coming to not only accept but also celebrate my disability has fundamentally changed the way I live. It has changed how I see myself and how I choose to use my energy, and perhaps most importantly, it has given me a unique perspective and vantage point from which to view the world and provide a counterpoint that I hope is of help to others. Pride doesn't deny disability. In fact, it's just the opposite. Pride acknowledges and embraces disability as an attribute rather than a deficiency. It simultaneously recognizes a new and valued perception of disability and rejects society's views.

With luck, families of disabled children will be exposed early to this alternate and empowering view. Hopefully they learn that devaluation is not inherent but rather is socially constructed, and that it can be questioned and challenged. Understanding this creates the opportunity to differentiate their perceptions and values about disability from the prevailing perceptions and values of an ableist society and participate in the creation of a new social order. Just as many African Americans discovered black pride, and others have discovered LGBTQ+ pride and Aboriginal pride, so too, do many disabled individuals and families discover disability pride. In my life this has made all the difference.

Silent Calm

When I realized that I had the right to be disabled, it was as if my body and I shook hands, and for the first time in my life, I felt a silent calm descend upon me. I now saw my body as an ally, not a foe. I recognized that over the years, and through all of the therapy, my body was doing everything within its power to accomplish what I and others were demanding of it. Seeing my body as an ally gave me a new sense of empathy, and I actually apologized not only for what I'd put it through but also my lack of appreciation for all its efforts. I began to applaud the part of me that had fought against the cure and rejected the pacemaker. Never again would I wage war against my disability. Never again would I apologize for my diversity.

I began to appreciate the innate wisdom of that seventeen-year-old boy who refused the cure. Somehow, somewhere deep inside, I'd known that cerebral palsy did not make me abnormal. The way I walked, talked, and moved was simply a personal difference, an attribute or trait like hair colour, height, or weight. I had an inherent right to be exactly as I was and I was not obligated to play down or reduce my differences. Cerebral palsy, I knew, was an integral part of me, something that helped define me, not something to be hidden or eradicated. The profound existential calm resulting from this realization has remained with me ever since.

Until that night in the bar, I had blithely accepted the assumption that disabled people needed to adapt to society. For the first time, I was asking why society had not adapted to me.

CHAPTER 2

THE RIGHT TO BE DISABLED

Emma's Story

I'd been working in the field of community living supporting people with intellectual disabilities and their families for almost fifteen years before I heard the phrase "the right to be disabled." It was 1990, and the venue where I first heard it was a staff training event jointly sponsored by the organization I worked for and the local school district. The presenter was Norman Kunc, a disabled activist, speaker, and writer from Toronto. I remember being riveted by the ideas…and the speaker. Norm and I have now been married for almost three decades. Some people hear an interesting message and take it away with them. I went one better; I took the message *and* the speaker away with me!

Norm and I like to joke that we did not fall in love in the conventional way. We describe it as falling "in recognition," and that recognition was immediate. However, it took me an additional twenty plus years before I understood much about what that actually meant and why that's the way we'd always described our meeting. I know now that it had a lot to do with "the right to be disabled" but at the time I had no idea that this phrase had anything to do with me.

I was excited about the ideas like the ones you've just read in Norm's story above. I saw important implications for the work I was doing and for the people I was doing the work with. At that time, in both schools and human service organizations, we were working from the premise that the less disabled a person appeared, the more they would be valued. Norm's bold assertion that people had the right to be disabled and should be under no obligation to minimize or hide their disabilities caused me to question and rethink much of what we'd been doing and why we'd been doing it.

These days, the idea that people should be "normalized" has fallen out of favour. Sometimes people in schools and human services get offended when we suggest that their goals are still to make people look, behave, and function more normally. They protest this claim as hyperbolic and overstated. And it is true that few people talk about "making people more normal" anymore because it isn't seen as politically correct; instead, we usually frame it as "helping people be the best they can be." However, despite this more palatable spin, many of the practices—therapies, resource rooms, work preparation, and life skills programs—continue to work from a premise that some form of remediation and rehabilitation remain a prerequisite for full school and community involvement (see more about this in Chapter 8).

As I thought further about Norm's assertion that people have the right to be disabled, I began to make even more connections. Remediation, I realized, isn't just reserved for disabled people. Everyone gets to experience its tyranny at one time or another. Take for example the diet and self-help industries with their brutal message that no one is ever good enough and that everyone is obligated to take part in some vast project of self-improvement. We've probably all felt the sting of implied inadequacy at one time or another. It's not that there's anything wrong with engaging in some self-improvement. A healthy diet, some exercise, and perhaps some improved communication skills are probably beneficial to most of us. However, in our society it seems that self-improvement often becomes a harmful obsession based on almost unachievable and artificial standards rather than a rational decision based on health, happiness, and better relationships. As Norm mentioned, asserting that we have the right to be exactly as we are doesn't mean we never do anything, just that we take some time to think about *why* we're doing whatever it is.

When I heard Norm defiantly assert that people had the right to be disabled and should live their lives unapologetically, it had a huge impact on my thinking. However, in order to unpack how this idea influenced me and the extent of that impact, I need to provide a little background context and tell you a few stories about me.

Passing in the Outsider Lane

My family will tell you that I was an activist almost before I stopped using diapers. I'm pretty sure my first words were something along the lines of "That's not fair." My nickname growing up—and I hated it for reasons I'm sure you can appreciate—was "the crusader." As a young teenager, I protested Vietnam, Amchitka, and nuclear weapons. I marched in marches and rallied in rallies. I boycotted certain foods and eschewed goods made in sweat shops, supported immigrant rights and championed women's issues. Although my family was unfailingly supportive, patient, and affectionate, and often agreed with my causes, they were also often overwhelmed by my single-tracked intensity. *Obsessive* was the other word applied to me from the beginning.

At the ripe old age of nineteen, I got a job working in a group home with ten people who had intellectual disabilities. I promptly added disability rights to my collection of causes. For the next decade or so, I continued to work in what is now known as the community living movement and continued my advocacy efforts with all the passion I could muster. We closed institutions, built group homes (and then closed them in favour of more individualized living situations). We helped people find jobs and worked hard to support self-determination. Advocacy for other people was my life; it was how I defined myself and where I got a sense of self-worth, and I didn't question any of it.

When I met Norm, my life abruptly changed. A couple of months after we got married, he convinced me to quit my day job, which had by that time evolved from forty hours a week of direct support into more than sixty hours of labour relations, and to work with him as a trainer, speaker, and consultant. Overnight, my high-pressure, frenetically paced life downshifted abruptly. Suddenly there weren't any more middle-of-the-night phone calls or brush fires to extinguish. It wasn't that I wasn't busy, since we had a hectic schedule of speaking dates, flights, and hotels, but the work I'd taken on had a different pace, and it didn't come home with me at night. Most people would have been pleased by a change like this, but I felt weirdly set adrift.

In the silence that followed, I began to take stock of my life. The spaces I'd filled with frenetic activity were eerily empty, and for the first time in years I had time to really think. For much of my adult life, I'd been engaged in an exhausting practice of pretending to be much more competent than I sometimes felt. I'd pushed away some of the problematic memories of my school, adolescence, and early adulthood, and worked very hard to conceal and mitigate the multitude of sensory issues I struggled with in the hopes that nobody would notice.

I'd always been aware that I was different, but I didn't know why. From a very early age I knew that I didn't respond emotionally, cognitively, or even physically to things in the same way as others seemed to do. I didn't always get the jokes, and my literal-mindedness and social awkwardness often resulted in unexpected humiliation. (We don't need to talk about the time I thought a jackalope was a real thing, or how it took my girlfriends to tell me when some guy was handing me a line).

In the quiet spaces of my new life, I was confronted with a Pandora's box of memories. School was the place where I first recognized the significance of my differences. At home I'd been indulged in my many passions, and my unusual habits mostly went unremarked. However, at school it quickly became apparent that I just didn't fit. I was the kid who stared out the window for hours and mostly avoided contact with the other kids. I found it difficult to complete tasks, and my homework was never done. While I liked English and art and drama well enough, and I liked some parts of history, I was completely unable to grasp math. It wasn't until recently that I heard the word *dyscalculia* used to describe a learning disability in math I have had a lifelong and intimate relationship with.

PE was particularly tough. I recently found an article called "PE Doesn't Stand for Physical Education, It Stands for Public Embarrassment" (Casey & Goodyear, 2014). I didn't even need to read the article; the title was enough to make me laugh out loud in recognition (something I can do now but couldn't then). I was ridiculed by both teachers and my fellow students in PE for my very obvious spatial issues. I have trouble locating myself in space, conceptualizing things in three dimensions, and following physical directions. Left and right confusion or a poor sense of direction doesn't even begin to describe it. I literally have to decode a new movement backward before I can put it together again and try it out. Even then, I have to repeat that process over and over because I'll probably forget how to do it between one session and the next. My success rates in the physical world are notoriously spotty. I've often joked that I am regularly ambushed and assaulted by inanimate objects and am often decorated with inexplicable bruises.

I have a visceral memory of running up to the vaulting horse in ninth grade PE and abruptly stopping in front of it like a horse refusing to jump a fence. I had absolutely no idea what my body was supposed to do. I was (and still am) totally unable to grasp the rules of any team sport, and this was a problem since soccer and softball were both a big deal in my schools. As a result I spent a lot of time randomly running after the other kids without any idea what I was supposed to do or hiding in left field desperately hoping that the ball would stay as far away from me as possible. I was often in the wrong place at the wrong time and regularly got hurt as a result.

To make matters worse, I was socially awkward. My stilted use of language was inspired by books. I spent months after reading English novels and watching English movies imitating what I thought was a Cockney accent and using those accents and turns of phrase and scripted movie lines in random social settings. Like school. Or in front of my parents' friends. This definitely marked me as odd. My tendency to use big words earned me a lot of teasing and a persistent label: "the walking dictionary." In my quest to figure out what was expected of me, I'd fixate on certain people with laserlike intensity, trying to work out how they managed to navigate the world so effortlessly. Then I'd obsessively copy them. In one particularly cringe-worthy case, I even tried to *be* the girl I'd fixated on, writing her name in my exercise books and onto my rulers. Suffice it to say this didn't go unnoticed. Lucky for me the girl in question was quite gracious about it, but lots of the other kids were not.

While my teachers (and others) were sure I was smart, they had no idea how to help. Instead, because I was obviously hyperlexic (I could read in two languages by about the age of three, and when I got to school I could both read and write far above grade level), the problems they saw were viewed as something I did on purpose. I was lazy. Noncompliant. Obsessive. I talked too much or not enough. They said I wasn't trying. How could they know that I didn't have any idea where to start or even what trying was? If the work didn't engage me, I was literally unable to do it. Even today, Norm jokes that I am the proverbial light switch—either on or off, with no in between.

I internalized these descriptions of myself, promptly incorporated them into my self-image, and then resolutely set out to make sure no one else would find out about them. As I grew up, I shifted into an exhausting adult enterprise best described as "passing."

Through two failed marriages and an aborted college degree, I continued to posit deficiency squarely within myself and work hard to make sure no one knew exactly how deficient I was. I carefully avoided the things I wasn't good at and emphasized those I could do well. But all the time I was asking myself, "What's the matter with me?" After all, I wasn't good at relationships, because I never really understood what was expected of me. I was hypersensitive to touch, light, smell, and sound. I startled easily. I didn't finish things. All my life I've struggled with an unpleasant physical buzz that feels like I'm plugged into an electrical socket. I had strange habits like rubbing my fingers together, typing on an unseen imaginary keyboard, moving air around inside my mouth, and vibrating my hands. I smiled too much or not enough. I talked too much or couldn't talk at all. I annoyed people by interrupting them and had a notoriously low tolerance for boredom and small talk. I focused on subjects that were interesting to me but had difficulty shutting off to listen to others. I had a hard time understanding social cues, which often resulted in embarrassing and sometimes even dangerous social exchanges. Accusations of "taking up too much space" and having "warp-headed ideas" were confusing and hurtful.

But still I soldiered on. I didn't tell anyone about my childhood experiences or that I'd quit school after failing tenth grade, or how I continued to struggle with sensory and social issues. For the longest time I actually thought everyone experienced the world the way I did and that my failures were my own fault. Why did other people seem to cope with an overwhelming world and incomprehensible human behaviour so much better than I did? As for disclosures about my failures at school, I figured they would make people reassess me in negative ways and could be career-limiting, so I carefully made sure no one knew.

Everything Worth Knowing about Advocacy I Learned from Belly Dancing

Most things we try to erase from our memories will come back to haunt us. The year I quit my job was my moment of truth. After an entire adult life of hiding behind a facade of super competence and strong verbal abilities, I was confronted with the issues I'd tried so hard to pave over. And this time they weren't going away.

It was precisely at this moment that I met Lynette. A friend invited us out to dinner at a local Greek restaurant. It was a busy Friday night, and the scheduled entertainment included a belly dancer. From the moment Lynette entered the room, I was mesmerized. Who was this engaging woman with dark curly hair and expressive eyes? I took in the exotic costume, a combination of red and gold, sequins, tassels, veils, and finger cymbals. I listened to the unfamiliar music and watched her fluid movements. How did she manage to communicate sensuality, self-respect, and humour all at the same time? The artist in me did a double flip. The magpie in me could think of only one thing.

That's what I want. I want to be her. (And I want all those shiny things.)

I got Lynette's phone number and found the courage to call. Within weeks I was taking belly dance lessons. In typically obsessive style, I immersed myself in a world of costume, music, and movement. I had no idea what this would—literally—put in motion.

From the first lesson, I was plunged into something so oxymoronic that I can describe it only as "a crisis of liberation." I'm not sure why I hadn't seen it coming, but I know I probably should have. After all, what is a spatially challenged person doing in a dance class? And not just any dance class, a dance class that asks dancers to use muscles and master complicated movements we seldom use in the Western world. Movements like belly rolls, shoulder shimmies, and snake arms. Movements that involve isolating and moving one part of the body while keeping everything else still. And later, the added complication of dance steps performed while trying to balance swords or canes or baskets on my head.

I slammed face first into every area of incompetence I'd ever had. And publicly! Spatial issues, body issues, fear of discovery. If my instructor (the beautiful Lynette or the elegant Shamani) demonstrated a walking three-quarter shimmy to the right, I shimmied to the left. If an elevation change required an isolation that started in the hips and traveled to the shoulders, my shoulders were followed by hips. It was a relentless struggle. Some days I couldn't believe my own determination in the face of such public humiliation. But it was more than my newfound passion for Middle Eastern dance, the costumes, and the shiny objects that kept me in the room. I'd begun to suspect that there were larger and more important lessons to be learned in the dance studio.

Gradually, with an enormous amount of practice, patience, support, and encouragement, I began to learn. Neuroscientists tell us that the brain is plastic. New synaptic connections can be made at almost any time in our lives. I began to understand the truth of this in a very concrete and observable way. I could almost feel those neurons changing. My body began to teach my brain lessons I'd been unable to learn in any classroom.

Dance class raised a lot of questions for me. It was precisely during this time that Norm's words began to take on an odd and unexpected personal significance. Perhaps, I wondered, "the right to be disabled" might actually relate to me, too. If so, was it possible that I might also find a way to embrace my idiosyncratic way of being in the world without the contortions I'd previously relied on to mask myself? Were self-acceptance and pride actually available to people like me?

As I continued to try to make sense of what I was experiencing, I simultaneously began to reclaim the hidden story of my childhood and question the way I'd previously framed it. Perhaps my inability to fit in wasn't my fault. Maybe I wasn't deficient. And further, perhaps there was a reason or a diagnosis for what I'd been experiencing. During this exploration, Norm and I went to see Dr. Gabor Mate, who wrote a book about ADHD called *Scattered Minds* (1999). We both suspected that perhaps what I'd read in his book might explain a few things about me. It was a relief when Dr. Mate confirmed my suspicion and agreed that I did have ADD (possibly without the H). When I told him about my experience with dance, he shook his head and laughed. "Wow," he said. "You really know how to pick your therapies!"

Finding My Place

Life continued, and although the ADD diagnosis explained a few things, it didn't explain everything. It wasn't until Norm and I began a doctoral program that more of those proverbial dominoes fell into place. We were doing a joint dissertation that involved looking at how both physiotherapy and compliance-based behavioural therapies could implant an identity of deficiency in the recipients. (Beware the commercial: that's another story we will fill out in our next book!) I was beginning to research and read the work of Autistic women. The more I read, the more resonant what I was reading became. I'd read parts of a book or blog post aloud to Norm, and he'd say, "Hmm… that sounds exactly like you!" I'd continue to read, and the hairs on the back of my neck would sometimes literally stand up. The sense of recognition I had was profound—it was like coming home. And yet it was also confusing. Over the years I'd met a lot of Autistic people, and I'd always had a perplexing sense of familiarity. I was drawn to them, and they to me, but I didn't really get why this attraction was so strong. Norm had always joked that I was "the Autism magnet."

As I read further, I began to understand why it was hard for me to make sense out of that familiarity. After all, most of the commonly held views about how Autistic people operate in the world favour a male perspective. The female experience of autism is vastly underresearched, and as a result, many of us aren't diagnosed as children and often don't recognize ourselves in the conventional literature or the pervasive social stereotypes. One of the jokes in adult Autistic communities is that the prototype of an autistic person is an eight-year-old white boy who lines up his toys, loves trains, is a math whiz, and has meltdowns in the grocery store. Many girls and women have a hard time relating to this description. (I'll confess that as a child I did line up my toys, though, and I do love trains, although the math thing continues to elude me. And as for meltdowns? Well, yeah, those too).

I'd never thought about the possibility that I might actually *be* Autistic until I was exposed to a female—and nonbinary—perspective. It was exciting and changed everything about the way I'd previously understood myself.

This new understanding put me on a further quest to make sense of my experience. I began to look for some official confirmation for what I was already suspiciously sure of. My doctor smiled when I told her I was seeking a diagnosis. She said, "What you're saying makes sense to me, and it sounds like you already know, so why do you need a diagnosis?" She was probably right, but perversely I still wanted that confirmation.

In the end I received the piece of paper with the diagnosis, and it actually did prove to be a further step in reclaiming my past and better understanding some of my present experiences. Receiving a diagnosis of autism as an adult has been an even greater relief than my first diagnosis of ADD, and although people wonder why I wanted to be so labelled, it has been a benefit, not a problem. Like Norm, I have been able to relocate the problem. I now understand that the problem isn't in me; it's in a society that demands conformity and uniformity and does not fully value difference.

If any "therapy" might have helped in my early years, it would not have focused on remediation but would likely have involved movement. Many Autistic adults report that movement helps regulate and smooth out some of the more difficult aspects of disability. I've heard people describe how aikido, gymnastics, karate, swimming, walking, and running have been life-saving activities. (Interestingly, like me, many—but not all—report that solitary activity is most helpful and that team sports remain confusing and problematic). Over and over, what I hear vehemently is that conventional, compliance-based behavioural therapies don't help. In fact, many Autistics report that the post-traumatic stress they experience as adults is directly related to the therapies they experienced in childhood. Most specifically, these were the therapies that required them to tamp down and mitigate important coping mechanisms like hand flapping and spinning, and transformed the things they loved into rewards contingent on "good" behaviour. Many of these therapies were experienced as frustrating, damaging, and cruel. It is for this reason that I am actually grateful that I managed to avoid a formal diagnosis as a child. As difficult as some things were for me, I've seen the negative effects of the regimes of compliance-based behavioural therapy that so many others like me have experienced, and I count myself lucky that I flew under the radar for so long.

Could I have used some help in learning to work with my body and brain as a child? Absolutely. But what I really needed was support and mentorship, not remediation. I needed someone who understood what it was like to live in my skin. It is through my association with disabled people, the Neurodiversity movement, and most particularly Norm, that I have learned that I am not broken. I, too, have the right to be disabled. I don't need to be fixed. I've learned that there's a difference between simply resigning myself to my limitations versus learning to accept and work proactively with them, and there's a difference between challenging myself to learn and grow versus trying to "fix" myself through remediation. I'm also in the process of learning that I can ask for what I need, and I am not required to perpetually engage in that exhausting and soul-killing activity called "passing." I can take the time I need to decompress after social encounters, and I can ask for the fluorescent lights to be turned off. I can carry and unapologetically use the fidget spinners, stim toys, dark glasses, and other props that help me keep myself together in public. I can encourage the audiences I speak to to use Deaf and Autistic friendly flappy applause (because you don't have to be Autistic to appreciate the fun of flapping). I couldn't have gotten to this place of happy self-acceptance without this community. And strangely enough, I'm not sure I could have gotten there without my experience with dance.

Although many of the experiences recounted by other Autistics resonate for me—at times rivetingly so—and although I am now the proud owner of two separate diagnoses, ADD and Autism, I admit I am still somewhat uncomfortable identifying as disabled. I recognize that I have not experienced the same underestimation and social and systemic discrimination as Norm and others who have observable disabilities have faced. For my whole life I have had the luxury of being presumed (mostly) competent (if a little strange) because I was able to hide the areas of my incompetence. Today, as for most of my adult life, my differences are tolerated as idiosyncrasies. Even during childhood, the frustration vented on me by adults was because they saw me as underperforming rather than incompetent. I am well aware that this is largely because of my strong verbal abilities. In this society, the ability to speak and write well is highly valued, and it is possible to use those skills to cover up other things that are either missing or would be seen as abnormal or deficient. That those abilities have allowed me to "pass" and hide what I don't do well is problematic in its own right, since many others don't have that luxury, but it has meant that for the most part I've been able to sidestep societal prejudice. This is, as I am well aware, the definition of privilege.

So I come to this work as a veteran, an ally, and an accomplice. It probably helps that there are points of intersection between my experience and the experiences of others—those with physical and intellectual disabilities as well as other Autistics – but what is most important is the way in which we work together to construct, deconstruct, and reconstruct our experiences; challenge conventional approaches and dominant narratives of disability; resist pejorative labels; and celebrate our differences. Identifying with a larger group of disability rights activists is both an act of solidarity and of self-preservation.

John McKnight, the friend and colleague Norm mentioned earlier, says that we are all like glasses of water that are half full. By this he doesn't mean that some of us look on the bright side of life and others don't; what he means is that all of us have things we do well and things we don't do well. And, as John says, that's the way we're supposed to be. In any community there will always be people who can do the things we can't, and because there will be things we can do that others can't, we will have all the bases covered. It's a tragic mistake to spend our lives desperately trying to fill ourselves up, to make ourselves perfect. Almost thirty years later, I understand that what Norm said about the right to be disabled on that fateful day we first met applies to me, too.

Postscript

I'll never be a great dancer, but I learned to dance and actually went on to perform with a troupe for awhile. I even got paid once. Along the way I learned a few valuable lessons that have little to do with dance. I learned how important movement can be for people like me. I also learned that the most unconventional paths are sometimes the most effective. All the remedial therapy in the world wouldn't have given me what five years of belly dance class did. The most well-intentioned of therapists could not have given me more support than the women I met through the dance community did. I discovered that it was OK to learn things differently and that I was capable of learning and growth.

After my experience with belly dance, something I was not immediately good at, once again I began to reevaluate the work I'd been engaged in. In special education, day, and vocational training programs and in therapy we ask people to "out" their areas of incompetence over and over again. We notice the stress, but we misunderstand where it's coming from. We call it "disability related" or speculate that it is the result of laziness, stubbornness, or worse, task avoidant behaviour. What we miss, or at least what I'd missed, is the constant, low-grade humiliation that people suffer when they are forced to continuously and publicly expose their so-called deficiencies and work hard to fix them.

As I mentioned, when I first heard Norm speak about the right to be disabled I immediately began to question these practices. However, it took me longer to understand how complicit I'd been. After all, how supportive is it to insist on remediation programs that focus almost entirely on a person's weaknesses? Why, in the name of help, do we ask people with physical and developmental disabilities to spend their days doing things they either aren't good at or can't do at all? "Touch your nose. Quiet hands. Don't drool. Stand quietly in line. Do up those buttons." Professionals have a litany of absurd demands, all in the name of remediation. And when people rebel, we're shocked. Our response to rebellion is then to label the rebel as deviant. We call it "challenging behaviour" or "noncompliance" and seldom look at the context in which people "behave." Then we try to remediate their protests and resistance, too. Perhaps it is important to remember, as Reverend Martin Luther King Jr. once said, "A riot is the language of the unheard" (Rucker & Upton, 2006).

It is not entirely amazing that these insights came later and only after I recognized commonality with the people I was supposedly "supporting." It is not surprising either that these insights were unavailable to me during the time that I aligned myself with the professionals. The process of "othering" always relies on distancing. When we lack self-awareness, it allows us to engage in remediation with the unquestioned belief that we know people better than they know themselves, and we know best about what they can and can't do and what they should and shouldn't do.

The lesson I'd learned that hit me the hardest was one I wish I'd been aware of years ago. I'd have been a better friend and a better ally. I saw that the advocacy I'd been engaged in was, at its essence, false. It was little more than benevolence. As the perpetually competent person (or at least the person arduously putting forward that fable), I was doing nice things for people, who then by default were the less competent ones. My own vulnerability stayed carefully hidden. This pseudo-advocacy was risk free and had the added benefit of making me feel good about myself. I never bothered to decode the messages I was sending or ask how it felt to receive the help I was offering.

For the first time I began to understand the difference between advocacy and self-advocacy. Advocacy is something you do for others that does not ask much of you. You can remain in hiding, and stay invulnerable. You can feel good about yourself and get a lot of kudos from others without ever having to change. Self-advocacy is when you understand that the world we should be advocating for is a world that will encompass all of us, just as we are. If I had my way, anyone engaging in advocacy should first have to publicly do something they aren't good at. Klutzes should try figure skating, and the shy types should join Toastmasters.

Today, I prefer the word *activist*. I am rethinking the notion of advocacy itself, even though I fully recognize and appreciate its history of reclamation and voice. The early etymology of the word tells us that it actually means "to plead." I don't want to plead for my right or the right of others to show up as fully human anymore. I will simply take my place in the world and resolutely work to ensure that others can do so as well. We all have the right to be who we are, but for disabled people this assertion takes more work and more resolve. It requires interrogating the premises and practices imposed by a society that devalues and often even fears difference. The right to be disabled is a rallying cry to a place of pride, freedom, self-determination, and, last but not least, celebration.

The ironic counterpoint to all the stories of dysfunction and deficit that surround my childhood and much of my adult life is that, when left to myself and my all-consuming interests, I am often absurdly happy. My inner life was and continues to be rich and interesting. I like myself. The things that others called obsessions—the way I can lose myself in the visual world, lights, and colours; the immersion in ideas, words, and books; the pleasure in my own company and solitude—continue to be a source of unmitigated bliss and elation for me. I have a happy marriage, and most amazingly of all, I have raised two beautiful human beings to successful adulthood.

I have never had a serious job that did not involve relationships with disabled people. My safety and happiness have always been tied up with theirs, even though I did not recognize for the longest time that this advocacy was forged in self-recognition. It is interesting and probably quite telling that I was married twice before to non-disabled, neurotypical men and neither relationship worked out. I have now been married to Norm for almost three decades, and we work exceptionally well together. It remains true that it is mostly through my association with disabled people that I have learned to talk back to the messages of deficiency I'd received. With their assistance, I now understand that I am not what I often thought I was: a bargain-basement version of a human being. I am not broken.

The stories we tell about our lives and the stories others tell about us are created interactively and relationally. Unfortunately, stories of dysfunction often take precedence and push the stories of happiness and competence to the margins when we take on the gargantuan tasks of self and other remediation. As I am learning to question the validity of what has been expected of me and what I've expected of myself and move into a place of self-acceptance, gradually and quietly an alternative and preferred story has begun to emerge. It is a story of pride and belonging. Norm calls this the "silent calm," and that is what it feels like to me, too.

Chapter 3

NORMALCY/ABNORMALITY: THE BIRTH OF A FALSE BINARY

We learned a lot about the way society defines both normalcy and abnormality during a conversation with a friend about homosexuality. It started off innocently enough. Our friend said that he believed that homosexuality was abnormal. It was, he asserted, a mutation of what normal people should be. We disagreed. We told him that we saw homosexuality as a normal expression of the diversity of human beings. We soon found ourselves embroiled in an argument about what constitutes normalcy.

Norm

I asked what I thought was a rhetorical question. "All right, given that I have cerebral palsy, would you consider me normal or abnormal?"

His answer was swift. "Abnormal, of course." I was momentarily nonplussed. However, he continued. "Now don't get me wrong, I don't think that disability should be a basis for unfair treatment or discrimination. Prejudice against disabled people infuriates me, but the fact that you have cerebral palsy means that you're an abnormal human being. Obviously, some people can't help being abnormal, and they should be given equal rights, but that's not to say they're normal."

I was initially taken aback by his comments, given our friendship, but I pursued this line of reasoning. "OK, if you lost a leg as a result of a car accident, would that make you an abnormal human being?"

The answer seemed obvious to him. "Of course it would. Normal people have two legs."

I pointed out that such an accident wouldn't make him a different person.

"Of course I'd be the same person," he responded, "but I wouldn't be normal."

Knowing he did a lot of renovation work on his house, I pushed the point further. "If you accidentally cut off your baby finger with the skill saw, would that make you abnormal?"

"Yes," he said. It was becoming clear that the bell curve of normalcy was decidedly steep and small for our friend.

I couldn't resist. "OK, your wife has had a hysterectomy. Do you consider her to be an abnormal woman?" At that point, the quality of the discussion deteriorated. As you might guess, neither of us changed our views on homosexuality.

Norm and Emma

Normal is a word that often appears in day-to-day language, and although politically correct people usually make "finger bunnies" in the air when they use it, we rarely question the idea. We glibly refer to normal ability, normal intelligence, normal weight, and a normal life, but when questioned, most of us must concede that we cannot really identify the criteria for the word.

While we may acknowledge that normalcy is a standard by which we are all, in some way, judged, we are led to a thorny question. What exactly is normal? How does normalcy get defined, agreed upon, and accepted in our society? How do we decide who is normal and who isn't? Perhaps normalcy is actually a mirage. As soon as you attempt to get close to it, it inexplicably disappears.

Normal as Ideal

Our friend seemed to imply that to be normal was to be somehow physically perfect. Having a normal body meant having a complete body with every part intact and functioning. Presumably, the same would be true for the mind housed in such a body. This idea of normalcy seems plausible enough at first glance but becomes problematic the more we look at it.

Let's look at intelligence, for example. Very few of us, if any, are academically excellent in every area. Some of us have good linguistic abilities but lack in mathematical aptitude. Others have wonderful memories but poor directional skills. Does this mean we're abnormal? It must, if we subscribe to the idea of normal as a form of perfection that involves everything working without a hitch. Obviously, in such a view, only a genius would be considered normal, and even that is debatable when you think about Beethoven's deafness and Einstein's famous spatial difficulties.

Likewise, only elite athletes would be considered to have physically normal bodies. Most of us could work forever and never have the stamina of an elite runner or the agility of Michael Jordan. Does this mean the rest of us are abnormal? Within this rigid definition, a person would have to be a brilliant, congenial, musically and artistically gifted Olympian athlete simply to earn the title of normal!

Of course we all know that there are no physically or intellectually perfect people. Everyone experiences some physical difficulty or limitation, from migraines to trick knees. Many of us spend time each day searching for lost glasses and car keys. It's clear that everyone can identify something that would make them abnormal under this narrow definition. (And the ones who say they can't are probably liars!)

So, normal as ideal clearly misses the mark. Once again, under this lens the idea of normalcy proves to be a mirage.

Normal as the Majority

Most of us would object to such a hyperbolic and narrow definition of *normal*. Instead, when pushed, we maintain that normalcy is actually about determining what's average. In other words, normalcy means our bodies and minds work in the same way that most bodies and minds work. This is also the statistical definition of normalcy—two standard deviations on each side of the mean. To be fair, our friend in the above example would probably have argued that he was normal not because he was perfect but because he was like the majority of people.

Again, this idea seems plausible at first. We don't assume perfection; we assume similarity. There's a range, we say. But there are problems with this definition as well. We know, for example, that the majority of people on earth are people of colour. Does this mean that white skin is abnormal? Men in Western society are typically seen as more emotionally removed than women. Since women make up 51 percent of the population, does this make emotional closeness the real norm?

Jim Iseldyke, an educational theorist, suggests that 70–80 percent of the human population could be defined as having a learning disability if assessed by current measures. Does this mean it's normal to have a learning disability? Again, the concept of normalcy shows itself to be frustratingly elusive.

Normal as Functional Ability

So if normalcy isn't exactly about perfection and isn't exactly about the majority, then what is it? Some people think it simply means having a reasonable ability to function in daily life. I (Norm) become aware of this criterion every time I'm required to take the ubiquitous health certification form to my doctor to certify to some agency that I do, indeed, have a disability. The question the doctor must answer invariably reads, "Does the individual have a physical disability that permanently prevents her/him from independently doing activities of daily life?"

This question implies that disability is abnormal because it might impose unusual limitations. The operative word is *unusual*. Thus, our friend might have argued that having cerebral palsy was abnormal because it consistently prevents or hinders me from doing certain routine activities. In this view, because blindness limits a person's ability to see, that person should be defined as abnormal; likewise those with intellectual disabilities are abnormal because they struggle with cognitive limitations. Non-disabled people assume that these limits undermine or interfere with a person's quality of life. This, then, is a working definition of abnormal for many people.

But perhaps the discussion isn't over. Scores of people are seen to be abnormal despite their ability to complete the routine activities of daily living. For example, the vast majority of LGBTQ+ people are able to walk, talk, feed, and dress themselves. In fact many women would argue that some gay men are far better at dressing themselves than are most straight men! Similarly, individuals who are very tall or very short are equally capable of completing ordinary tasks. So again, just when the concept of normalcy seems within our grasp, it slips through our fingers and is gone.

What, then, is normalcy? Can it be defined at all?

Abnormality as a Measurable and Observable Difference

Most of us believe that disability, like gender, is a real, measurable, physical, intellectual, or sensory deficiency or limitation located inside a person's body. For example, most people assume that because someone has difficulty walking, they therefore have a disability. But if disability is simply about limitations, why are some limitations not considered to be disabilities? Not all poor eyesight, for example, is considered to be blindness. Yet this distinction also seems obvious. Disability, as we already noted, is assumed when a limitation is severe enough to impede a person's ability to carry out daily living activities.

But upon closer examination, it becomes clear that even this isn't necessarily the case. For example, we have a friend who suffers from migraine headaches. When a migraine hits him, he is completely debilitated. All he can do is lie in a dark, quiet room for several days and wait for the pain and nausea to pass. On the other hand, although I (Norm) have always had cerebral palsy, it has never debilitated me to the same extent that migraines do to our friend. Improvisation and a host of adaptive devices enable me to do most of the things I want to do, and although many things are probably more time-consuming and require more effort than would be true for most people, I have always managed reasonably well.

So why is cerebral palsy considered to be a disability when migraines are not? Some conditions, it seems, are seen to be a normal, albeit unfortunate, part of human experience; whereas other conditions are seen as aberrations of what human life should be. In a nutshell, people are not *supposed* to have cerebral palsy, whereas migraines are seen as unfortunate but not uncommon or even abnormal.

Perhaps it might also be argued that cerebral palsy is a disability because it is a visible condition. After all, people can readily see an unusual gait, cane, or wheelchair, so it therefore follows that those who walk differently or use mobility devices should be designated disabled. Because those who have migraines are not easily detectable out in public, they manage to elude such descriptions. This should make a clear distinction, but again, under examination this assumption also crumbles. What about all the invisible conditions that are also designated as disabilities?

Consider epilepsy. Migraine headaches and epilepsy are both neurological conditions. Although it is difficult to ascertain which condition is more debilitating, we have very different narratives for each. As noted, we see migraines as a normal if unfortunate condition that afflicts some people. This is not the case with epilepsy. In our society, we see epilepsy as more than a normal neurological condition. We see it as an atypical abnormality in the brain. Even though both conditions are neurologically based, migraines are seen as a normal condition, whereas epilepsy is seen as an abnormal condition. It is difficult, if not impossible, to point to some objective criteria that accounts for this difference. It is also interesting to note that despite being almost undetectable (except during a seizure), epilepsy is a designated disability.

Once again we circle back to understanding that a condition becomes a disability not when it is debilitating, severe, or visible but when it is somehow deemed to be abnormal. As we have seen, the criteria for this designation are arbitrary and elusive. They shift and change. However, once a person is designated as disabled or abnormal, there are further ramifications. Decisions are made.

A Categorically Different "Kind" Of Person

Unfortunately, it's not just the particular condition that is seen as abnormal. It goes much further than that. In fact, the person who *has* the condition is seen as abnormal. Having a condition that has been labelled as abnormal or a disability causes that person to be viewed as a categorically "different kind of person." For example, someone who has epilepsy is commonly referred to as "an epileptic." We have no corresponding term for people who have migraines. We don't call them "migrainetics." While we will likely feel sympathetic toward a person who deals with migraines, we do not see them as a different type of person in the same way we do with a person who has epilepsy.

It becomes clear that the meaning of disability goes far beyond a description of limitations. Disability is a judgment about the way people *should be* masquerading as a description of how people *actually are*. The most insidious part of this attribution of abnormality is that not only does society see disabled people as fundamentally different, but even disabled people internalize this idea and come to define themselves as categorically different.

If we are going to adequately understand the subtle yet significant meaning of disability, perhaps we have to understand the origin, meaning, and history of the notions of both normality and abnormality. Where exactly does this idea come from? Most people assume that the concept of normal has always existed. In fact, this is not true.

Origins, Meaning, and History

Lennard Davis, a disability studies scholar, points out that the concepts of "normal" and "normalcy," "normality" and "norm," and "average" and "abnormality" became part of the English language only in the mid-nineteenth century. Davis (1995) writes:

> The word "normal" as "constituting, conforming to, not deviating or different from, the common type or standard, regular, usual" only enters in the English language around 1840. (Previously, the word had meant "perpendicular"; the carpenter's square, called a "norm," provided the root meaning.) Likewise, the word "norm" in the modern sense has only been in use since around 1855, and "normality" and "normalcy" appeared in 1849 and 1857, respectively. If the lexicographical information is relevant, it is possible

to date the coming into consciousness in English of an idea
of "the norm" over the period of 1840-1860 (p. 24).

Davis goes on to explain that the concept of normal or average entered
European culture with the birth of statistical mathematics. Initially
designed as a tool to help understand what is prevalent in society, the
statistical approach soon took the concept of normal from a broad
and general description to a much more specific way to describe an
individual.

Adolphe Quetelet (1796–1847), a French statistician, astronomer,
mathematician and sociologist has the dubious honour of having
transformed the concept of normal from a descriptive idea to an
imperative. At that time, astronomers were using the science of
probability and statistics and the "law of errors" primarily to plot the
position of stars. In order to correct for possible errors in plotting the
location of a star, astronomers would simply plot its position in the
middle of all the sightings. Quetelet blithely extrapolated this notion to
human beings through something he called "social physics" and saw
this as wonderful way to define normal human features such as height
and weight. In this way, he sought to identify what he referred to as
the "average man". In the blink of a moment, the human community
was divided into two categories: normal and abnormal. The wide
range of *what is* immediately became a very narrow notion of *what
should be* (Davis, 1995).

Further extrapolations were made. The idea that it was possible to
determine and define normalcy was soon suggested as a remedy for
a host of social problems. Among other things, it gave rise to the
eugenics movement in the late nineteenth and the first half of the
twentieth centuries. The ability to define normalcy was believed
to be the first step toward creating a "better society." Remediation,
sterilization, and even extermination were put forward as possible
solutions for crime, poverty, chronic sickness, and mental deficiencies.
Intellectuals and politicians heralded eugenics as a feasible way of
achieving a Utopian society, free of miscreants and defectives. Western
society was well on the way to implementing a eugenics approach
when the Second World War broke out. It was only when Hitler used

the precepts of eugenics as the rationale for his "final solution" that the idea fell out of favour with the rest of the world. Unfortunately, it continues to arise without being adequately questioned in campaigns like the quest to eradicate Down syndrome in countries like Belgium and Iceland.

Traits, Subjectivity, and a Few Examples

In their book *The Unexpected Minority*, authors Gliedman and Roth (1980) offer a humorous example of the subjective nature of disability. The story goes like this: a British diplomat was having dinner with a colleague while visiting a remote part of Africa when they were interrupted by a knock on the door. The diplomat's colleague answered and briefly talked with a very small man. After he returned to the table, the visiting diplomat commented on how well "dwarves" [sic] seemed to be integrated into the community. His friend chuckled and pointed out that the man at the door was not a dwarf. In fact, all the people in this village were of a similar height.

Of course, the case could be made that simply because all members in a community have the same trait does not necessarily mean that the trait is normal. In this example, it could be argued that just because everyone in the village was short does not mean it is normal to be that short. After all, most people in the world are not. In another example from the early twentieth century, everyone in a large community on Martha's Vineyard used sign language because almost everyone living there was Deaf. In the context of that community, it was normal to be Deaf or to use sign language. However, once again, in a larger context, it is not.

Let's use yet another example. Until recently many cultures have defined left-handedness as abnormal. In some cultures left-handed people were considered frightening and morally corrupt and have even been accused of being possessed. It is interesting to note that the word *sinister* comes from the root word *sinis*, the Latin root for "left."

The right hand is considered holy in many religions, whereas the left hand often represents evil. Religious art and symbolism consistently show Christ, Buddha, and various Hindu gods using the right hand for blessing, whereas Satan is usually depicted as left-handed. In Satanic ceremonies known as the Black Mass or the Witch's Sabbath, the left hand is not only used to curse but also replaces the right hand in mirror-image rituals where the right hand would be used in Christian services.

Buddha describes the road to Nirvana splitting into two paths: the path to enlightenment goes to the right and the path to evil to the left. In Hinduism, right-handed tantras (Daksincara) are seen as more spiritually evolved than left-handed tantras (Pancamakara). The evil Yetzer Hara, in Judaism, is associated with the left side, whereas its opposite number, the Yetzer Hatov, is based on the right. In Islam, the left hand is considered unclean. There is a practical rationale for the custom of eating with one hand and performing personal hygiene with the other, but it is clear that practicality is not the only issue. If it were, it would presumably be fine to do things the other way around. But in some cultures, it remains unacceptable to eat with your left hand and clean with the right.

In Medieval times, left-handed people were sometimes presumed to be witches and put to death. More recently, left-handed students, most notably in Catholic schools, were humiliated, forcibly restrained, and even hit by teachers in an attempt to make them use their right hands. Is this bias in favour of right-handedness simply an expression of religious belief, or did the idea of left-handedness as a negative attribute come directly from a perception of normalcy as uniformity? Is it actually the result of imposing an arbitrary belief of "what should be" on to the reality of "what actually is"?

In our quest to define normalcy, we come to a metaphorical fork in the road. If we decide that normalcy can be defined as uniformity, we take one path. Deciding that normalcy is diversity puts us on another. In the example of hand dominance, presuming that all people should be right-handed catapults us down the "normalcy as uniformity" path. This causes a number of foreseeable consequences. Now left-handedness is a deficiency rather than a difference. A person is not seen as capably left-handed; they are seen as lacking in normal right-handed skills.

If we pursue this line of thinking to its hyperbolic end, it would follow that giving birth to a left-handed child would be viewed as a tragic event. We can then easily imagine support groups springing up around these individuals and their families. Social workers would be charged to help families "grieve the loss of their right-handed child." Fathers would begin to doubt their virility. Mothers would scrutinize their habits during pregnancy and early parenting, wondering what misdeed caused their child to be left-handed. Rehabilitation therapists might encourage parents to tie their child's left hand behind his or her back in order to discourage its use. (This example is factual, since parents and teachers in the not-too-distant past were actually encouraged to do this.) Researchers would publish empirical studies demonstrating that left-handed children placed unbearable strain on families, thus creating a greater likelihood of divorce among their parents. Siblings of left-handed children would feel starved for attention or attempt to compensate for their inadequate brother or sister by becoming the perfect child.

Again, this sounds ridiculously overstated. However, in a publication called *The Left-Hander Syndrome*, author Stanley Coren (1992) claimed that left-handers could expect a shortened lifespan. He believed this was primarily because of stress and injury due to coping with a right-handed world. Needless to say, his methodology and results have been challenged in the years since publication, but just when we thought we had relegated these attitudes to the distant past, it is interesting to note the relatively recent 1992 publication date.

Fortunately, present-day society has largely chosen the other path, in which left-handedness is viewed as an expression of diversity. Supports are commonplace. Most appliances have doors that can be installed on either side. There are left-handed mugs, left-handed golf clubs and baseball mitts, left-handed scissors, left-handed keyboards, and left-handed tools. We see the variation of hand dominance in much the same way we see differences in height and hair colour. From this perspective, the idea that only right-handedness is normal is exposed as false. We have come to realize that the problem was never about deficiency; it was devaluation. Supports replace remediation, and rather than trying to make everyone right-handed, we are now working to ensure that left-handed people are not disadvantaged or inconvenienced.

Unfortunately, we have not done the same for disability as we have for left-handedness. In most societies we have consistently chosen the path that defines disability as abnormality. However, if we recognize that normality and abnormality are nothing more than socially created distinctions, we are offered another perspective. In this view it is possible to speculate that a disability is not what we have assumed it to be: a definable biological reality existing within the body or brain of the "disabled" person. Instead, we can come to see that it is little more than an arbitrary distinction that flows directly from the attitudes a society holds toward it.

Perhaps these examples, rather than suggesting answers, actually provide us with the next question. Is it actually context that defines normalcy? To address this question, it is necessary to give a brief (and hopefully) accessible description of social constructionist theory.

Social Constructionism (It's Not That Complicated…)

Shortly after the Second World War, Michel Foucault (1980), a French social theorist and philosopher, pointed out that abnormal people were not, as most of us believe, the exceptions in an otherwise normal population. He maintained that we had, in fact, gotten it backward. Most of us begin with the unquestioned assumption that the majority of people are normal. When exceptions arise, we define them as abnormal. In this light, normalcy appears to precede abnormality. However, according to Foucault, human beings are neither normal nor abnormal; they are simply diverse. He pointed out that different cultures make different decisions about what is acceptable and then go on to impose a criterion of *what should be* onto *what is*. Foucault maintained that the concept of abnormality originates with those decisions and not in the specific traits of particular individuals. Ironically, in Foucault's analysis, it is the absence of abnormality that makes us normal. In other words, once abnormality is defined, normalcy is, by definition, whatever is left over.

Discussing Foucault's ideas about the origin and nature of abnormality may seem like a useless esoteric academic and philosophical exercise. After all, we might argue that most of us do not immediately categorize people as being either normal or abnormal; we recognize that people have a range of traits, abilities, and limitations. Defining someone as abnormal seems simplistic, hyperbolic, and probably rude. However, just because we reject the concept intellectually does not mean that it has been rendered irrelevant. Unfortunately, the idea that some people are abnormal still persists and has serious consequences in the lives of disabled people and those who are otherwise marginalized. The creation of a class of people defined as abnormal has served as a justification for many problematic decisions—everything from persistent segregation and lack of opportunity to eugenics and extermination.

The idea that a disability is not an abnormality in the body (although disabled bodies are undeniably diverse) but is actually a social construction may initially be a strange and confusing idea. Most people do acknowledge that prejudice exists towards disabled people; however, while we may intellectually understand that disability is a fluid concept that changes from culture to culture and is continually redefined in courtrooms and professional conferences, the idea that a disability is, as Barry Allen (2005) puts it, an impairment "implanted" in the body (p.93) may strike us as a foreign notion. A closer look at the narratives we use to navigate our worlds can provide us with a helpful way to cut through the confusion of this discussion.

What's a Narrative, and Why Is Understanding the Way Narratives Operate Important?

In university, I (Norm) often used visual metaphors to help me understand complex philosophical concepts. The visual metaphor I used to describe the way dominant social narratives operate in our lives was the memory of travelling through the Tokyo subway system at rush hour. I lived in Japan for three months during the year I took off between finishing high school and beginning university. I would often spend my days exploring different sections of Tokyo and then returning to my friend's home for dinner. Sometimes, I would get caught in rush-hour foot traffic, and that's when the adventure would begin!

North Americans who visit Japan invariably return with a new definition of what a crowd is. This new definition transcends what we in the West experience in shopping malls on December 24. It is more like what would happen if a sporting event audience exited the stadium using only one quarter of the exits. A person doesn't just walk in a Tokyo rush-hour crowd; they are forcibly carried along. It feels much like being swept down a swift river. In order to turn left or right, a person needs to begin veering in that direction well ahead of the turn.

Narrative, or discourse, is like that Tokyo rush-hour crowd, only in this instance we can substitute language for walking. Instead of being physically carried along by the movement of others, we are conceptually carried along by language. The collective social narratives we hold are hugely influential in shaping our understanding of the world. In order to more fully describe how narratives operate in our lives, consider this piece we've airlifted from Emma's upcoming book *Talk to Me: What Educators Can Learn about Deescalation from Hostage Negotiators.*

> When most people hear the word *narrative* they understand it as another word for a story; whether an oral history, a biography, novel, blog or even a work of non-fiction. Sometimes the word *narrative* is interpreted as an autobiography, or the story of our lives. While these are all good examples of a particular use of the word, in this book I am going to use it differently. The narratives I want to talk about are the pervasive social stories that operate underneath our conscious awareness, and influence our ideas, attitudes and actions.

Winslade and Monk (2007) define narratives as the complex, socially constructed cultural and personal stories we all use to bring coherence to our lived experience. In other words, they are the stories that help us make sense of our lives and the world around us. These stories, they noted, do more than describe. They work below the surface as a framework that supports us in actively constructing our perceptions. They are the stories we carry with us that we use to make decisions about what is right and wrong, what is true or false, real or not, about who we should be, what we should do and what others should be and do.

These narratives are created relationally. They come from what we have learned and assimilated from our families of origin, through our education, religious communities, and through the cultural groups we are part of. They also come down through the ages in the form of allegory, fable, cautionary tales, historical accounts, religious tracts and even morality plays. We internalize the messages contained in these stories and are guided by them. Within these narratives are a series of unquestioned norms that "shape… choices, values, feelings and actions" (p. 30) and, perhaps most important in the context of the discussion that follows, shape "what we expect of ourselves and others around us" (p. 30). Like fish in water, we are so familiar with these stories that we rarely question their origins. We take their veracity for granted, and we come to regard them as simply "common sense." But are they?

Although it might seem that these narratives represent obvious truths, in fact, they are simply a series of culturally generated assumptions. After all, these stories differ widely from society to society, from community to community, and even from family to family and individual to individual. They are fluid, and change over time. Take, for example, the role of women in western society. It's only been 100 years since women gained the right to vote in Western societies. Before that, women were seen as unable to make the rational decisions necessary to do so. But today women not only vote, they run for office and are elected. What changed? Did women somehow evolve? Of course not. What changed was the *narrative* our society holds about women's capabilities and competence. Understanding the shift in this example allows us to recognize that narratives are far more fluid, changeable and subject to challenge and contradiction than we might immediately recognize. Consider another example.

We are all familiar with the cartographical map of the world, and it is a common assumption that mapmakers show the world accurately. In all modern maps of the world, north is at the top of the map and south is at the bottom.

But is this representation accurate or is it an arbitrary rendition of what the world looks like? In 1979, Australian Stuart McArthur challenged this view, and developed what he called the Universal Corrective Map, sometimes known as the "upside down" map. The slogan McArthur attached to the map was "Australia: No Longer Down Under."

Although many believe this map corrects a Eurocentric view of the world and a bias favouring the north, in fact early map makers all over the world—including Europeans—drew their maps the way McArthur did. There were many other conceptualizations and representations of the world reflected in the way maps were drawn at different times in history. Some showed east at the top or, even more confusingly, with all views pointing inward. So which is the right way? Perhaps there isn't one. After all, if we look at the world from outer space the idea of up, down, north or south becomes ludicrous. Obviously, there is no "upside down" or "right side up" from that vantage point. However, most of us become disoriented when we see McArthur's map, since it contradicts a universally accepted narrative we've uncritically carried since childhood.

It's undeniable that life would be easier if there was only one overarching narrative—or map—of what is real and true that we all agreed upon. It's likely we'd rarely be in conflict with one another. However, the truth is that we live in a world rampant with multiple conflicting narratives. There are no singular stories that describe reality in complete or definitive ways and for every story there is at least one other story that contradicts it, if not many. Not only do we hold personal narratives that do not line up with the stories of others, each of us are also walking repositories of multiple and competing narratives that we try desperately to sort through and reconcile. We may have been raised, for example, to believe that women should stay home and raise their children. However, we may now also believe that women should be financially contributing members of society. This contradiction of narratives can result in considerable personal stress as we try to align them and live accordingly. Consider the following quote from Alice Morgan (2000), a Narrative Therapist from Australia.

Our lives are multistoried. There are many stories occurring at the same time and different stories can be told about the same events. No single story can be free of ambiguity or contradiction and no single story can encapsulate or handle all the contingencies of life (p. 8).

However stressful, complicated and contradictory they may be, we need narratives. These social stories give us the ability to organize and interpret our experiences. Without them, we would be adrift in a sea of incomprehensible and unmanageable incoming data. Narratives help us sort through the chaos and create cognitive order for ourselves. However, the narratives we live by can become problematic if we mistake them for unquestioned objective reality. We risk becoming rigid and dogmatic, believing that anyone who disagrees with us must be wrong. Thus, learning to question and even replace unhelpful narratives can allow us to choose those that are most useful and discard those that are not. The more lightly we hold our narratives and the more we learn to question them, the more opportunities for action and influence become available to us. When we understand that the narratives we hold are arbitrary and can change, we open up space to consider alternatives (Van der Klift, 2019 in press).

Changing the Narrative

The narratives we hold about what's normal have consequences for disabled people. They are not simply stories. In our society they are transformed into imperatives. At the point of diagnosis, a disabled person becomes the repository for society's belief that everyone should be normal. In a split-second, the disabled person is transformed from just a child to a child in desperate need of remediation. Decisions about treatment, surgeries, therapy, and placement are quickly made, most often without the input of the disabled person. This holds true not only for children but also for people who acquire disabilities later in life. Stringent courses of rehabilitation are suggested and often enforced.

Understanding the way narratives operate in our lives and influence the way we see the world, define reality, and shape our practices can open the door to alternatives and possibilities. What if we didn't have to think of the world and other people in terms of binaries like normal and abnormal? How would our practices change if we understood disability to simply be another expression of what's normal in the range of human experience? Perhaps making this change in narrative would open up space to consider alternatives that go beyond linguistics; changing the narrative has the potential to significantly improve the lives of disabled people in real and tangible ways.

Chapter 4

LANGUAGE AND IDENTITY

Emma

It's puzzling that in human services, schools, and even families, a lot of terms are used to describe disability without ever saying the word *itself*. Disability is most often couched in euphemism; we say that people have "special needs" or are "physically challenged" or "differently-abled." These linguistic contortions are sometimes amusing (consider "speciable needs" and "speciability" as particularly ridiculous and cutesy examples), but perhaps we should be concerned that these terms are not nearly as benign and kind or even as humorous as we may think. However well-intentioned those who use these terms may be, refusing to directly acknowledge disability may have unexpected consequences. Consider the following story.

Several years ago we attended a conference keynote given by a prominent local celebrity. She proudly told the audience that she had never told her eight-year-old son he had Down syndrome and that neither he nor his siblings were aware of his differences. Both of us were appalled. What, we wondered, is so shameful about Down syndrome that it couldn't even be said out loud, much less acknowledged with any kind of pride?

We're sure that the intention of the keynote speaker was good. It's likely she thought she was shielding her child from what she believed might be a painful shock to his self-image. She likely also believed she was shielding him from potential teasing. However, is this apparent kindness misguided? What are we actually telling our children when we refuse to acknowledge their disabilities? Our silence speaks volumes and may even do the opposite of what we intend. It may be that we are contributing to the very societal stigma we believe we are resisting when we treat disability as something to be hidden and ashamed of.

It is dangerous to assume that disabled children are unaware of their differences. Many, if not all, disabled adults tell us that they knew they were different from a very early age. When we don't acknowledge what our children already know, we forfeit the ability to assist them to develop the skills they will need to challenge and contest ableist messages from society and navigate a world not set up for them. We also indirectly teach them to hide their disabilities and take on the arduous task of "passing." Even if by some remote chance we are successful and our children are truly unaware of their disabilities, we should ask ourselves if we are leaving them unprotected from the schoolyard bullies who will have no compunction about being the first to tell them that they are different and that their differences are abnormal and wrong. The shock of that moment is potentially far more damaging than acknowledging disability directly in the first place. Instead of protection, perhaps we should be doing what our friend and colleague Dave Hingsburger calls *target hardening*, a phrase he borrowed from law enforcement. In this context, what he means is helping our children learn the strategies they will need to protect themselves and refuse the problematic identities they have been assigned (Hingsburger, personal communication, 2018).

To be fair to the keynote speaker, it's likely she'd been influenced by decades of indoctrination that say that labels are bad and encourage us to be politically correct and morally sensitive by avoiding them at all costs. She'd likely seen the posters and T-shirts that exhort us to "label jars, not people" and was probably encouraged to use "people first" language as a way to distance her child from the stigmatized label. "I'm a person first" is the rallying cry in many circles. Not a bad sentiment at first glance, but what lies underneath? Is it still the pervasive notion that disability is a negative, undesirable attribute and ought to be firmly separated from the person, hidden, diminished, and even denied?

It is important to understand that simply noting that someone has Down syndrome or Autism or cerebral palsy is not the same as labelling them. These are actually neutral descriptions, much like saying that someone is black or white or Aboriginal or Asian or LGBTQ+. Many members of marginalized groups talk about the irritation they feel when people say, "I just don't think of you as black, or brown, or LGBTQ+." What the people who make these remarks often view as a compliment actually feels like dismissal and insult to those on the receiving end. The reason, they tell us, is that being black, or brown, or LGBTQ+ is an integral part of their identity. To pretend that it isn't there is to diminish its importance and even to imply that it is something shameful.

What might happen if instead of denying disability, we encouraged the development of pride and a sense of solidarity in our disabled children? From this position, we can help them to develop the strength they need to go forward in what is often a disability-hostile world. The first way we can accomplish this is to acknowledge and honour their identities as members of a rich and vibrant disability community. We can introduce our children to positive disability history and positive disabled role models. For many disabled adults, the moment of discovering a community of others who understood their issues is described as a significant, pivotal moment in their lives. For both Norm and me, finding these groups and individuals was profoundly life-changing. We learned about pride. Pride is an inoculation against bigotry and prejudice, and its power must not be underestimated.

As mentioned, terms like Down syndrome, Autism, and cerebral palsy are not in and of themselves either stigmatizing or problematic. However, there are other so-called descriptors that actually *are* damaging and can affect a person's reputation and sense of identity in profound and lasting ways. Terms that label someone as a behaviour problem are particularly troubling in this context. They are often contained in the acronyms we use to describe people: diagnoses or descriptors like "oppositional" and "behaviour disordered." Others, like "noncompliant," are more informal and have little to do with diagnosis but can nonetheless also have equally difficult ramifications. Let's look at several terms we often hear used to describe people whose actions we either do not understand or do not approve of, then look at some typical responses, and examine how these terms can influence lives in negative ways.

Five Problematic Descriptions

1. Resistant

Perhaps you've heard people labelled this way. "She's resistant!" In this context, the word *resistant* seems to imply an overarching identity. In other words, this is not just what she *does*; it's actually who she *is*. When we hear someone called resistant in such a globalizing way, it should raise an immediate question in our minds: Why is a verb that is commonly used to describe an activity now being used as a noun to describe a person? Is she herself really *innately resistant*, or is she actually *resisting something*?

We've probably all been called resistant at one time or another. Try to remember the last time someone accused you of being stubborn or refusing to comply. Can you remember what it was you were resisting and why? Wasn't it most often something that felt legitimate and real—something worth fighting for? In most situations, we probably believed that we were resisting something either unfair or wrong. It's important to remember that no one resists for no reason. None of us do.

If we reframe resistance as the act of struggling against something we believe to be unfair or wrong, the word takes on new meaning and reverts to its original usage as an action word. It doesn't presume a general identity of pigheadedness but instead describes someone trying in whatever way they can to solve a problem or to right an injustice. In this view, we might even begin to see resistance as part of an honourable tradition and not a negative character trait. For example, people in the Resistance Movement during the Second World War are now seen as heroes. In her book *Possessing the Secret of Joy* (1992), author Alice Walker talks with great eloquence and passion about the importance of resistance and its role in developing identity and pride. Susan B. Anthony, an American suffragette, was also an abolitionist and actively fought against the oppression and slavery of African Americans in pre–Civil War America. She once famously said that "resistance to oppression is obedience to God."

In 1965, author Darrell Trent quoted a much older and perhaps familiar statement that often shows up in internet memes today. He said, "One man's terrorist is another man's freedom fighter." https://en.wikiquote. org/wiki/Talk:Terrorism This quote frames resistance in two starkly different ways and implies that we must consider both context and who is doing the describing when we think about the nature of resistance. Unfortunately, this distinction is not often considered in the context of schools and human services. Disabled people protesting their lives and treatment are most often treated like terrorists, not freedom fighters. They are often placed on restrictive behaviour plans, sedated, and in too many instances even restrained and secluded.

What might change if we recognized that the person we call noncompliant or resistant may actually be trying to resist the way they've been described and treated and the system imposed upon them—a system of rules, regulations, and behaviour plans that often feel arbitrary, mean-spirited, and confining? We seldom ask people to explain their actions or to help us create alternatives that work for them. Instead, in too many situations, plans and interventions are created without any meaningful input from the person upon whom they will be imposed.

One of the pitfalls of working in education and human services is that we do not necessarily see resistance as a reasonable response to a difficult situation but instead label it as obstinate noncompliance. Reframing resistance as reasonable opens up an opportunity to ask different questions, to change the way we respond, and even to enter into solidarity, helping to foster resilience and create positive change.

In this way we may even find *ourselves* described as resistant but, in the most honourable sense of the word, resisting the tendency to pathologize others. As our friend and colleague the late Herb Lovett often noted, when we see people through a different lens, it is possible to understand those labelled disruptive as social critics, the canaries in the coal mines of education and human services who tell us what's wrong with what *we're* doing. Being seen as a social critic with something useful to say is worlds away from being labelled noncompliant, or resistant, or that huge catchall, a behaviour problem.

2. Manipulative

This is a word I wish we could get rid of. Calling someone manipulative is not only unkind, it also tells us nothing about who the person is or what they're trying to accomplish.

It's likely that all of us have been accused of being manipulative at one time or another. However, is that necessarily a negative thing? Michel Foucault (1980) once noted that every action we take in the world exists in the context of power; we're always trying to achieve something. Whether what we're trying to achieve gets called either good or bad isn't really the point. We are simply trying to influence our environment to create positive outcomes for ourselves (and hopefully for others). This does not necessarily mean that we are self-interested egotists. Manipulation is a survival skill. It is how we've managed to stay on this planet as a species for as long as we have. Calling someone manipulative is probably stating the obvious, since life is a continuous process of manipulating variables to influence outcomes.

Perhaps you're thinking, "Yeah, I get how we all manipulate our environments, but what I'm talking about are the people who try to get us to do what they want in sneaky and underhanded ways." Consider this: What if being straightforward and asking for what you want rarely achieved results? This is a sad reality for many disabled children and adults. Many have been called demanding when they ask directly for what they want and need, and many have even been punished for those requests. Many have learned that the only acceptable disabled person is a quiet, non-demanding, compliant person. What one person labels as manipulative or underhanded may be another person's only way to influence their environment and those around them. We could, in fact, see manipulation as an ingenious adaptation to a system that often refuses to acknowledge more direct attempts to create change.

When we rely on words like *manipulative* to describe people, we risk dismissing them and their concerns and missing important information that could help us understand what the person is doing and why.

3. Just for Attention

Another way in which legitimate conflicts are often discounted between non-disabled and disabled people is when non-disabled support workers and teachers claim that the person is "just doing (whatever it is) for attention." Like the terms *resistant* and *manipulative*, this phrase needs a closer look. After all, we could argue that all human beings look for attention, whether we call it that or not. We are, at our heart, relational beings. We want and actively seek out each other's attention; we want to belong. In this context it's easy to understand that doing something for attention is not necessarily a negative thing at all!

It is an unfortunate reality that for people with disabilities there is often another insidious belief at work just beneath the idea that people do things "just" for attention. Have you ever heard someone say that bad attention is just as reinforcing as good attention for "these people"? I know I have, and too often. This assumes that the person has nothing important to say but is simply acting out in order to get a reaction—any reaction. Therefore, it might follow that we should not give the person the satisfaction of believing that their actions have had any impact on us. This often leads to behaviour programs and strategies like planned ignoring.

Planned ignoring is based on the idea that it's legitimate to use attention as some kind of reward and that it makes sense to withhold attention when someone is asking for it in ways we call inappropriate. I've seen many a behaviour plan that includes some instruction for support staff or teachers that looks like this: "Staff will ignore Josie when she continues to ask for more coffee (or whatever it is that Josie wants) even after she's been told to stop." It's often followed with further step-by-step instructions to "Tell Josie that you will be ignoring her and walk to the other side of the room, turn your back, and wait until she stops engaging in the behaviour." If we truly believe that people do things just for attention and that furthermore this is a bad thing, we might come to the conclusion that it is not only efficacious, but ethical to use our attention as leverage to change Josie's behaviour. If she doesn't have access to us and our attention, we might surmise, she will stop engaging in the behaviour we don't like. It seems to make a certain kind of sense.

But think about your own life. How might you respond if you were really trying to get something across to somebody, and their response was to say, "I don't like the way you're saying this, so I won't listen to what you're trying to say and I'm going to ignore you"? Anyone who has ever been on the receiving end of the silent treatment will know that it does little to cause us to rethink our actions. Instead, our response is often resentment, anger, and a deep sense of being misunderstood. For most of us, there are generally two ways we respond to being ignored: we either escalate or we shut down. If we do the first and get more upset, it's likely that things will get even worse for us. We may lose relationships and privileges, or even find ourselves restrained or segregated in some way. The second response is more difficult to decode because it might be mistaken by the other person as positive. It may seem as though we've accepted our punishment and actually learned from it. But is that really true? Unfortunately, when we shut down, we're likely thinking, "What's the use in trying to communicate with this person? They aren't interested, and they don't care."

The danger in these strategies is that if we're the ones doing the ignoring and someone escalates in response, we might feel justified in "upping the ante" and moving on to more punitive responses. If the person shuts down, however, we may feel that we've been successful and fail to notice the sadness and hopelessness the ignored person feels.

Does this mean we can't help someone find alternative ways to elicit attention from others? Of course we can. For example, I once knew a young nonspeaking man who'd recently left an institution. His way of gaining attention was to hit the person he was trying to engage with across the back with a stiff, extended arm. Because he was strong and often had the advantage of surprise, this approach often resulted in shock, pain, and distress for the receiver—not a good thing. Over time, we were able to help him find other ways to get our attention, like shoulder tapping. I'd like to tell you that this strategy was unilaterally effective, but I'd be lying. The truth is that he found the reactions he got from others really funny, so sometimes going for the startled reaction was difficult for him to resist. However, that doesn't take away from the point that assisting someone to learn alternative methods to engage is much more effective (and kind) than escalating a cascade of punitive responses.

Ignoring can be misused and can be used well. Does this sound like I've just contradicted myself? Not at all. For example, sometimes just being present and alongside someone who is upset without trying to mould or change them can be the best thing we can do. Not remarking on someone's unusual behaviour is a courtesy we routinely offer our friends but often seem to believe we cannot or should not do with the students we are teaching or the people we are supporting. It's as if we believe that if we don't immediately move in to correct someone's behaviour that means we are condoning it. We will, as it were, be letting them "get away with bad behaviour." We worry that unremarked and uncorrected behaviour will lead to an escalation. Once again, if we think of our own lives, it's easier to understand that this is likely untrue. Having a friend to sit with us during a difficult time without trying to change us or even trying to make things all better can help us find the resources to manage ourselves. It is important to note that letting a difficult exchange go unremarked is not the same as ignoring someone.

Helping someone to access alternative communication devices is not only often successful, it is essential. When communication is difficult, attempts to gain attention may reflect frustration about not being able to make ourselves understood. It is critically important for us to assist someone to find as many ways to communicate as possible, and it is equally critical for us to hone our ability to interpret unconventional ways of communication. The right to communicate should be seen as a fundamental human right.

4. Passive-Aggressive

When a person shuts down, this is sometimes misunderstood as passive aggression. In other words, the person is seen as deliberately provoking us by being indirect or stubbornly refusing to cooperate. Even if the lack of cooperation is deliberate, we must ask ourselves why someone would respond in this way. Is it because they see no other way of ensuring that at least some of their needs get met? Or that they are registering their distress in the only way they think is available to them?

It isn't just disabled people who acquire this negative and damaging designation. We are all vulnerable to labels like *passive-aggressive*. As some anonymous person once said, "Catch any of us on the wrong day, and you might see us engage in so-called challenging behaviour." I've often heard people describe coworkers and bosses as passive-aggressive, and it's never a positive attribution.

Just imagine for a moment that it's you who is on the receiving end of this label. Imagine that there's something you really object to going on in your workplace or between you and your partner or family members. Despite your concerns, you may believe that you don't have the power to do anything about the situation. In fact, you worry that voicing your objections might be a severely career-limiting move or lead to the loss of important relationships. So, given the context, it's plausible to imagine that you decide that your only option under the circumstances is to put your head down, quietly soldier on, and try to ignore the situation as best you can. However, your coworkers, bosses, or family members might easily misunderstand the change in your behaviour as passive aggression. If you've ever been subject to that label or another one like it, you were probably outraged, and you likely wanted to say to your accusers, "If you just knew what's happening to me, you'd understand my response."

5. High- or Low-Functioning

People sometimes ask what's wrong with using terms like *high-functioning* and *low-functioning*. These terms are used not only in the formal literature but also informally by therapists, educators, support workers, and parents. Many people assume that they are simply descriptive terms and that using them helps us understand something meaningful. But how meaningful are they and exactly what do they describe? And perhaps most importantly, what are the consequences of characterising people in this way?

First, it's important to notice that these terms don't give us much useful information. Does high-functioning imply that someone has greater capacity, whereas its opposite implies incapacity? Those are pretty broad categories. If this is what's implied, are they seen to be static and unchangeable traits located within the person, or are they simply arbitrary social constructs? I would argue the latter. For example, we know people who describe the strange existential experience of finally accessing a reliable communication system and suddenly finding themselves magically transformed from someone everyone thought was low-functioning to someone now considered high-functioning. In these instances, nothing changed except the perception of others. Capacity was always present, just not immediately accessible or noticeable to others. Autistic writer Ido Kadar (2012) describes the frustration of living in "a body with a mind of its own" (p. 17) and being continually underestimated by teachers and others simply because he was unable to reliably use speech or manage his fine motor functions. This frustration must never be underestimated. Kadar recounts agonizing and infuriating memories of professionals speaking over him and talking about him and his capacities (or the apparent lack thereof) right in front of him. However, once he was able to access a communication system that worked for him, those who had considered him low-functioning were forced to reconsider their judgements. Perhaps it would have been wise to reconsider those judgements long before they were proven wrong. As Anne Donnellan points out in her seminal journal article *The Criterion of the Least Dangerous Assumption* (1984), we must always presume competence.

Functioning labels are not only inaccurate, but what is worse is that they actively reproduce a social order that puts one group over another. We've often heard parents (and even some disabled people themselves) proudly assert that they or their sons or daughters are high-functioning. This appears to be an effort to create distance between themselves and those who are labelled lower functioning. Unfortunately, in this way, the credibility that people hope to achieve happens at the expense of others. It perpetuates a hierarchy that values one group over another.

While this designation seems to offer a sense of superiority, does it always grant the credibility people expect? I have personally experienced being discounted and dismissed when I disclose that I'm Autistic by people who say something like "Well, yes. But you are so *high functioning* that you can't possibly know anything about my child who is much lower functioning".

Many disabled adults describe the frustration of this experience. If we are able to communicate at all, regardless of how profoundly our disability affects us, parents and professionals claim that we do not represent the "severity" of the disability that their children/clients have, and therefore not only are our experiences irrelevant, we do not have the right to speak up. I would argue that this is a tried and true tactic used to silence many marginalized groups, and is accomplished through what we might call "the manipulation of similarities and differences". In other words, when you cannot speak and appear profoundly disabled, you are dismissed as merely "one of them" and not credible. When you speak up or otherwise distinguish yourself as competent, then you are dismissed as the exception and also deemed not credible.

In this way, the manipulation of similarity and difference renders some stories almost "untellable". We must ask ourselves, if no one who is able to speak is allowed to, and those that can't speak don't, whose story remains? Unfortunately, the story that remains is one that foregrounds the opinions of professionals and parents over the lived experience of disabled people. This is not only dangerous, it is actually tragic. It means that the opportunity for adults with disabilities to provide valuable insights and advice for the next generation of disabled children and their families is lost.

Every time we fall prey to the seduction of false binaries like high and low functioning, we perpetuate a dangerous idea of better and worse and a hierarchy in which some people are praised and others are punished or simply overlooked. Unfortunately, these clumsy attempts to understand difference by categorizing people into false binary descriptions have consequences that can be far-reaching and seriously damaging. Real decisions and actions flow from these labels. Although it is irritating for those considered high functioning to be discounted, for those labelled low-functioning, the result can be much more disastrous and include everything from punitive therapies and restrictive educational decisions to decisions about where a person should live and how much independence they can expect to have.

The Problem with all of these Labels

When descriptions like these are attached to anyone—ourselves or the people we teach or support—they are difficult to overcome. However, the consequences for non-disabled people are usually not as dire as they can be for those with disabilities. When non-disabled people are accused of being resistant, manipulative, passive-aggressive, or even doing things for attention, it doesn't usually have any long-term implications. However, for many disabled children and adults, these labels—both formal and informal—stick like Superglue and can result in files as big as coffee tables that follow them throughout their lives. The teachers, support workers, and others who read these files come away at best with a false idea of who the person is and at worst a sense of fear and dread that can lead them to respond punitively to almost anything the person does or says. Too often, the consequence of carrying this kind of reputation is a life spent in the confines of a variety of "behaviour plans."

When we use the language of dysfunction to describe someone, we're implying that "this is all you are." It implies that this is not only who you are in this moment, but this is forever who you are. The problem with words like *manipulation, resistance,* and *passive-aggressive,* and even the idea of doing things for attention, is that it's as if the entire person could be summed up and neatly described in this way. But it's worth wondering whether these words might be little more than a sophisticated form of name-calling, not a reasonable way to describe someone. Perhaps these words are simply the result of our frustration at dealing with a person who does things we don't understand and we don't always appreciate. It's fair enough to say we are frustrated, but to take the extra step of blame and name-calling is more than unkind; it can have dire and often devastating consequences.

People trying valiantly to manage within systems that often fail to take their needs and preferences into account are often simply trying to improve their lives in the only way they feel is available to them. It's often difficult for those of us who do not live within restrictive systems and are not subject to behaviour plans and other programs to understand how oppressive they can be. Many disabled people are denied much of the agency, independence, and respect that most of us take for granted. It's problematic if we presume that the people we are supporting have the same degree of control over their lives that we do. The sad fact is that for many, if not most, this is simply not true.

I have heard educators and support workers say, "But we do everything to make sure the person we're teaching/supporting is treated well and given lots of choices and autonomy, and they still continue to act out! We don't understand." It is critically important to remember that people had lives before they met us, and sometimes the people from their pasts were abusive. Trauma is the proverbial gift that keeps on giving. Dave Hingsburger argues that it is not an exaggeration to suggest that all disabled people have experienced trauma at some time or another, and many continue to experience it in their interactions with bullies on the street, in the schoolyard, and even in their classrooms and homes (Hingsburger, personal communication, 2018). Actions we take that we assume are benign may be interpreted by a person who has had previous experience with bullying and abuse as threatening and scary.

This discussion inevitably returns us to the issue of power. Nietzsche (1977) once noted that one of the perks of having power in a relationship is that the person with the most power gets to name things. In other words, if I have more power than you, and you act in a way that displeases me, I get to label your actions a behaviour problem. Take as an example how this dynamic works if you are a parent. Suppose you and your significant other are having an argument. It's likely you will call the disagreement a conflict. However, if your children talk back, argue with you, or act out, you are unlikely to call their actions "interpersonal conflict." Instead, you might refer to them as behaviour problems. In a relationship of equal power, it's unlikely that any of us would label our partners as having behaviour problems (unless we really want to escalate the situation), but it seems fair to label the kids that way. It's essentially a seniority issue and indirectly points to the power relationship. The same dynamic operates between teachers and their students and even support workers and the people they support. Whoever has the most (acknowledged or even unacknowledged) power in the relationship retains the privilege of defining the problem.

When we raise this issue with support staff, they sometimes protest, saying that they do not have, want or actively wield power over the people they support. It is important to remember that while you may not be on any kind of overt "power trip", the role itself implies a power differential that is difficult to overcome. Children in schools and individuals receiving support in service agencies are acutely aware of this difference in status. When we refuse to acknowledge this power difference, we are acting in a way that denies the privilege we have.

Language and Identity

The way we describe people is seldom lost on them. It can affect a sense of self in powerful, unexpected, and damaging ways. A heartbreaking illustration of how a negative self-image can be implanted in a person and how quickly it can occur comes from a story told to us by our colleagues and friends Rich Villa and Jacque Thousand. Several years ago Rich helped include Christine, a teenage girl with Down syndrome, into a regular high school. Christine participated fully and enthusiastically in all school activities and was on the cheerleading squad. She was so successful in the regular school that an opportunity was arranged for her to talk about her experiences at the annual Down Syndrome Congress conference.

Christine's first presentation was scheduled at the beginning of the conference, and she was her usual confident, funny, bossy self. A member of the audience interrupted to ask a question, and Christine responded by scolding them. "Be quiet," she said. "This is my workshop!" The audience roared with laughter. At the end of her session, she got a standing ovation, and word of Christine's self-assured panache spread through the conference like wildfire. Everyone wanted to be in her second workshop. The conference planner had to think fast, quickly switching rooms to accommodate a larger audience—a ballroom instead of the smaller breakout room Christine had initially been assigned. Even so, when it came time for her second presentation, there was standing room only, and people lined up in the hallway straining to hear.

In the hours between her first and second presentations, Christine attended a series of keynotes and workshops she thought might be interesting. The presenters were doctors, researchers, and special educators talking about their specific expertise with Down syndrome. In each session she heard people like herself described as low-functioning, sub-normal, unable to generalize skills, and socially immature. Presenters warned that many people with trisomy 21 were more vulnerable to Alzheimer disease than most other people (something that has been disproven). They discussed surgeries, heart issues, and speech abnormalities and listed all the limitations Down syndrome imposes on the lives of individuals and their families. The way in which Christine heard herself described in these sessions was demoralizing, disheartening, and painful.

When she arrived in the ballroom for her second presentation, it was as if she'd transformed into an entirely different person. She slowly climbed onto the stage of the packed ballroom and faced a supportive, smiling audience full of anticipation to hear what else this confident young woman might say. Christine walked up to the microphone with her head lowered and spoke in a quiet voice. "Hello, my name is Christine. I have Down syndrome, and I'm stupid."

Appalled by this development, Christine's parents and friends rushed to her and frantically coached her back to a more upbeat mood. She went on to talk about some of her high school experiences, but unfortunately she wasn't completely able to regain the confidence and spark of that first workshop.

Only a few short hours of listening to professionals describe her in medicalized and demeaning ways had done their damage. Just that fast, Christine had adopted a new and decidedly negative view of herself. In this way it could be said that an identity had been "implanted" in her from the outside in. She'd been robbed of her natural ebullience, optimism, and humour, and her sense of self and agency had been effectively replaced by a dysfunctional description that she'd quickly internalized and believed.

Hilde Lindemann Nelson (2001) calls the process that Christine went through "infiltrated consciousness" (p. xii) or "doxastic damage—the damage of distorting and poisoning people's self conceptions" (p. 106). In other words Christine took what she'd heard to heart and believed it. Nelson goes on to say that "a person's identity is damaged when she endorses, as part of her self-concept, a dominant group's dismissive or exploitative understanding of her group, and loses or fails to acquire a sense of herself as worthy of full moral respect" (p. xii). Identity, she contends, is a complicated mix of the way we see ourselves and the way we are seen by others. It is for this reason that those of us who hold the power to name things must be cautious of how we speak about - or to - those we support.

Stephen Madigan, a friend, colleague, and narrative therapist living in Vancouver, outlines four important questions we should ask ourselves before we take on and believe any description of a person. We have adapted them here.

What is the story being told? (Is it a story that could damage a person's sense of self or result in restrictions and sanctions being placed upon them?)

Whose story is it? (Is it the person's story, or is it our interpretation based on what we think we see?)

Who is telling the story? (Is the disabled person telling the story, or is it the professional version?)

With what authority? (Is it assumed that the professional assessment is the more accurate story?)

(Madigan, 2011, and personal communication)

An old African proverb says, "Until the lion has a history of its own, the tale of the hunt will always go to the hunter." If the stories that are given the most credibility are the stories that professionals tell, we are effectively taking the next dangerous step in saying we know people better than they know themselves. Too often the stories told by disabled people about their experiences are dismissed as merely anecdotal—one-off descriptions that are rendered irrelevant and therefore have little effect on policies and procedures. In our society we are enamoured with the idea that truth is contained only in empirical evidence. While no one is arguing against the rigorous use of the scientific method in understanding many important issues, it is often less than helpful in trying to understand individual experiences. Empiricism can become problematic when applied to human behaviour and can actually reinforce power dynamics, serve to silence dissident voices, and obscure disconfirming evidence.

The stories and the language we use to describe each other are much more important than we sometimes recognize. They have the capacity to influence real lives in profound and far-reaching ways. Language actually *does* things. It influences the way we think, the decisions we make, and the actions we take, and we should never take their power and influence for granted. The great Brazilian philosopher, educator, and activist Paulo Freire (1970) once noted that language is never neutral, and as Sara Cobb (2013) points out,

> "Stories matter. They have gravitas; they are grave. They have weight. They are concrete. They materialize policies, institutions, relationships, and identities that circulate locally and globally, anywhere and everywhere" (p.3).

CHAPTER 5

DO YOU KNOW WHERE OREGON IS?

Norm

I thought it was going to be another routine flight to a speaking engagement in Portland, Oregon. I had a stopover in Boston, so when the agent asked me where I wanted my bags sent, I absentmindedly said Boston rather than Portland. I realized my error at the departure gate and tried to correct the problem with the gate agent. Directing my baggage to the wrong destination proved to be a fortunate accident.

When I told the agent that I had mistakenly checked my bags to Boston and that they needed to be checked right through to Portland Oregon, he said, and it wasn't a question, "You mean Portland, Maine."

I corrected him. "No. I'm going to Portland, Oregon."

"But you have a ticket to Portland, Maine."

I immediately realized the problem. My travel agent had accidentally booked me to the wrong Portland. It was a simple oversight that I hoped could be easily fixed.

"Why are you going to Portland?" he asked.

I wasn't exactly sure why he needed to know this, but I told him anyway. "I'm speaking at a conference."

"What type of conference is it?" The agent was skeptical.

I began to see where this was interchange was headed, so I began using multisyllabic words. This is often helpful when I feel underestimated.

"It's an interdisciplinary conference on disability rights and inclusive education."

"Are you sure," he asked me, enunciating carefully, "that the conference isn't in Portland, Maine?"

"Yes, I'm sure it's in Oregon. I've been dialling the 503 area code for the last two months, and 503 is the area code for Oregon, not Maine."

And then, incredibly, he asked "Do you know where Oregon is?"

I held back the urge to confront him. It would, I realized, only complicate the situation. My goal was to get to Portland that evening, and it was already two thirty. I swallowed the implied insult.

"North of California, south of Washington State." I hoped my sarcasm wasn't too obvious. "Look," I went on, "I'm a professional speaker, and I'm giving a keynote speech at an education conference at nine o'clock tomorrow morning. I need you to change my ticket to Portland, Oregon."

Unbelievably, he wasn't done. "Do you have any letters or brochures about the conference?"

It was humiliating, but I showed him the correspondence and contract. Clearly this was the only way he'd believe me.

He sighed deeply. "The ticket is going to be more expensive."

My patience was quickly evaporating. I slammed three credit cards on the counter.

"Take your pick," I said, trying to control my irritation. "Visa, Diners Club, or American Express?"

He finally consulted his computer and told me that my only option was a three thirty flight to Chicago that connected to Portland, Oregon. The flight, of course, was at a different terminal, and I had to go back to the check-in counter to buy a new ticket.

I suspected that I'd likely have to repeat this interchange with the new agent at the check-in counter. Thinking ahead, I asked this agent to help carry my bags, knowing that the ticket agent would be more inclined to believe him than me.

We rushed to the check-in counter, where he explained the situation, dropped off my bags, and left. It was now two forty. I knew I'd need at least ten minutes to get to the other terminal, ten minutes for security, and five minutes to get to the gate. I could just manage.

However, my escape to the gate was undermined by the new agent. She had inch-long glossy fingernails and, despite my urging, plucked lazily at the computer keys, manicured forefinger by forefinger. It was now two fifty. With luck, I could make the end of the boarding process. I continued to glance pointedly at my watch. Unfortunately, she was oblivious to all of my nonverbal cues. Finally, she finished. Holding the ticket in the air beside her ear, she began giving me instructions in a loud, slow voice.

"OK. This is your new ticket. Put this ticket in your bag. Go out to the big glass door, and get on the bus with the big red number one in the window."

I interrupted, "I know how to get to terminal one. Just give me the ticket, please."

Undeterred, she continued. Detailed instructions for security were followed by step-by-step directions to the gate. I briefly considered trying to snatch the ticket out of her hand but concluded that if I missed, my credibility would be further minimized. This would undoubtedly lead to an even longer delay. She finally handed the ticket to me at three o'clock, and I managed to get to the gate by three thirty-five. Luckily, the flight was late boarding, so I made it, not exactly unscathed, to Oregon.

Norm and Emma: Is it Just Ignorance?

When we share these experiences with others, we are often told that these are not examples of prejudice against disabled people; they are instead the actions of well-intentioned but uninformed people. These people, we're told, mean well. They just don't know any better. But is this a correct interpretation?

There is a double standard regarding the prejudice directed against disabled people and the prejudice directed against other marginalized groups. If a person acts on the presumption that women are less intelligent or capable than men, this is seen as an expression of blatant sexism. Likewise, if a person acts on the presumption that people of colour are less intelligent or capable than white people, this is seen as an expression of outright racism. But if a person acts on the presumption that disabled people are less intelligent or capable than they are, this is seen as a lack of education.

Why are people seen as not knowing any better when they are disrespectful towards disabled people but are told they should know better when they are disrespectful toward women and people of colour?

We believe this double standard arises out of some confusion between sympathy and prejudice. It is largely assumed in our society that if we feel sympathy toward another person, we cannot, by definition, be prejudiced toward them. Sympathy precludes prejudice. In simple terms, being sympathetic means having nice and compassionate thoughts toward someone, whereas being prejudiced connotes having mean thoughts toward them.

When you have a disability, however, you find out very quickly that sympathy and prejudice are not mutually exclusive. In fact they often come wrapped together in the same insidious package. As an example, a friend told us that she received a sympathy card after giving birth to a beautiful daughter with Down syndrome. In the midst of her excitement and joy over having a new baby, she felt slapped in the face by her friend's card. The frustrating part of merging prejudice and sympathy is that it is almost impossible to confront the prejudice. Had she confronted her friend about the insulting nature of the card, her objection likely would have been dismissed. When people mean well, they generally don't question their actions. It seems that a prevalent belief is that intention trumps impact. In other words, if I mean well, then any negative impact my actions have on you are mitigated and become your problem. Unfortunately, benevolent people often suffer from an absence of self-doubt. Any objection to their intended benevolence is typically seen as ingratitude or deliberate misunderstanding.

It is this unconscious conflation of sympathy and prejudice that made those interchanges with the airline agents so difficult. Sympathy and benevolence, despite the best of intentions, can often be expressions of prejudice. However, for the purpose of this discussion, let us assume that the sympathy and benevolence are as innocuous as many believe them to be. What we find is that even with this constraint, it is possible to expose the airline agents' prejudice.

Ignorance, by definition, most often implies an absence of education or information. To assume that these airline agents were completely unaware would imply that they had no presumptions about disabled people at all. It would be describing them as empty vessels. However, if they'd been truly unaware (a cultural impossibility), then you might reasonably expect them to recognize Norm as a competent adult once he began speaking to them in a coherent manner.

However, this was clearly not the case. Despite an adult vocabulary and rational conversation, they persisted in treating him like an unaccompanied minor who required their guidance and supervision. Their attitudinal vessels weren't empty; they were full. So full, in fact, that there was no room for any alternative information.

The problem wasn't that the airline agents didn't know *what Norm was capable of*; the problem was that they firmly believed that he was *incapable*. The first is ignorance; the second is prejudice. They may have felt sorry for him; they may have been genuinely trying to help, but their sympathy and desire to help were completely unrelated to their underestimation. Sympathy, benevolence, and prejudice can coexist. They often do.

Being Polite

In the face of prejudice, we are often encouraged to be understanding and patient. Criticizing or becoming angry when people (perhaps unintentionally) insult disabled people is often seen as unjustified and even mean-spirited. We've often wondered why disabled people are encouraged to adopt the demeanour, if not the responsibility, of monks when everyone else is given the right to confront and question insult and underestimation.

When women or people of colour are confronted by bigoted comments or actions, their anger is not only seen as justified; it is seen as the necessary first step in changing the dialogue and foregrounding social justice. Encouraging members of these groups to be patient and understanding in the face of sexism and racism only perpetuates the bigotry. Yet when disabled people become angry, they are seen as maladjusted; the presumption is that they "have a chip on their shoulders" and are projecting their anger at being disabled onto non-disabled people. What should be understood as a political interchange is transformed into evidence of personal dysfunction.

At times feminists who challenge male patriarchy have been accused of projecting their anger about being women and their desire to be men onto the men that insult them. However, this Freudian idea of "penis envy" has become outdated, and most people don't believe it anymore. Yet the same claim is still seen as unquestionably legitimate when it is levelled against disabled people. All disabled people *must* want to be non-disabled. Even if the people who object to our anger acknowledge that that those airline agents probably carried prejudicial attitudes towards disabled people, they still often insist that we should refrain from directly confronting the prejudice. They claim that polite, non confrontational discussion and education is the most effective way to change erroneous perceptions. Unfortunately, history tells us unequivocally that this is seldom the case.

Adam Kahane, a renowned international mediator who worked extensively in the Truth and Reconciliation process in South Africa, spoke eloquently about the perils of politeness. In his book *Solving Tough Problems* (2004, 2007), Kahane wrote:

> Politeness is a way of not talking. When we are being polite, we say what we think we should say: "How are you?" "I'm fine." We do not say what we are really thinking because we are afraid of a social rupture: "How are you?" "I'm terrible." When we talk politely, we are following the party line, trying to fit in and so keep the social system whole and unchanged, even though the whole may be diseased or counterfeit... When somebody speaks personally, passionately, and from the heart, the conversation deepens.

> Politeness maintains the status quo… As long as the status quo is working, we can afford to remain polite. But when we see that the status quo is no longer working, we must speak up. (p.56)

Kahane's comments led us to realize that many of the people who urge us to be polite and non-confrontational are people who are probably afraid of conflict. They aren't necessarily encouraging us to avoid confrontation because confrontation isn't the best way to change perceptions; they are encouraging us to avoid confrontation because conflict makes them uncomfortable, and they wish to reduce their own anxiety.

Many people prefer to view prejudice towards disabled people as ignorance rather than bigotry, and suggest that the best response is education. However, the uncomfortable truth is that in many instances no amount of educational intervention is adequate to effect the necessary change in attitude. Most often, it simply engenders defensiveness or outright denial: "That's not what I meant!" Those who would have us endlessly turn the other cheek might do well to notice that the status quo is simply not working for disabled people.

With this understood, we were still left with the question of how to respond effectively to interchanges like the ones with the airline agents. Kahane is right: being polite isn't efficacious; it is naive at best and an abdication of responsibility at worst. Not to mention the fact that it accomplishes nothing. Perhaps one of the most perceptive and concise answers to the question of how to proceed effectively came from a university friend who was working his way through a master's degree in social and political thought by being a bouncer in a pub. During the day he attended classes and engaged in thoughtful and measured dialogue. However, later at night he could be seen putting disruptive patrons in half nelson holds and escorting them out of the pub. When asked about this apparent contradiction in his behaviour, he chuckled and said, "It's true that you can only foster insight through dialogue. But first you have to get their attention!"

We recently objected forcefully to an action taken by a prominent person—an action with potentially dire consequences for some members of the disability community. In the public discussion that followed, those of us making the objection were accused by one individual of violence. This accusation was perplexing since no threats were ever made. It seemed that our accuser believed that *any* form of criticism or disagreement could be categorized as damaging and counterproductive, even violent. Her argument reminded us of that old adage that many of us heard from our parents: "If you can't say something nice, don't say anything at all."

Unfortunately, as Kahane and our university friend so eloquently pointed out, saying nice things isn't always effective. It can result in a lack of necessary clarity and thus miss the mark entirely. In fact, in the instance above, our subsequent ability to have a fierce but respectful conversation with the person concerned resulted in a change of heart and a different action. But first that person had to know exactly what the problem was and why we objected so strongly.

Does this mean that we are advocating for wholesale rudeness or personal attacks? Of course not. Respect and clarity are not mutually exclusive. Confronting the status quo is not always a comfortable activity, but it's necessary, and it can be done well. This is what we try to do even though we acknowledge that there have been times when frustration and fatigue have caused us to lash out unproductively. There are also times where we have simply sighed and let an insult or slight pass because the energy it takes to deal with the situation just seems too much. Like many other disabled people, we get tired of the responsibility of continually being required to educate the public and take on and confront societal bigotry. However, while we understand that we are under no obligation to continually engage in the process of such education, we also recognize that our ability to step away from it is a luxury that disabled people can ill afford. We recognize that when we have the courage to speak out about injustice, we don't do it only for ourselves. We pave the way for the others who come behind us. Every time we note the absence of a ramp or the presence of some other barrier to our full inclusion, and every time we call out condescension and underestimation and bring it to the attention of someone who has the power to make a change—whether structural or attitudinal—we make the world just a little more accessible for the people who follow.

CHAPTER 6

IN SPITE OF MY DISABILITY

We wrote this article (Van der Klift & Kunc, 1995) long before Emma received her first diagnosis (ADD) in 1999 or her second (Autism) in 2017. Colleagues and friends have suggested that we amend it accordingly. This is our attempt to do so. We wish to acknowledge the earlier publication here with thanks to the Association for Supervision and Curriculum Development for permission to republish.

Norm: Emma and I were invited to speak at a conference on inclusive education. After one of our workshops, a young woman approached Emma. On the verge of tears, she explained that she had a ten-year-old son with cerebral palsy. "Until today," she said, "I never thought about the possibility of marriage or even a loving relationship for him with anybody but his family. Seeing you with Norm has changed all that. Thank you." Emma smiled and reached out to touch her shoulder.

Then came the kicker. "I think it's amazing that you love Norm in spite of his disability."

Amazing? In spite of my disability? I overheard and felt insulted, overwhelmed by the implications of her comment. One more time relegated to the subhuman. Not a real man.

I was filled with an overpowering urge to educate this woman—through retaliation. I tried to invoke my undergraduate training in rhetoric and debate as I approached her. A suitably caustic response was forming in my mind. Luckily, Emma saw my approach in time. She could tell by my increased spasticity that I'd overheard and was in revenge mode. She stepped deftly in front of me, blocked my path, and said to the woman, "I don't think you understand. I don't love Norm in spite of his disability, I love Norm. Period. His disability is part of him. I can't imagine who Norm would be without his disability." The woman walked away, obviously confused.

Emma turned to me and said, "Feel like a double scotch?" We left in search of the bar.

Emma: It's not actually that simple, and unfortunately the scotch doesn't really help. The truth is I never get used to it. A quick karate chop to the esophagus. A sharp smack on the psyche. There is so much that people don't see when they are under the influence of negative views about disability. They don't notice the reciprocity and mutual support inherent in our relationship. They seem to think I'm some kind of secular saint.

Norm: Needless to say, Emma saved me from weeks of self-recrimination and guilt, to say nothing about how I might have wounded that woman. To be fair to myself, I'm usually more understanding than I would have been that day. I know there is no excuse for retaliation, especially as vicious as mine was going to be. Nevertheless, the phrase *in spite of* reveals the difficulty this woman had seeing me as a real person. In her mind I still seemed to be a collection of abnormal speech patterns and involuntary movements. Trapped behind an opaque wall of cerebral palsy, it was probably impossible for me to correct that vision, let alone explore what we might have in common.

Situations like this happen all the time. Unwarranted assumptions and inferences get made about who I am as a person or what my life is like, and they are made solely on the basis of my disability. Many people, for example, assume that all people with cerebral palsy have a limited intellect. Therefore, when they meet me, they assume an intellectual disability. Some people think cerebral palsy is a disease, so they don't want to touch me in case they catch it. Still others see me as a charity case, someone to feel sorry for. All of these are problematic. When they assume I have a limited intellect, yes, they underestimate me, and that's a problem. But they are also saying something about how they view people with intellectual disabilities that makes it even harder to respond effectively. I have no interest in raising my hand to say, "Um, not me. My mind's just fine," because that effectively throws my brothers and sisters with intellectual disabilities under the proverbial bus. And likewise, when they see me as diseased, what does that say about people with other disabilities and illnesses? It gets messy and difficult to respond without a great deal of explanation—much of which doesn't appear to make much difference and only engenders defensiveness.

Emma: Assumptions and inferences. Polite words for prejudice and bigotry.

Norm: When people first meet me, they tend to see me as nine tenths disability, one tenth person. What they see as paramount are the things that mark me as "different"—the way I walk, speak, and move. The disability expands in their eyes, taking up more space than is warranted and thereby throwing a shadow over me and my life in the same way that a shadow on a sundial widens in the afternoon light. My disability is perceived as being more influential than it actually is.

Let me counter that view for just a moment and describe how I see myself. First, I'm a white man who grew up in Toronto, Canada. My father was Polish; my mother was English and Serbian. I have an older brother and sister, nieces, and nephews. Our family is Anglican, but I grew up in a predominantly Jewish neighbourhood. I did an undergraduate degree in humanities and a Master of Science degree in Family Therapy. I like sailing and used to compete in local and regional regattas. I'm married to Emma, and I live in New Westminster, British Columbia. Our children are grown up and have productive and interesting lives of their own. These days we live in an apartment in a wonderfully diverse neighbourhood where having a physical disability and using mobility devices doesn't stand out much. Emma and I have our own business as writers, speakers, and consultants. We operate an online training platform called Conversations that Matter. We share a passionate interest in social justice and conflict management. I enjoy computers, classical music, jazz, chess, and food. (We are unabashed foodies.) For many years I played the drums, although I have to admit, not particularly well. I have an uncanny ability to remember phone numbers and jokes. I also have cerebral palsy.

Emma: I have an affectionate recollection of Norm and our son Evan. In this remembered vignette, Evan is about five years old. The two of them are repairing the brass fireplace surround—an odd, rickety thing I moved from house to house for years simply because I liked its funny almost-art-deco shape. Unfortunately, in addition to its charm, it had a way of mysteriously losing its stabilizing screws and tiny nuts and bolts on a regular basis.

In this memory Norm is replacing the screws laboriously, but since fine-motor control is not his strong suit, it's a difficult task. "Would you help me, Evan?" he asks. After explaining what has to be done, he watches as Evan carefully, with his tiny fingers, tightens the nuts on each of the bolts.

"I know why you need me," Evan says proudly, "it's 'cause you're wiggly, right?"

"That's right, Evan. I'm wiggly." It's an unusual though apt description of cerebral palsy.

"I'm not wiggly," Evan goes on, "but I'm not too strong yet, either. You're wiggly, but you're strong. You can pick up big, heavy things." He walks away, musing about this apparent paradox.

Norm: Cerebral palsy is a small part of who I am and what my life is about. I've become so accustomed to making daily accommodations for my disability that I often forget I have one. When it does come into my awareness, I simply see it as part of my life. I honestly don't think about my disability that much. This doesn't mean that there aren't very real frustrations involved in navigating daily living tasks. It also does not in any way take away from the very real challenges that disabled people - including me - face on a daily basis, but it does point out that an obsessive focus on what I can't do limits me in more ways than the actual disability ever does.

The "in spite of" comment not only implied an exaggerated view of my disability, it also presumed a deficiency within me. The inferences people make about my disability reveal more about their stereotypical views about the *idea of disability* than about the limitations of disability itself. It seemed that, for this woman, I was simply a defective adult, a grown-up version of her defective child. I was abnormal, deserving of kindness and sympathy yet still fundamentally "different." Slightly beneath her words, the unspoken insult was clear. Why would anyone marry a man with a disability? He's ugly, he's broken, and he's not quite fully human. What could he possibly offer anyone? He'd be a burden. And if I were married to him, would others think that I couldn't do any better?

Emma: When I tell people this story, or one of hundreds like it that centre around the deliberate or accidental insensitivity of non-disabled people, I am both amused and distressed at the reactions I get. "You have to understand," they say. I always know what's coming when I hear that phrase. I usually want to sigh when I hear it. Sometimes "understanding" is very tiring, especially when you "have to." "She didn't mean it," they go on. "She just doesn't know any better. In fact, she does it to everyone."

It's true. I actually do know that lots of people who do or say silly things don't mean to be offensive. I understand that people are often just trying to be nice, or helpful, and operate out of a set of assumptions based in myth, misinformation, or lack of information. And I also know that unfortunately some people really do treat almost everyone (with the possible exception of those they perceive as more powerful— and that's a story unto itself) with condescension and a lack of respect.

I sometimes wonder if the people who listen to my stories think I don't know these things. Maybe that's why they feel that it's their personal responsibility to edit my experience and provide me with a more "balanced" interpretation of events.

Have I lost my perspective or become unkind? I hope not. I do my share of embarrassingly ignorant things. Most of the stories I tell are not without humour and perspective. I try not to blame people or fall prey to evil oppressor/victim stereotypes. So why the knee-jerk reaction? How come the ten-minute sermons I routinely get reminding me to offer up the other cheek?

It occurs to me that there's more going on here than meets the eye. There's a message underneath the message. When people ask me to understand the ignorance and prejudice of others and swallow my pain, they're asking me to be quiet. They're saying, "It's not really like that. You're imagining things. You're overreacting. You're paranoid."

I guess I can't accept that it's OK for people to continue not to know any better. Silence and compulsive understanding never did much to challenge or change the status quo.

There are also times when I am encouraged to take another approach: the one we discussed in the last chapter. I'm told I should take the opportunity to educate people. Besides being a tiring enterprise, there is another problem with this approach. Many people assume that those who don't know any better are empty vessels into which new information can be poured, rectifying the situation efficiently once and for all. Unfortunately, as we noted earlier, people are not empty vessels. What is assumed as simple ignorance is often evidence that the vessel is already full of stereotypes and biases. These are not as easily corrected as we might hope.

Norm: I'm sometimes asked, "You've accomplished so much in your life with a disability; have you ever wondered where you would have been if you hadn't had cerebral palsy?" The answer is obvious. I'd be a drummer in a blues band. I work on social justice because I can't do triplets on a ride cymbal.

An overstatement, obviously, yet it's truthful enough to engender a moment of existential reflection. Would I have followed a life of speaking and writing about human rights issues if the world of musical composition and performance was open to me? I honestly don't know. I do know that, given a choice and knowing what I know now, I would choose to live with cerebral palsy. This statement invariably evokes bewilderment and skepticism among non-disabled people. They are firmly convinced that I would be better off—and hence, prefer - to live a non-disabled life. What they fail to understand is that cerebral palsy is an integral part of who I am. My identity is the product of my history. My history is that of a person with cerebral palsy. If I didn't have cerebral palsy, I wouldn't be me; I'd be someone else. Frankly, I like who I am. I like my history. I like my life. I'm not sure I'd sacrifice who I am for the sake of normal movement and speech.

Many people assume that living with cerebral palsy means that I am endlessly confronted by my body's limitations. Actually, this is not my experience. Having cerebral palsy means living a life in which innovation, improvisation, creativity, and lateral thinking are essential. In practical terms, it means knowing which cup fits snugly into the sink drain and doesn't tip over when I pour coffee. For a long time, when I was walking, it meant finding the same challenge and enjoyment in finding my balance on an icy sidewalk that my friends found mastering Tai Chi. These days it means finding the most accessible parts of the street—the curb cuts that don't collect water and the places where wheelchairs and scooters most easily move. It means being ever conscious of the number of drinking straws in my possession in the same way that a smoker is always aware of the remaining number of cigarettes. It means paying attention to breathing and articulation, like a jazz singer crafting a phrase. It means bracing my wrist on the table before I grasp a glass of beer or a cup of coffee in the same way that Emma braces her left hand when she threads a needle. As far as I know, Emma does not long to be a brain surgeon every time the eye of the needle eludes her thread.

Emma: When we first wrote this piece, I loudly asserted that I didn't have a disability. And it remains true that I do not have a physical disability. What we weren't talking about at that time was something that we both recognized but hadn't yet put a name to. There were parts of our lives and relationship that were puzzling, and in the process of trying to understand those things, I acquired an ADD diagnosis and later an Autism diagnosis. Surprising to many people is that this was not negative. In fact, it has been tremendously helpful for both of us—an "aha" moment that explained and put much of my life and our life together into perspective. Receiving a diagnosis and connecting with other Autistic people has helped us engage in thinking and rethinking our relationship and how we work together.

Years ago, when we first discussed this issue, we talked about the need to negotiate both a personal and a professional relationship, and how this has presented us with some interesting dilemmas. This is still true. Who does what? What's a fair division of labour? Even back then, before I realized that I'm Autistic, we understood that conventional solutions to the fairness dilemma just didn't seem to work for us. We knew we had to reinvent the rules of reciprocity, and that also remains true. We continue to live our lives like street theatre; we're always improvising. We change the rules or make up new ones as we go.

For example, cooking is difficult for Norm. It isn't that he can't, but it requires an inordinate amount of effort, planning, balance, and innovation. At the right time, cooking can be a challenge, an interesting problem to solve. Mostly it's arduous and time consuming. On the other hand, I love to cook. It's cathartic, creative, and different enough from what I do for a living to provide me with a much-needed reprieve. It's also my passion. So I cook. I also clean (more or less). Norm does the lion's share of grocery shopping now that he has a scooter. He takes care of office and travel trivia and returns more calls than I do, since phone calls are not easy for me. He has an inexplicable passion for excel spreadsheets and has created intricate bookkeeping formulas that have allowed him to do all of our monthly and yearly bookkeeping in an amazingly short time. These are things I have no talent for, let alone interest in.

Sometimes our roles appear deceptively traditional and gender-specific; sometimes they don't. For example, I read a lot. Norm reads less. I'm primarily a divergent thinker; he's more convergent. I become overwhelmed by the sheer volume of what I've read; Norm has an incredible ability to create coherence out of chaos. (Example? We once had an argument over the telephone when we were in different cities. The next day Norm called me back and said "Honey? I don't want you to take this the wrong way, but I created a matrix to explain our disagreement". The worst part? He was actually right!)

Rather than undertaking lifelong remediation with each other, we use our differences in complementary ways. I still can't believe that a valuable part of our work together involves the luxury of reading! I read and highlight. Norm synthesizes. We both write. Our work is stronger. We're happier. Our strengths are utilized, and our weaknesses seem more irrelevant. Interestingly, our continued collaboration has helped me to become more organized, and Norm is reading more.

In the quest to figure out what equality means, many of us confuse it with symmetry. The commonly accepted definition of *fair* seems to be a tidy thwack down the middle of everything. It's as if we believe that equity can be mandated, maintained, and meted out by an exacting and humourless accountant. We've taken a longer view. We know it isn't about treating people the same, ending up with a carefully balanced sheet at the end of each day. It's about quality of life, negotiation, interdependence, and long-term relationships. We've learned that giving means contributing what you can where you can, without obsessing about what you don't have or can't do. We know that what we get back is often unexpected, generous, and complementary. It creates a different kind of climate. Life is less structured and more fun. Imagination, flexibility, and humour are a bigger part of our lives, things few of us feel we have enough of.

Would I have learned these things if Norm weren't physically disabled? Would I have even figured out that I'm Autistic? And if I had figured it out, would I have developed the sense of pride that I've learned from him and our other disabled friends? I'd like to think so, but I'm not sure. Working on the pragmatic level, solving problems that relate to physical differences has helped both of us learn skills we can translate and use on a more conceptual level. It's not just about how to manage daily life with a disability. It's bigger than that. It's a whole new way of thinking about how we orchestrate our relationships and live our lives.

One-answer thinking seldom works for us, and I don't think it works for a lot of disabled people. So we've learned to look for multiple alternatives to the usual ways of getting things done. As a result, when solutions can't be found with conventional and jaded modalities, we're remembering to look for different ones. Even if the old answers fit, we're more inclined to wonder if those are the solutions we really need or just the ones we're used to. We are looking for wider spaces and new models large enough to hold us, and synergistic and complementary enough to sustain us. We are always reshaping and reinterpreting our lives. I wouldn't have it any other way.

Postscript

We have long ago embraced the notion that life is long and contribution is fluid and complex. As we age, we recognize that our experience adapting to disability has uniquely prepared us for any new adaptations we might need to make to support each other going forward. For example, I (Emma) broke my patella in four pieces recently. Needless to say, the break and the subsequent surgeries compromised my ability to accomplish a lot of what I usually do. Without missing a beat, Norm and I stepped into innovation mode and together figured out how we could accomplish the things that needed to be done in our daily lives. Although parts of this innovation process were undeniably difficult and frustrating, just as many were satisfying and even hilarious. (Example? Watching Norm figure out how to put the duvet into the duvet cover). After this incident we believe even more strongly than before that innovation delivers what rehabilitation promises.

CHAPTER 7

WE DON'T KNOW WHAT
WE'RE HANDING YOU

This article is reprinted from our website and is almost twenty-five years old. We thought it might be worth recycling since the issues it addresses continue to arise, and in the context of an increasing trend worldwide to endorse and legalize the use of assisted dying and euthanasia, including the relatively recent Canadian decision, we felt it was particularly relevant. The criterion for who should be eligible for physician-assisted suicide threatens to creep in ever more dangerous directions with every passing year, especially as it relates to disabled people. For example, here in Canada we are once again before the courts with proponents of assisted suicide petitioning the court to expand the criteria to include not only those with terminal illnesses, but those with mental illness and/or disability. Canada currently has the most liberal laws of any country in the world, and even the supposed safe-guards we have in place are eroding quickly.

Emma

Last week we received word that my husband has been nominated for an honorary doctorate. I caught myself wondering for a brief moment what the physician who attended his birth more than forty years ago might have had to say about this. If this momentary musing seems confusingly unrelated to the event, I assure you it is not. Let me explain. In some ways, one event is about potential; the other is about its realization. At both events you might expect to hear words of congratulation. Certainly, at least in some circles, the honorary doctorate generates all kinds of it. However, that was not the case for Norm more than forty years ago. In fact, at the time of his birth, the doctor had few words of congratulation, little of the expected happy small talk. Potential wasn't discussed. Instead, Norm's doctor told his parents, "We don't know what we're handing you."

That line used to infuriate me, probably because the doctor used the dehumanizing *what* as opposed to the more accurate *who*. While I still take exception to that word, it seems to me now that the most important part of the sentence might in fact be contained in the first three words. "We don't know" he said. It's an unusual admission for a doctor, and in the light of recent events, I've come to wonder if Norm might not owe his life to it.

Here's why. In direct contrast to Norm's family doctor, Peter Singer, an American bioethicist, seems to think he pretty much does know what's being handed to parents at the point of birth. In his controversial pro-euthanasia book, *Rethinking Life and Death: The Collapse of Our Traditional Ethics* (1994), Singer advocates the infanticide of babies with what he calls "clouded prospects"—either at birth or during the first twenty-eight days of life. Later, just in case the "prospects" are a little too difficult to gauge that early on, he hedges his bets by speculating that this period might even extend to include the first five years of life.

Exactly what is a "clouded prospect," according to Singer? Reading further, we realize that he's not just talking about children who may not survive birth, the first month, or the subsequent five years due to catastrophic disabilities. Initially at least, he's referring to infants with Down syndrome. But he doesn't limit himself. We are led to conclude that the term *clouded prospectus* a nauseating euphemism for disability.

Although Norm's doctor wisely admitted his inability to make predictions about the future with any accuracy, it's clear that Norm wasn't considered a very viable specimen at birth. For one thing, although he was a big baby, the damage done to his brain by the forceps used to deliver him suppressed the two reflexes most critical for infant survival, crying and sucking. For the first few months of his life his mother and grandmother had to feed him with an eyedropper and watch him with a level of vigilance that the parents of babies who are able to communicate their needs or distress through crying never have to consider. It was also increasingly obvious that he would have significant motor impairments. It was unclear what effect, if any, had been made on his cognitive abilities. The official diagnosis? Cerebral palsy of uncertain severity. All in all, a "clouded" prognosis. A good candidate for Singer's approach? Probably.

Too many of our friends with intellectual, developmental, or physical disabilities tell stories about doctors and other professionals who, like Singer, thought they could predict for the long-term. Many of these physicians and other professionals went on to paint sensationalistic worst-case scenario pictures for the still-shocked and uninformed parents during the vulnerable moments directly following the birth of their disabled children. Often parents described feeling pressured into decisions they later regretted on the basis of these supposedly credible future portraits. After all, these were doctors. These were experts. They should know what's possible and what the best course of action is, shouldn't they?

In fact, it is important to acknowledge that there are countless individuals with disabilities who are living testimony to the fact that doctors and professionals do not know and did not accurately predict their potential. Most doctors, when pushed on the subject, will acknowledge that they are seldom able to predict time of death accurately for any patient, and many will admit that they have been shocked by some patients' longevity. This, of course, doesn't even begin to acknowledge other issues like whether a disabled child will be able to walk, or talk, or go to school, or have a good quality of life. A documentary on CBC's *The Passionate Eye* (2019) showed a child born with only a very small amount of brain matter go on to increase his brain size and relate with his world normally and almost on schedule with other children of his age. What this tells us is that it is not possible to predict an outcome, and we shouldn't try.

While scores of disabled people are still subjected to problematic and sometimes downright cruel remedial treatments that include incarceration in institutions, segregation, unneeded surgeries, and painful physical and behavioural therapy programs, the legal options presented to parents do not currently include infanticide. However, if so-called ethicists like Singer get their way, that could all change. It's appalling enough to know that Singer (who incidentally wrote the chapter on medical ethics for *Encyclopedia Britannica*) is out there advocating infanticide. Unfortunately, we also know he's not alone in his opinions. For example, in the Netherlands, a country with widespread euthanasia, assisted suicide, and mercy killing, Singer's colleagues are busy petitioning the Supreme Court for the right to legalize infanticide.

It's open season on children with disabilities. When a mother who drowns her six-year-old in the bathtub because he was Autistic claims a mental breakdown, she gets two years of probation in a halfway house, and then the Autism Society of Canada responds by hiring her to become its fund-raiser! When Robert Latimer is charged and convicted in the death of his twelve-year-old disabled daughter, Tracy, the public won't rest until the appeal process renders him blameless and offers him a pardon. He is a gruesome folk hero. The Appleby family in Kentucky pleaded undying (pardon the black pun) "love and caring" for their intellectually disabled daughter and sister; after they lovingly and caringly facilitated her death by neglect and starvation in a back room of the family home!

The value our society places on disabled people is shockingly clear. Faced with a growing number of child murders perpetrated by parents upon their disabled offspring, the public seems unable to respond with the clarity reserved for the parents who murder their nondisabled children. As a society, we seem both unable and unwilling to decide the morality of this issue. In fact, the public begins to look suspiciously like the proverbial deer caught in the headlights—stunned moral relativists unable to mouth anything better than weak platitudes about not being able to judge what goes on in someone else's family and the effects of overwhelming stress on the parents of children with disabilities. Words like *mercy, compassion, caring,* and *love* are readily bandied about in connection with these deaths and met with noises of sympathy and support. Sympathy and support for the murdering parent, that is. Not for the dead child.

For Norm, as for many individuals with disabilities, the road from birth to the present has been circuitous and at times difficult. However, if you ask him to describe the difficulties he's faced, he'll tell you that few of them have to do with the physical limitations of disability. While those limitations do exist, the most painful elements of his life have to do with the attitudes and assumptions of non-disabled people. To sum it up more succinctly, bigotry and prejudice are the primary problems. But even if he'd had the ability to predict these potential problems at birth, would he really have wanted to be spared them? He emphatically says he would not. Spare us instead from the kind of empathy that believes it is walking in another person's moccasins while in fact it is reacting to a barely submerged set of prejudices, faulty assumptions, and unfounded inferences about the quality of life possible for someone with a disability. Spare us instead from the lethal benevolence of those who would seek to alleviate suffering or even the appearance or possibility of future suffering with a final solution.

Unfortunately, we the public are guilty of more than mere sloppy thinking. To the extent that we continue to accept arguments of mitigation for the murderers of our disabled citizens, we become complicit in these and every subsequent so-called mercy killing or infanticide. When we mistake homicide for care and compassion, we help to create a climate where these and other atrocities become possible. Don't forget that the Action T4 program, which facilitated the murder of 200,000 Germans with disabilities during World War II, was precipitated by the "mercy killing" of a disabled child by his father, a German farmer.

So, harking back to Norm's inauspicious birth, and viewing it in the context of his life since then, it seems fitting to ask: Who could have predicted? Who is presumptuous enough to believe they can look ahead and make final life and death pronouncements about anyone's future quality of life? The honest doctor—or parent, for that matter—is obliged to say he or she doesn't know who that infant will become or what will constitute a meaningful life for that individual. We cannot make decisions like these for others, unthinkingly based on societal prejudices and beliefs about disability that continue to lurk under a misleading overlay of compassion and empathy. We must ask ourselves: Is it really better to kill the baby than challenge the society? Better admit, then, that we kill our humanity in the process.

Today, while Norm and I sit on our sailboat and toast each other and our wonderful life with a glass of not terribly expensive but pretty nice wine, let doctors, professionals, parents, and caregivers hear the resonance of that toast: "To life!"*

- Please note that this is not an argument in support of anti-abortion. Both of us are committed to choice. Our concerns are with selective abortion based on disability as an expression of eugenics and discrimination.

PART 2

INCLUSION

CHAPTER 8

THE NEED TO BELONG: REDISCOVERING MASLOW'S HIERARCHY OF NEEDS

Originally published in: Villa, R., Thousand, J., Stainback, W. & Stainback, S. Restructuring for Caring & Effective Education. Baltimore: Paul Brookes, 1992.

By Norman Kunc and amended in 2019 by Emma Van der Klift and Norman Kunc

Newtonian principles of physics were regarded as true until Einstein demonstrated that they didn't provide an adequate explanation of the laws of nature. Similarly, Freudian analysts believed that a woman's accusation of being sexually abused by her father (or others) was a neurotic fantasy stemming from something they called an "Electra complex." It's only recently that therapists have come to understand that women were accurate in their accounts of being abused. In every field of knowledge, anomalies such as these arise and call current practices and "paradigms" (i.e. world views) into question and necessitate the creation of new paradigms and related practices. It is precisely through this process that a new body of knowledge emerges. Over the past several decades, such a process has taken place in the field of special education. Anomalies have arisen that seriously call into question the validity of segregating students with specific physical, intellectual, or emotional needs. Moreover, these anomalies demand that new paradigms be created and embraced.

The Special Education Paradigm: Skills as Prerequisite to Inclusion

In the United States, P.L. 94-142, the Education for All Handicapped Children Act of 1975 was initially seen as a meaningful step toward including children with physical, intellectual, and other disabilities within regular classrooms. However, this legislation and its embedded concept of least restrictive environment (LRE) still gave credence to the continued existence of segregated, self-contained classrooms. Lip service was given to the idea that students would be integrated as much as possible, but the underlying paradigm supporting the maintenance of something called "the continuum of services" still suggested that students with severe or even moderate impairments would be best served in segregated settings. The rationale for this was simple; students needed to learn and demonstrate basic skills (staying quiet in class, using the washroom independently) before they could be allowed to enter regular classrooms. This educational paradigm can be represented as follows:

STUDENT --> skills --> regular classroom

This continues to be the foundation for the pervasive practice of placing students with moderate or severe disabilities in segregated, self-contained classrooms or programs. The curricular premise of these programs is that basic skills instruction needs to take place before disabled students are deemed "ready" to transition to inclusive settings. Some students, viewed in this way, are seen as unlikely to ever meet the criterion of "ready", and as a result, segregated classrooms are often still seen as a necessary educational option that must be maintained to meet the needs of "some" students – those who may never learn the appropriate skills or behaviours. These practices are also part of the way in which human service organizations often provide services to adults with disabilities. Segregated living situations, employment readiness programs, day and lifeskills programs are based on a similar paradigm.

Anomalies in the Segregation Paradigm: Lack of Progress

This continuing belief in the need for segregation has created a situation in which students with intensive physical, intellectual, developmental or emotional disabilities enter the school system at the age of 5 or 6 and are immediately placed in self-contained classrooms or programs in which life skills, age-appropriate behaviour, and social interaction with other students are the primary goals. It is common for these students to stay in the school system for 15-18 years and despite the commitment of hundreds of thousands of dollars and the best efforts of their teachers, many fail to master the requisite life skills or emulate what is considered appropriate behaviour and remain socially isolated throughout their school years. These students are seen to have not progressed at a rate that allows for a successful transition into community life (Lipsky & Gartner, 1989., Stainback, Stainback, & Forest, 1989., Wagner, 1989). This often consigns these students to lives of limited opportunity as they transition to adulthood.

Although teachers and teaching assistants may be fully committed to helping students acquire basic skills, many of these students seem puzzlingly disinterested, unwilling, or incapable of learning what they're being taught. Even more distressing, those who do master certain skills often fail to retain them or cannot replicate them in situations outside the classroom. For example, a student taught to make a bed in the segregated setting may prove unable to generalize that learning enough to master making a bed at home. As a result of what is perceived as an inability to learn, many "graduates" of self-contained classrooms enter directly into sheltered workshops or segregated prevocational training programs where they must continue to practice the same basic life skills they were taught at school – sometimes for decades. The sad result is that many people with disabilities, deemed unable to make a successful transition into community life, spend their years continuously preparing for a life in the future. In this way, they are modern versions of Sisyphus pushing the proverbial rock up the hill only to see it roll back down again. It is not uncommon to see 65 year old adults still attending employment "readiness" programs.

Most often the lack of progress is blamed on the student. They are seen to have such severe disabilities that they are incapable of learning or generalizing what is being taught. However, over the years we are finding that this notion is losing credibility. Increasingly, we are questioning the validity of de-contextualized learning. For example, teaching someone to make a bed that isn't theirs in the resource room at 1 o'clock in the afternoon is a ridiculous premise. In addition, research and experience show that students in segregated programs *are* learning, but the problem is that they aren't necessarily learning what we are trying to teach them. For example, take five students who exhibit one unusual characteristic each and put them together, and soon you will have five students exhibiting five unusual behaviours. This tells us that indeed these students are capable of learning – just perhaps not what we are intending them to learn.

We have seen growing documentation of students who seemed incapable of learning appropriate behaviour and skills in segregated settings who go on to achieve these seemingly unattainable goals once included into regular classrooms and community settings. The fact that people are learning much more in inclusive settings should cause us to question the paradigm of segregation. It seems plausible, given these findings, to suggest that the adherence to current paradigms within special education and adult services has resulted in the creation and maintenance of what might be called "low-expectation immersion" scenarios. Why should it surprise us that students immersed in an environment where little is expected of them go on to live down to these low expectations? It is yet another example of the self-fulfilling prophecy.

A far more reasonable explanation for the lack of progress than the severity of a disability has to do with motivation. After all, there are very few, if any, rewards or payoffs for learning new activities in segregated environments. In schools, students don't *pass* low-expectation immersion and exit to general education: they can't even *fail* it. In fact, they are sometimes even punished for being successful. A mindless adherence to developmental milestones often results in enforced failure for some students. For example, I have seen situations where students have been required to stack blocks in an effort to improve fine motor control. When the students successfully complete this task, they are *rewarded* by being given smaller blocks. With every set of smaller blocks, the task becomes more difficult until it is entirely beyond their capability. We ask children and adults to spend their days doing tasks that are meaningless, difficult and discouraging, and then we wonder why so little learning takes place or why they object to our demands through what is then deemed "inappropriate" or "challenging" behaviour.

Maslow's Hierarchy of Needs:
A Paradigm for Motivating Learning

To summarize, segregated programs and classrooms have failed to teach students the social or academic skills they need to succeed. Environments where individuals are required to endlessly learn, practice and re-learn meaningless tasks have not proved successful in preparing them for community life. This understanding challenges the validity of segregation as an educational practice and requires us to consider adopting new ways of thinking -- paradigms that take into account what motivates a person – any person – to engage and want to learn.

Educators and support staff have a choice. We can either continue to blame the lack of progress in segregated environments on the severity of a particular disability, or we can have the courage and integrity to seriously question whether there is, in fact, a more effective way to prepare students with disabilities for life in the community after graduation, and to provide more relevant and inclusive support throughout their lifespan.

In the 1980s, when I (Norm) first started thinking seriously about these issues, it was becoming increasingly apparent that a different paradigm was needed. We recognized that practices of the past were founded on an old set of beliefs. As mentioned above, segregated practices were founded on the notion that before an individual could be included in a regular environment they would need to learn the skills that would help them to be successful. However, with the advent of inclusive education and a move to more community-based support models, more and more educators and support organizations have questioned these ideas and recognized that perhaps we need to reverse this order. What is needed instead is to abandon the emphasis on skills as a prerequisite and place the person in a regular setting (with appropriate support) with the assumption that they will learn what they need to know in an environment where those skills actually make sense. The rationale is that the urge to belong, to be "one of the kids" or part of the larger community provides the motivation to learn new skills, a motivation noticeably absent in segregated situations. Consider the following story.

> Many years ago I was involved with a group of people assisting disabled students to access inclusive classrooms in their neighbourhood schools. One of the young people we were working with – let's call her Mary – was a student transitioning from a segregated school into a regular 9th grade classroom in a local Junior High School. Mary had remained segregated because she'd been deemed too disabled for consideration in a regular school – primarily because she had not yet mastered the skill of using the washroom independently. Initially, her educational assistant would try to take her to the accessible washroom. Mary rebelled. She wanted to go to the regular girl's washroom. Once in the girl's washroom, she headed directly into the stall. At that point it was easy to help Mary learn to use the washroom independently. Much to the amazement of

the inclusion team and Mary's teachers, within a month of attending her neighbourhood school, Mary was able to use the washroom independently. Not only had she learned this skill, but she'd learned to wash her hands and then brush her hair after leaving the stall. Why? The answer isn't that complicated. Because that's what the other girls were doing, and Mary wanted to belong.

Of course Mary (and her teachers) required support in making this transition successful. However, support is only part of the reason Mary was able to learn not just this skill, but many others. All people learn best when they are in environments where they feel valued and they feel that they belong. The endless readiness programs Mary had experienced told her that she wasn't good enough to belong (don't let anyone tell you that disabled children and adults don't understand that this is why they have been exiled), so once she was in the regular classroom her desire to fit in was the catalyst for all kinds of learning. The new paradigm illustrated by this story can be visually represented as follows:

**STUDENT ==> regular classroom ==> skills
(with support)**

This paradigm, with its recognition of the importance of belonging, is not a new concept introduced by the inclusive education and community living movement. In 1970, Abraham Maslow pointed out that belonging is an essential human need that has to be met before it is possible to achieve a sense of self- worth.

Maslow divided and prioritized human needs into five "levels." Individuals, he claimed, do not necessarily seek the satisfaction of a need at one level until the previous "level of need" is met. The five levels of need identified by Maslow were Physiological, Safety/Security, Belonging/Social Affiliation, Self-Esteem, and Self-Actualization. They are represented as a pyramid in Figure 1.

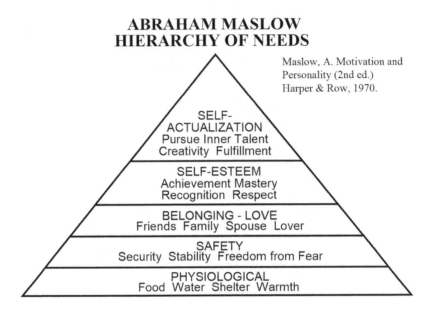

Figure 1. Maslow's hierarchy of human needs. (From Maslow, A. (1970}. Motivation and personality (2nd ed.). New York: Harper & Row; reprinted by permission of Harper Collins Publishers.)

Maslow maintained that our most basic need is for physiological survival: shelter, warmth, food, drink, and so on. Once these physiological needs are met, individuals are able to address the need for safety and security, including freedom from danger and absence of threat. Once safety has been assured, the need for belonging or love, which is usually found within families, friendships, membership in associations, and within the larger community then become a priority. Maslow went on to stress that only when we are anchored in a sense of belonging do we develop self-esteem. He claimed that the need for self-esteem can be met through mastery or achievement or through gaining respect and recognition from others. Once the need for self-esteem has been met, we will then develop a new restlessness and the urge to pursue our unique gifts or talents. As Maslow stated, "A musician must make music, an artist must paint, a poet must write, if he [sic] is to be at ultimate peace with himself. What a man can be, he must be. He must be true to his own nature" (p. 48). Maslow referred to this final level of need as "Self-Actualization."

The majority of us would likely agree that it is important for a person to develop a sense of self-worth and confidence. However, in our society, especially in the field of education and human services, it has been assumed that a sense of self-worth is best developed through personal achievement. However, what Maslow suggests is that self-worth can arise only when an individual is grounded in a sense of belonging and community. He made a powerful argument that belonging is one of the central pillars missing from our educational structure, and I would argue, also from the service system many people access after leaving school:

> If both the physiological and the safety needs are fairly well gratified, there will emerge the love and affection and belongingness needs.... Now the person will feel keenly, as never before, the absence of friends, or a sweetheart, or a wife, or children. He will hunger for affectionate relations with people in general, namely, for a place in his group or family, and he will strive with great intensity to achieve this goal....he will feel sharply the pangs of loneliness, of ostracism, of rejection of friendlessness, of rootlessness.

> We have very little scientific information about the belongingness need, although this is a common theme in novels, autobiographies, poems and plays and also in the newer sociological literature. From these we know in a general way the destructive effects on children of moving too often: of disorientation: of the general over-mobility that is forced by industrialization: of being without roots, or of despising one's roots, one's origins, one's group: of being torn from one's home and family, and friends and neighbours: of being a transient or a newcomer rather than a native. We still underplay the deep importance of the neighbourhood, of one's territory, of one's clan, of one's own "kind" one's class, one's gang, one's familiar working colleagues...

> I believe that the tremendous and rapid increase in...personal growth groups and intentional communities may in part be motivated by this unsatisfied hunger for contact, for intimacy, for belongingness and by the need to overcome the widespread feelings of alienation, aloneness, strangeness, and loneliness, which have been worsened by our mobility, by the break-down of traditional groupings, the scattering of families, the generation gap, the steady urbanization and disappearance of village face-to-faceness, and the resulting shallowness of American friendship. My strong impression is also that some proportion of youth rebellion groups -- I don't know how many or how much -- is motivated by the profound hunger for groupness, for contact, for real togetherness.... Any good society must satisfy this need, one way or another, if it is to survive and be healthy (p. 43).

Belonging -- having a social context -- is requisite for the development of self-esteem and self-confidence. This is why Maslow placed self-esteem above belonging in his hierarchy. Without a social context in which to validate a person's membership and value in the community, self-worth is not internalized.

Despite the essential importance of belonging as a precursor to the development of self-esteem and motivation, it is interesting to note this is not typically something that those who work in special education pay much attention to. We have practices and programs to support physiological needs (e.g., subsidized breakfast and hot lunch programs), safety needs (e.g., traffic, sex, drug and health education), learning structures to build confidence and esteem (e.g., co-operative group learning, mastery learning models with individualized objectives and performance criteria, esteem building curricular units) and specialized learning practices in many curriculum domains. Yet, creating caring communities has not been a priority in the overly tracked, segregated, and often exclusive and exclusionary schools of the 20th – and now the 21st - century. This is similarly true for many of the organizations that take over support once disabled children leave school.

It isn't just the Disabled Kids: Inverting Maslow's Hierarchy: the problem with having to earn the right to belong

Despite the wealth of research and personal experience that gives validity to Maslow's position, it is not uncommon for educators and others to work from the premise that achievement and mastery rather than belonging are the primary if not the sole precursors for self-esteem. Our educational system – and arguably much of our western society – is built on this premise. The purpose of education is seen as the process of imparting knowledge. In schools, despite a recent rise in discussions about culture, it is still seen as a secondary concern, a "soft" issue eclipsed by more pressing "hard" curricular issues like standardized testing and global competition. As Figure 2 illustrates, the result is that we have inverted Maslow's hierarchy so that belonging is transformed from an unconditional need and right into something that must be earned, something that can be achieved only by the "best" of us.

Figure 2: The inversion of Maslow's hierarchy of human needs in 20th century education.

In education, despite evidence to the contrary, there is an assumption that children who come to school have had their physiological and safety needs met at home. We know that for many students, this simply isn't so. And then, upon entering school, despite the fact that they may have arrived at school hungry, cold or not feeling safe, we expect them to immediately buckle down to the tasks at hand and learn the curriculum. It's taken for granted that successful mastery of school work will foster a sense of self-worth, which in turn will enable students to join the community as "responsible citizens." In this way, we require children to earn their right to belong without taking into account what else may be occurring in their lives.

I have often heard the claim in the field of education that an effective way to bolster student self-esteem is to provide students with opportunities to experience success. Efforts are made to ensure that the school work is easy enough so students have little difficulty completing the work correctly, with the assumption that this will foster trust in their abilities. It can be argued that students do actually develop some sense of self-worth in this way. But in the process, they also learn another perhaps unintended lesson; that their worth as individuals is contingent upon being able to jump through the prescribed academic, physical, or personal hoops.

Casualties of the Inversion of Maslow's Hierarchy

The view that personal achievement fosters self-worth is by no means limited to the field of education. The perception that we must earn our right to belong permeates all aspects of our society. It is an unfortunate truth that in our culture we tend to value uniformity. Because uniformity is often the criteria for belonging, we tend to exclude people we perceive as different. This exclusion manifests itself in overt racism and classism, but also in smaller and less recognized ways. Body image and weight loss are examples of the insidious ways in which people feel driven to earn the right to belong. Reinforced by the messages contained in weight loss commercials, most dieters engage in a form of self-talk that reflects the inverted hierarchy of needs. "If I lose 50 pounds and go from a size 16 to a size 10 (achievement), then I will feel better about myself (self-esteem), and perhaps then I will be able to regain the lost romance in my marriage and be more valued in my community (belonging)." Similarly, one can see how the prevalence of workaholism also corresponds with the inversion of needs. The reasoning goes something like this, "If I work 60 hours a week (achievement) then I'll be assured that my work matters (self-esteem), I will be respected by my colleagues and won't be fired (belonging)."

When we live in a society that holds belonging as something we must earn through academic or physical achievement, through appearance, and through a host of other socially valued criteria, we become a society of tyrannized individuals. We no longer believe that belonging is a fundamental and inherent right of all human beings. Unfortunately our schools are a reflection of the larger society, and therefore continue to unthinkingly perpetuate this belief.

When a school system makes belonging and acceptance conditional upon achievement, it essentially leaves students with two options. A student can either decide that they will pursue acceptance through achievement (sports, academics or appearance), or they will decide that they are incapable of attaining any of these expectations. While we tend to honour students who strive for acceptance through achievement over those who we believe are just giving up, in either case, there are potentially serious negative consequences for all of them.

The Problem with Gifted Programs

Maslow's hierarchy of needs not only reminds us how essential it is for people to live within the context of a community if they are to thrive, but also reveals that the need for self-actualization is present in every person. However, in our current education system it is sometimes assumed that only a minority of students are gifted, have an individual calling or are capable of self- actualization. But is it possible that this minority has been artificially created to a large degree by the fact that most schools only see those students with exceptional academic, athletic, musical and artistic abilities as deserving of the opportunity to develop their talents? Students with gifts in non-traditional areas are often relegated to the world of the average and mediocre: their requests for special considerations that would allow them to pursue their unique gifts (whether those are auto mechanics, cooking, or a fascination with nature) are seen as self-indulgent fantasies or "special interests." As a result, only a few privileged students are granted the luxury to work and concentrate in the areas in which they naturally excel. Ironically, children identified as "gifted and talented" are often also relegated to segregated gifted programs. It is also sadly ironic that many students who graduate these programs report experiencing isolation and alienation, and recount instances of bullying and ridicule where they are treated as nerdy social pariahs or even "brown nosers." This reveals that even when we grant students the opportunity to self-actualize it is often done at the expense of their sense of belonging.

School Dropouts

It is fairly easy to see how students who see themselves as incapable of achieving excellence develop a sense of personal unworthiness and even hopelessness. As mentioned earlier, our society - including most of our schools - highly values academic achievement, physical prowess, and attractiveness. Students who do not excel in at least one of these areas often feel devalued and misunderstood. These are the students who, quite understandably, are more likely to drop out of school. Unfortunately, when they remove themselves from the school environment they sometimes enter into other, often more dangerous situations in which they may then come to feel that they have found value.

Gangs

Some students turn to gangs to find that sense of belonging. Here again, Maslow's hierarchy of needs provides a framework for understanding why gangs have become so popular among today's youth. It can be argued that teenage gangs satisfy each level of need in Maslow's hierarchy. When youths join gangs, their physiological needs are met: food, shelter, warmth, and even their quasi-physiological needs, such as sex, heroin, and crack are also met. They are provided with a sense of safety in the knowledge that if they are ever harmed by another individual or group the other gang members will retaliate. Members describe a strong sense of belonging within gangs, and in this environment, belonging is not contingent on achievement but instead on "wearing the colors" or receiving the requisite tattoo. After passing an initiation ritual, the sense of belonging provided by gangs is close to unconditional. Given this acceptance and inclusion, the individual's feeling of self-worth naturally flourishes. Anchored in this newly found sense of inclusion and self-worth, many youths begin to focus on those areas in which they can excel, such as understanding the technicalities and loopholes within the criminal code, mastering martial arts, developing knowledge and skill in using firearms, stealing cars, extortion, and so on.

It's ironic that some school districts try to tempt youths away from an environment where they are experiencing unconditional inclusion and acceptance back into school. It is not entirely surprising that such efforts are often unsuccessful, since schools are environments where belonging and acceptance are conditional and must be earned. To make things even more difficult, these youths are asked to return to a context where they know they have already failed. Maslow would be unsurprised that these individuals refuse the invitation to re-enter school. The tragedy within our education system is that we see the continued membership in a gang as the result of a student's moral deficiency or the result of bad parenting rather than acknowledging school structure and an intrinsic educational ideology as a causal factor.

In the context of this discussion, it is important to note that the sense of belonging young people gain in gang membership is at its heart false and dangerous. The belonging experienced in these dangerous and hierarchical groups can probably best be described as a sense of allegiance. The difference between belonging and allegiance is easily overlooked, but important. Belonging is based in a sense of security and fellowship, while allegiance is most often about having a common enemy. This is an important distinction. It reveals that the desire to belong will often lead people to settle for a fraudulent facsimile.

However, if we agree that belonging must precede achievement, then we must face the credible and deeply disturbing proposition that inner city gangs, despite their inherent dangers, are sometimes experienced by their members as healthier environments for human beings than schools. It is shocking to even entertain the idea that schools may be more damaging to adolescent development than gangs, but if we do not, then there is little hope for change.

Perfectionism and Suicide

The repercussions of conditional belonging are not limited to those students who fail to excel. There are negative consequences for the "achievers" as well. When students strive to become shining scholars or all-star basketball centers, they learn that their value is dependent upon maintaining these standards of achievement at all costs. As a result, many students wake up each morning to face a day of ongoing pressure to remain "good enough to belong." They worry that if they blow a test, miss the critical lay-up shot in the last seconds of the game, or wear the wrong kind of running shoes, their status among their peers and possibly within the school will be sacrificed.

Tragically, a growing number of adolescents find that the endless demand to be "good enough to belong" is beyond them and they end the struggle by taking their own lives. As we begin to recognize the problems of living in a world of conditional belonging, we can better understand why students who commit suicide frequently are the high achievers - those we least expect. While Maslow's hierarchy of needs may not provide a complete framework for understanding and dealing with this issue, I believe the absence of belonging in our schools and communities is a contributing factor to teenage suicide. LGBTQ+ groups report a distressingly high suicide rate and attribute this to a sense of isolation, loneliness and a school environment that remains conducive to bullying.

It is true that most "student achievers" do not take their own lives. However, we cannot minimize the stress these students feel. Teachers are aware of those students who are "perfectionists"; obsessively driven to avoid even a slight error despite reassurance from family and teachers that their worries are unwarranted. Anxiety is something that students, teachers, counsellors and therapists tell us has become an overwhelming issue in school communities. Here again, it is important to step back and see the student within the context of both school and a society that repeatedly gives the message that they must earn the right to belong. When community, acceptance, and belonging -- some of the most primal human needs - are held out as the rewards for achievement, we cannot expect students to believe any of our assurances that they will be "accepted as they are." In fact, if we're being honest, we don't even believe that for ourselves as adults. Everything in our society screams out that belonging is almost totally dependent on maintaining a veneer of competence and continuing to strive for perfection.

Segregation: forcing people to earn the right to belong

Let's go back to the issue of segregation and its fallout. Perhaps the most glaring example of an educational practice that forces individuals to earn the right to belong is the maintenance of segregated special education classrooms and programs. The practice of making segregated environments the intermediary and prerequisite step toward inclusion explicitly validates the idea that belonging is something that must be earned, rather than an essential human need and right. What is only implied to non-disabled people is made very clear and explicit to disabled people. Although the stated intent of segregation is to help individuals with disabilities learn skills and so-called appropriate behaviour, the very act of removing and sequestering them away from others teaches them directly and explicitly that they are not good enough to belong as they are, and that the privilege of belonging will be granted only if and when they have acquired an undefined number of skills.

The tragic irony of self-contained environments is that as soon as we take away an individual's sense of belonging, we undermine their capacity to learn the skills that will enable them to belong. This is the painful "Catch-22" that confronts students with disabilities -- they can't belong until they learn, but they can't learn because they are prevented from belonging. This injustice is compounded by the fact that the lack of progress they make in a segregated setting is then seen as further evidence used to justify the need for segregation.

It has been argued that segregated environments, although possibly inappropriate for students with minor or moderate disabilities, are absolutely necessary for those with severe or multiple disabilities (e.g., Jenkins, Pious & Jewell, 1990). This line of reasoning has resulted in a cruel and insidious form of emotional abuse. Placing these individuals into segregated, self-contained classrooms or programs not only excludes them from their peers and the community, but ensures that their isolation will be permanent. What we know is that segregation is the proverbial "gift that keeps on giving." When students are segregated at school, it is almost a foregone conclusion that they will remain segregated throughout their lives.

It is common practice within segregated classrooms and adult services to offer rehabilitative, communication, and life skill programs. Until the person demonstrates the ability to overcome the limitations of their disabilities and emulate normalcy, it's assumed that there is more work to be done, and that this work is best done in a cloistered setting. Despite the fact that the attributes that have led them to be segregated - physical, mental, sensory or severe learning disabilities - likely cannot be eradicated to the point where the person approaches some artificial standard of "normalcy", these programs persist. The unfortunate result is that what is learned is that not only are they not good enough to belong, but that they *never will be* good enough to belong.

Belonging Without Valuing Diversity: The Inappropriate use of Maslow's Hierarchy to Support Inclusive Education and So-called Inclusive Community-based Programs

There is a caution and a caveat important to those who might be inclined to use Maslow's hierarchy of needs as a rationale for including disabled people with intensive educational needs in general education programs. If we continue to believe and do not question the notion that the goal is primarily to minimize evidence of their disabilities, inclusive education will be little more than a more enlightened way to achieve the same goals as before. If the underlying assumption remains that children and adults with disabilities should be as "normal" as possible, we continue to give legitimacy to a world view in which uniformity and perfection are still the gold standard. If this is how we understand inclusion, we will have changed little.

All people are people. The idea that some of us are normal and others are deficient and therefore need to be repaired in some way is still a concomitant of a society that values uniformity rather than diversity. The potential of heterogeneous education lies in the possibility of redefining the very concept of "normalcy." When individuals are given the right to belong, they are seen as having a right to be exactly as they are in all their multifaceted diversity. When disabled children and adults are welcomed into our neighbourhoods and seen to enrich our communities, and when we reject the construction of rehabilitative hoops through which they must jump in order to become "normal enough" to belong, our communities are strengthened.

Good educators and support staff believe that it is their responsibility to help each person discover their individual strengths and capacities and then facilitate opportunities for them to concentrate and excel in those areas. Trying to mould people into carbon copies of each other with uniform abilities is a betrayal of the awesome wonder of each individual. Attempting to do the same to those with disabilities is no less a travesty.

Inclusive Education:
An Opportunity to Rediscover our right to Belong

Throughout my career, my motivation in advocating for the inclusion of students with severe disabilities within regular classrooms has come out of a sense of social justice. I believed – and continue to believe – that students in segregated classrooms or programs are being denied the opportunity to learn needed social and academic skills and prevented from developing friendships with their non-disabled peers. However, as time has passed, I have become increasingly alarmed at the severity of the social problems in our schools for *all* students. Academic averages are plummeting, the drop-out rate is increasing, and teen pregnancy continues to be a major social concern. Teenage suicide continues to increase at an exponential rate and now has become the second leading cause of adolescent death in the United States and in Canada. Violence, drug dependency, gangs, anorexia, anxiety and depression among students has risen to the point that these problems are now almost viewed as an expected part of high school culture. The job description for teachers now vacillates between being an educator and a psychotherapist, and at times even borders on that of benevolent sorcerer. University and corporate establishments continue to be vocal about the lack of preparedness of high school graduates. It is little wonder that principals are attending high-powered corporate seminars on crisis management rather than the more sedate presentations on curriculum implementation.

What we are witnessing, we believe, are the symptoms of a society in which self-hatred and isolation have become an epidemic. Feelings of personal inadequacy have become so common in our schools and our culture that we have begun to assume that it is part of what it means to be human. It is not hyperbolic to question whether our society will be able to survive if this self-hatred is allowed to flourish.

In attempting to counter this crisis, many supposed pundits of educational reform claim that we are in desperate need of an immediate return to values reflected in words like "standards," "achievement," and "curriculum." However, before we run full speed backward, grasping at these hard words and clutching them close, it may be wise to pause, if only for a moment, to consider that our social malady might stem not from a lack of achievement, but from a lack of belonging.

Underachievement and unfulfilled potential in our society may not be the result of widespread laziness, as so many assume. It may in fact result from a pervasive sense of apathy, an apathy that so often accompanies the constant demand to be perfect. Perhaps what we need in our society (and especially our education system) is not more rigorous demands to achieve, but a collective effort to search for ways to foster a sense of belonging not only for students, but for staff as well. When we are able to rely on each other's strengths rather than expecting to somehow attain complete mastery in all areas, belonging will take precedence over achievement, and we may be welcomed into community not because of our perfection, but because of our inherent natural and individual capacities. Ironically, it is then that higher achievement is made more possible.

Inclusive education remains, more than twenty five years after this paper was first written, a very concrete and manageable step that can be taken in our school systems to ensure that all students learn that belonging is a right and not a privileged status offered some and withheld from others. We don't have to earn it – it is our birthright. If we want to create schools in which students feel welcomed and part of their communities, then we must begin by creating schools that welcome the diversity of all children.

The fundamental principle of inclusive education is valuing diversity and understanding that every person has a contribution to offer to the world. We have drawn narrow parameters around what is valued and exactly which contributions will be honoured. The ways in which people with disabilities can contribute may sometimes be less apparent: they often fall outside the goods and service-oriented, success-driven society. Unfortunately, this leads many to believe that no gift is present. From this premise, and often with the best of intentions, many educators set about to minimize evidence of the disability, believing that by doing so their students will move closer to becoming contributing members of society.

When inclusive education is fully embraced, we abandon the idea that children have to become "normal" in order to contribute to the world. Instead, we search for and nourish the gifts that are inherent in them. We begin to look beyond the typical, and in doing so, begin to realize the achievable goal of providing all children with an authentic sense of belonging.

As a collective commitment to educate all children takes hold and "typical"" students realize that "those kids" do belong in their schools and classes, typical students will benefit by learning that their own membership in their classes, schools and society are about basic human rights rather than academic or physical ability. In this way, it is conceivable that the students of inclusive schools will be liberated from the tyranny of believing they must earn the right to belong. It is ironic that the students who were believed to have the least worth and value may be the only ones who can guide us off the path of social destruction. We close with a true story that illustrates this point.

> Almost twenty years ago, Emma and I were asked to travel to Capetown, South Africa to visit a Jewish school. The principals of the middle and junior high schools had heard us speak to a Principal's Institute at Harvard University the previous year, and asked for our help as they went through the process of adopting an inclusive model in their schools.

> Geoff Cohen, the principal of the middle school, described their journey to inclusion as somewhat accidental. "I was coming out of a meeting one day", he told us. "A parent approached me and said 'Mr. Cohen, my daughter is blind, but I would like her to have a Jewish education. Can she come to Herzlia?' I admit that I was a bit preoccupied, so I said 'sure, why not?' It was only when I got home that I realized that I'd inadvertently committed us to inclusion!"

> After a somewhat panicked and lengthy discussion with the principal of the junior high school (also named Jeff Cohen) later that night, the two principals took this proposition to the school board. After hearing Jeff and Geoff's eloquent

arguments for inclusion, the school board agreed to try it for a year. If, they told the two principals, at the end of that year, school achievement scores went down, the project would be abandoned. If they stayed the same or close, they'd continue with inclusion.

At the end of the year, to the astonishment of all concerned (but especially the school board), scores had actually climbed. "We don't understand," they said to Geoff and Jeff. "We're pleased, but it doesn't make any sense. How is it that you can include much more diversity into the school community, put more demands on teachers and still see the scores rise?"

Jeff and Geoff said "We think there's a simple answer and a more complicated answer. The simple answer is that as a part of the preparation for establishing an inclusion program, we trained our teachers in differentiated instructional learning techniques, and that has made them better teachers for all the students. They are able to adapt curriculum to fit a wide demographic and a lot of different learning styles."

"The more complicated answer is this; before inclusion we were a school known for high achievement (Herzlia Jewish Schools are high academic schools – more than 90% of their students go on to ivy league universities). Students felt pressure to meet those goals. They felt that their membership in Herzlia was contingent on their ability to score well on tests. When we introduced students with different educational goals, it was as if everyone relaxed. Students began to realize that membership was not contingent on achievement. Without that pressure, they actually did better!"

In an email to us a year later, Geoff Cohen wrote the following:

"Like so many things, when one has lived with inclusive education for awhile, it simply becomes part of the furniture, part of the language, part of the culture – and life without it becomes unthinkable. We shall never look back."

CHAPTER 9

ABILITY & OPPORTUNITY IN THE REARVIEW MIRROR

Published in Sobsey, D., & Scorgie, K., Eds. (2018). *Working with Families for Inclusive Education: Navigating Identity, Opportunity and Belonging.* Emerald Publications. Reprinted with permission.

The last three decades have seen a huge proliferation of information and research on strategies that can be used to successfully support disabled children in regular classrooms. Many of these are useful and have facilitated better inclusive environments. However, from our experience as two adults with different disabilities who have experienced the school system in different ways and with different degrees of success, we believe that there is a central issue - an ongoing confusion about the relationship between ability and opportunity that we must grapple with in order to ensure that inclusive education truly lives up to its promise.

Ability and Opportunity

It is widely seen as self-evident in our Western culture that ability leads to opportunity. If you're good at something, the reasoning goes, then those skills, talents, and abilities will certainly foster opportunity. We rarely question this belief. When it comes to disability, fostering ability in both schools and human services has traditionally focused on teaching life skills as a prerequisite for entering the "regular" community. This approach fits with an equally unquestioned belief that improving a disabled person's ability is the best way to improve their quality of life and increase the likelihood of later opportunities. But is this necessarily so?

Indulge us in a quick exercise. First, think of five classical musical composers. Now, think of five famous artists.

It's likely that you thought first of composers like Beethoven, Bach, Mozart, Handel, and Tchaikovsky. Artists? Perhaps Picasso, Renoir, van Gogh, Matisse, or Michelangelo. It's likely that many, if not all, of the names you thought of were men.

If we believe that ability truly determines opportunity, it would then logically follow that women must have been devoid of artistic and musical *ability* for the last few centuries. Obviously, this is not the case. The reason why women have been so underrepresented is obvious. Until recently, women have not been afforded equal *opportunity* to develop and foster musical and artistic ability.

This simple exercise reveals an unfortunate truth: Opportunity is determined by social convention, not ability. That is, opportunity is not afforded to those who are most able but to those our society deems worthy of that opportunity. This has significant parallel consequences for disabled people and raises different questions as we continue the enterprise of constructing truly inclusive classrooms.

In the context of the preceding discussion, we offer our personal experiences.

Norm - When Ability is Seen to Precede Opportunity

Like many educators and other professionals working with disabled people, I had always just assumed that my abilities would largely determine my opportunities. I believed that the more things I could do, the more doors would open for me. So I focused early on becoming as nondisabled as possible. Improving my ability, whether that was learning to walk, improving my speech, or doing well in school, seemed to promise a better chance for getting a decent job, finding a meaningful relationship, and having a rich, enjoyable life. It wasn't until I left the segregated school that I began to question these assumptions.

At the segregated school, I had speech therapy twice a week for eight years. I'd sit in a small room with a speech therapist and read an endless stream of boring books out loud in what I called my "speech therapy voice." Prompted by the therapist, I'd dutifully pause at regular intervals to breathe, swallow, and articulate.

There was no doubt about it. For the duration of the 30-minute therapy session, my speech was dramatically more intelligible. However, it didn't make much difference in my life because, at the end of the session, I'd leave the speech therapy room and talk the way I usually talked. Everyone I knew at the segregated school and at home understood me and the "breathe, swallow, and articulate" mantra was only required in the speech therapy room; it seemed unnecessary in the rest of my life.

When I decided that I wanted to leave the segregated school and attend my neighbourhood junior high school, one of the most vocal opponents to this idea was my speech therapist. It wasn't that she was against integration; she was just worried that I would no longer receive speech therapy in the regular school. Although I was secretly delighted by the prospect of therapy-free days at school, she insisted that I was making a terrible mistake. She stressed that I had made substantial progress in speaking and that stopping speech therapy would prevent me from reaching "my potential"– that nebulous Shangri-la of functioning that always seemed to loom two years of therapy ahead of me. Having no desire to remain a segregated Sisyphus, I told her that speaking clearly was pointless… if I didn't have any friends to speak to.

The combined weight of my determination to go to a regular school, my parents' support of this goal, and the wary consent of school administrators outweighed the speech therapist's objections, and I entered my neighbourhood school. However, within days of being in my new school, I realised that the other kids and even some of the teachers were having trouble understanding me. I noticed that they would listen to the first three or four words I'd say. If they understood those first words, they kept listening. But if they didn't understand me, their eyes would glaze over. It was clear that they had decided my speech was unintelligible. I knew the exact second this happened. They always did the same three things: they'd smile, nod their heads vigorously, and then benignly say, "Yeah."

Translation? "I don't have a clue what you're saying."

I quickly understood that if I wanted people to listen to me, I needed to make my first words as intelligible as possible. That's when I developed my standard operating procedure for talking to a new person. I'd invoke the old speech therapy mantra: "Breathe, Swallow, Articulate." It invariably worked! Once the person came to understand me, I would gradually drop the speech therapy regimen and seduce them into my usual way of talking. I soon realized, however, that I needed to continue to do this with every new person I met, day after day, week after week.

By the end of my first year at the regular school, I would meet family friends and relatives who hadn't seen me since I left the segregated school. Astonished by the improved clarity of my speech, they would invariably say, "Norman, you're talking so much more clearly. What did you do?"

I'd say "I quit speech therapy!"

I usually get prolonged laughter when I tell this story in conference keynotes. But when I told this story to an audience of speech therapists in Sioux City, Iowa, they somehow missed the humour. In fact, some felt I'd discounted the importance of speech therapy. This isn't true. What I learned in speech therapy was useful. My *ability* to talk clearly was important. But it was my *opportunity* to attend a regular school that allowed me to put what I'd learned into practice.

This insight was reinforced when, later in university, I became affiliated with the Toronto Disability Rights Network. I met many powerful and articulate disabled activists. I was amazed to discover that most of them, despite their obvious capabilities, were either unemployed or drastically underemployed. I quickly realized that it was the lack of *opportunity* and not the lack of *ability* that posed the greatest threat to my quality of life. Clearly, my success in later education and employment would depend on my ability to navigate through a world of prejudice and social bias. I realized I would have to cajole, convince, or coerce people into giving me the opportunities that would afford me a chance to demonstrate my ability. When it came to improving my speech or physical ability, my success largely depended on what I did; I was ultimately in charge. But when it came to dealing with discrimination and prejudice, my success would ultimately depend on what others did. This seemed far more daunting, and to be honest, it scared me.

Emma - Opportunity is Not Enough

Let me add a little more complexity to this issue and talk about my life at school. I was born and grew up in the days before the words *Autism spectrum* or *sensory processing disorder* became public property. Had I been born a decade or so later, that label or one like it might have been applied to me.

Because I was undiagnosed and largely "flew under the radar", my experience was quite different from Norm's. I was never denied access to the classroom. It was never suggested that segregation was appropriate for me or that I should take part in remedial programs. In fact, there were no such programs in my schools. Arguably, I experienced all the opportunity I could wish for. However, the problem was that I lacked support. Because nobody understood that I was experiencing the classroom differently and coping with a laundry list of sensory and learning issues, I was largely ignored or treated with disdain and frustration. It is undeniably true that opportunity must precede ability, but unfortunately, opportunity without support is a set up for failure. So my experience was best encapsulated by the immortal words of Pogo. I was "surrounded by insurmountable opportunity."

I do not entirely blame educators for my experiences. I was certainly a child who presented baffling dichotomies. After all, how is an educator to understand a hyperlexic child who is reading existentialist literature at age 12 but is inexplicably dyscalculiac and cannot master the times tables or the simplest mathematical equation? I was a frustrating child to my teachers: single-tracked, focusing on something and then sticking in that track, often at the expense of getting other things done. Paradoxically, I was easily distracted and experienced great difficulty in getting my brain's motivational apparatus in gear if the topic didn't engage me. Norm often jokes today that I am the proverbial light switch—either on or off, no in between. My idiosyncratic and divergent learning style made conventional classroom approaches inaccessible to me, and my love-hate relationship with the spatial world made physical education an impossible enterprise. I was and continue to be a hybrid of sensory avoiding and sensory seeking. My sensory issues made concentration a challenge during times of overstimulation, and boredom a huge issue during times of understimulation.

So, school was a nightmare. The characteristics that simply bemused (and yes, sometimes irritated) my family were transformed by educators into personal failings. I became the sad recipient of much adult frustration.

My teachers knew I was smart and that I likely had the necessary ability to succeed, but they had no idea how to help. Instead, the problems they saw were viewed as something I did on purpose. The labels I collected were not medicalized. Instead, they were descriptions of volitional behaviour: lazy, noncompliant, obsessive. "Must try harder" and "doesn't pay attention" were part of a constant litany that followed me from my earliest academic experiences until the day I quit school in demoralized desperation at age 15.

Ability and Opportunity in the Rear-view Mirror

It is through viewing our educational experiences retrospectively that we have come to believe that inclusion needs to be viewed more broadly. It's our hope that we might consider how strategies tied to fundamentally flawed theoretical constructs can be turned on their heads and reconceptualized. If we believe that education is about outcomes, and life after school ends is certainly the outcome we most need to be concerned with, then we are challenged to find ways to maximize success for disabled students. Currently, we create remedial programs to bolster ability, firmly believing that this will lead to opportunity. And yet we continue to see adults who have 'graduated' these programs fall into segregated lives of unemployment, underemployment, isolation, and poverty.

Although improving ability may make a person's life easier in some respects, it probably won't make their life better. The significant obstacles confronting us are the lack of opportunities, not the limitations of ability. And in that context, we also need to think about the kind of support we offer in order to ensure that people leave school with a sense of confidence, competence, and optimism.

We are sometimes asked by both teachers and parents whether pull-out programs are ever justified. Norm spent most of his time at school in regular classes, but when it didn't make sense (i.e.: some sections of physical education), he would find a quiet place and work on homework. But because these alternatives to the regular curriculum made logical sense and were not associated with a Special Education program, Norm was always seen as belonging to the regular class. Unfortunately, many of the traditional "pullout" programs designed to help students with learning or behavioural difficulties are part of a Special Education program founded upon an ideology of deficiency. Unfortunately, in this view disabled students are seen as globally deficient and different, and therefore in need of remediation in segregated settings before they can be effectively reintroduced to the larger non-disabled community. Sadly, this ultimately leads disabled students to view themselves as broken and implants an identity of deficiency that is difficult to overcome in later years.

Emma was never offered the opportunity to leave the classroom. At times this might have been helpful in managing sensory overload. Again, being able to leave the classroom is quite different from more traditional time out and seclusion responses to children who are experiencing overwhelm. Helping a student learn to self-regulate by offering opportunities to experiment and learn about how their bodies and brains work is invaluable. These are the experiences that increase confidence and promote the ability to experience inclusive classrooms in positive ways.

The issue of pull-out is not about placement. It is about power and agency. In other words, does the student have some say in the process? Forcible exclusion is fundamentally disempowering. Working with students to craft innovative accommodations - even when they may include working in separate spaces for finite periods of time - empowers them to develop self-understanding and learn advocate for themselves and initiate the support they need. It is the ability to speak up for themselves and to initiate needed supports, and not the minimization of a particular disability, that will be essential skills they'll need in later life.

Swimming Lessons

When it comes to thinking about the difference between ability and opportunity, we've encapsulated our thinking into one simple metaphorical rule. It goes like this: No matter how good a swimming instructor you may be, you can never teach a person to swim in the parking lot of a swimming pool. And yet, this is what we've been trying to do in segregated programs. In my (Norm's) early years, I was stuck in the parking lot. Teachers with the best of intentions could not possibly replicate the nuances of typical experiences that I needed to know about through fabricated life-skills education. It was only after leaving the segregated school that I was able to learn the more complex rules of human interaction and the skills I'd need to be successful..

I (Emma) was in the pool, but spent most of my time drowning. Our friend and colleague Bill Page also uses a swimming analogy: he says, "never give swimming lessons when someone is drowning." So just being in the pool isn't enough, either. Opportunity must be accompanied by support. Sometimes this support is about fostering learning, but sometimes it is simply about providing safety. Bill reminds us that educators and parents have two roles; that of the swimming instructor, and that of the lifeguard. He suggests that we get into trouble when we don't understand which role we need to assume at which time. When I was drowning, it was not helpful for the teacher to be a swimming instructor, yelling directions from the metaphorical pool deck. What I needed was a teacher who was a lifeguard -someone to get into the pool with me and help me get to shallow water. Then later, after the overwhelm had dissipated and I was emotionally ready to engage, to help me learn the skills I needed.

Conclusion

To summarize then, as disabled people, we believe that it is both essential and ethical that disabled children are afforded the same opportunities as their non-disabled peers. Focusing on ability to the exclusion of opportunity is not only fundamentally unjust, it ironically undermines the very conditions needed to acquire those abilities.

Yet, it is equally important that those opportunities be accompanied by support and that educators take the time to work with the student to determine what kind of support will be most helpful.

CHAPTER 10

SEGREGATION VERSUS SOLIDARITY: RETHINKING THE UNCRITICAL COMMITMENT TO INCLUSION

This piece was originally published in Van der Klift, E., & Kunc, N. (2019). "Promoting Social Inclusion: Co-creating Environments that Foster Equity and Belonging, *International Perspectives on Inclusive Education*, *13*, 17–24. Reprinted with permission from Emerald Publishing Limited.

> Segregation: "the separating of one person, group, or thing from others, or the dividing of people or things into separate groups kept apart from each other" (*Encarta World English Dictionary*)

> Solidarity: "harmony of interests and responsibilities among individuals in a group, especially as manifested in unanimous support and collective action for something" (*Encarta World English Dictionary*)

In a conversation many years ago, a friend and colleague made what she thought was an embarrassing confession. "I've been an advocate of inclusive education for years. But here's the thing. I attended an all-girls school when I was growing up, and quite frankly, I loved it. Because there were no boys, girls were not overshadowed in typically male-dominated areas like science and math. I honestly believe I received a better education in that school than I would have in a public coed school. But," she went on, "you could say it was a segregated environment. Am I being hypocritical now when I advocate for inclusion?"

There is still confusion in both educational and human service circles about exactly what constitutes segregation. Passionate supporters of inclusion believe that any grouping of people with disabilities is automatically a segregated grouping and as such is stigmatizing and to be avoided. In this chapter we will argue that when disabled people come together in groups, those groups are not necessarily evidence of segregation. They may in fact be groups of solidarity. Specifically, we will make a distinction between the two kinds of groups and further suggest that an uncritical commitment to "absolute" inclusion may undermine the goal for the emancipation of disabled people.

Segregation versus Solidarity

Many proponents of full inclusion are understandably wary of any argument articulating the benefits of segregation. Those favouring congregated programs are often quick to seize any opportunity to justify their validity. Consequently, like two lawyers arguing a case, each side avoids arguments that could be used by the other. The unfortunate result of this adversarial debate is that we overlook the complexity of this issue.

If we view any gathering of people with disabilities as a segregated event, we must ask ourselves whether we would say the same for any other community group or educational institution. For example, would we frown on an ethnic, religious, or LGBTQIA+ group coming together to celebrate shared identity, holidays, parades, or other events? Would we consider traditionally black colleges like Spelman or all Deaf universities like Gallaudet to be examples of stigmatizing segregation? Of course not. After all, in most western cultures, the right to gather and be self-determined is encoded and enshrined in legislation as a basic human right.

Historically, however, the ability to gather in free association with the express purpose of celebrating shared identity has not often been available for disabled people. This is especially true for people with intellectual disabilities. Instead of "gathering together", they have been "gathered together" in segregated schools, classrooms, day programs and living situations that are non-optional. The rationale for this practice is firmly rooted in a remedial premise – namely that disabled people need both intervention and supervision. Under the following headings, we will examine some fundamental differences between segregated groups and groups of solidarity. To do this we will take the discussion beyond the educational context and simply compare and contrast groups. Later, we will make a few recommendations.

Enforced versus Voluntary

The first thing that distinguishes segregation from solidarity is choice. In segregation, being with others is not about individual choice, it's about placement; being placed with others deemed to be "of your own ilk" for fiscal and administrative convenience. It may be that the required support is seen as too expensive to be given "one to one", or it may be that the reasons for segregation are framed as a safety concern.

Solidarity, on the other hand, implies choice and agency. Groups are composed of people who choose to spend time together. They are often people who share common interests and goals.

Imposed Agenda versus Common Purpose

Over the years, both of us have been involved in disability related groups. Sometimes we come together to talk about societal issues, and to advocate together for better access; other times we come together to share stories and experiences or simply to enjoy the pleasure of each other's company. Anyone looking in might consider these groups segregated since they generally don't include any non-disabled people. However, there is a distinction. Our agenda is not imposed by others. We create it together. The group's purpose may be around advocacy and activism, or it may be the simple desire to hang out with people who understand our reality - where a paragraph of meaning can be transmitted in two or three words, a knowing smile and an uproarious laugh.

In contrast, segregated groups are often subjected to an imposed agenda – we know you better than you know yourselves, and we will determine what activities you should be engaged in.

Remediation versus Acceptance

Another vital difference is the goal. In other words, what's the reason for coming together? Regardless of whether it is a life skill, behavioural, or pull-out program, the overarching reason for a segregated group is to work on remediation. Inherent is the idea that the person is deficient and lacking something, either a tangible or an interpersonal skill. That the disability is seen as a problem to be fixed remains largely unquestioned.

In solidarity, people often come together specifically to challenge these notions and to contest ideas that posit them as inadequate or in need of repair. Instead, the problem is reframed as the consequence of living in an ableist society. In groups of solidarity, disabled people come together to collectively "talk back" to a society that tells them they need fixing. In fact, forcible segregation is often precisely what group members are protesting, and acceptance is what they are working towards. This is the fundamental difference between an all black educational institution like Spelman College and a finishing school, and an all Deaf university like Gallaudet and an institution.

Damaged Identities versus Positive Identities

When groups are created based on the notion that people are deficient and abnormal, it has serious implications for the development of positive identity. Despite best intentions, segregation reinforces the development and maintenance of what we might call "damaged identities" (Nelson, 2001), where people are seen as essentially inadequate, needy and lacking in skills. Unfortunately, even when this is not explicitly stated, the message is clear. You need remediation. You need supervision. A vicious cycle is put into motion; people internalize messages of personal deficiency, and their subsequent lack of self-confidence is used as justification for further segregation.

In contrast, participants in groups of solidarity understand that although they are members of a marginalized group, they can challenge these messages and, with the support of others who share this struggle, assume more positive individual and collective identities.

Shame versus Pride

Many proponents of segregation claim that providing a safe environment will not only promote the development of needed skills, but will also bolster self-esteem. This is founded on the belief that a cloistered environment will give the student the opportunity to foster a positive sense of self. Despite best efforts and intentions, the fact remains that it is segregation itself that undermines the development of pride. Students who spend time in the "sped" room know that they are seen as fundamentally different, and they understand that this means fundamentally "less than" their non-disabled peers. It doesn't matter whether this is called the "resource room", "the opportunity centre" or the "learning assistance program", both the disabled student and the other students understand it as a stigmatized environment.

In solidarity, there is pride. A sense of self can be redefined and embraced, and rather than apologizing or attempting to "pass" as normal, individuals and groups have the opportunity to assert the right to be exactly as they are, and that they are under no obligation to minimize evidence of their disability. Groups of solidarity counter the idea that there's something wrong with disability and instead label it as part of the normal diversity of the human experience.

Low Expectations versus High Expectations

In segregation, expectations are typically low. Far too many schools and life-skills programs spend hours on meaningless and repetitive activities. These activities are more about filling time than fostering learning. Life skills are often divorced from real life and the settings in which they would normally occur. In many instances, these "readiness" programs start early, and many people never graduate out of them. Most, if not all, segregated programs focus on what people can't do and are future oriented – working towards some goal that remains elusive. The curriculum is often either very easy or nonexistent. No one expects the disabled student to accomplish much, and that expectation becomes internalized so that disabled students learn to not expect much from themselves, either.

In solidarity, expectations are high. The focus is on strengths, not weaknesses. In addition, there is an acknowledgment that there is a higher social goal that transcends the myopic view of individual improvement. An example of this is the ADAPT movement, where people with diverse disabilities unite, act, encourage and hold each other accountable in their efforts to effect social change.

Benevolence versus Respect

Perhaps the most problematic feature of segregation is that it is often based on benevolence and paternalism, with the idea that people are vulnerable and need to be protected. Segregation is often justified on the pretext that keeping people in self-contained environments will help them avoid teasing and provide safety.

In contrast, there is a fundamentally equitable relationship between members of a group of solidarity; there is no relationship of "helper" versus "helpee." These groups are often good examples of interdependence. The skills of each individual enable the collective to function effectively. Implicit in interdependence is respect and valuing of the unique skills that each individual brings. So, as segregated environments are founded on inequity and benevolence, groups of solidarity are founded on reciprocity and mutual benefit.

Empowerment is not something that non-disabled people can somehow bestow on disabled people, but is instead a natural outgrowth of confidence as new skills are learned and incorporated. Instead of keeping people safe, they should be assisted to learn the skills and self-protective strategies they both want and need in order to manage in the world.

Non-Disabled Professionals versus Relatable Role Models

Schools, both segregated and inclusive, are almost universally run by nondisabled educators. As well intentioned as they may be, the unfortunate consequence is that few disabled students have the opportunity to meet powerful disabled adults in whom they can recognize themselves. We have long understood the need for relatable role models for other marginalized groups, but this discussion has been largely missing when it comes to people with disabilities.

For me (Norm), finding the Toronto Disability Rights group in my early twenties was a revelation. Here were articulate, powerful activists demanding the right to control their own lives. Perhaps for the first time, I was aware of having "a people" who understood both my struggles and my perspective. For me (Emma), finding the autistic Neurodiversity community much later in life was equally a revelation. After decades of "passing" as non-autistic, I met a group of people who shared many of my experiences. I found a community that encouraged me to have pride in my identity and enabled me to ask for the supports I need.

These experiences explain why places like Gallaudet University, Spelman College and perhaps even the girl's school our friend attended are not examples of segregation. These institutions are based on ideas of shared experience, solidarity, and social justice, and the role models are present, accessible, and relatable.

A Final Distinction: Social Justice

The most important distinction between segregation and solidarity is a focus on social justice. Segregation, despite an often stated commitment to improving the lives of disabled people, rarely - if ever -is rooted in social justice.

In contrast, groups of solidarity are often based on principles of justice, equity and fairness. The fundamental difference between these two approaches is the location of the "problem" In segregation, the problem is situated in the person's body or brain; in solidarity, the problem is situated in society.

Groups of solidarity promote and maintain healthy self acceptance and pride. When people come together to challenge negative stereotypes about themselves and to gain strength by spending time with others who are like-minded, social change happens. Conversely, when people come together at the behest of those who are not members of the group, people with credentials, influence, and power who have their own agendas and ideas about what group members should be doing, those gatherings will almost certainly have been hijacked and will devolve into groups of segregation. It has been argued that much of the disability rights movement, especially as it relates to people with intellectual or developmental disabilities, has been primarily led by non-disabled people. This should concern us. We would not expect a group of women focused on women's issues to accept being led by a man. No community of colour would accept being led by white leaders. Why do we believe that non-disabled people should speak for disabled people?

It's possible to tell the difference between a segregated group and a group of solidarity. The segregated group will almost always be based around deficits in its members, and will have been organized by a leader who is not part of that group. Groups of solidarity, on the other hand, are composed of those who have an immediate and firsthand understanding of the issues.

Does this mean non-disabled educators have no role? Not at all. Here are a few ideas.

Find Relatable Role Models and Teach Disability History

Can an inclusive school unintentionally foster another kind of segregation? We believe it can, and often results in what we might call "the segregation of one."" Students who have no access to role models or others who look, move, think or talk like they do will inevitably feel isolated and different, alone in their classrooms despite efforts to make them feel included.

Educators can help to counter this in several ways. First, pay attention to how disabled students are introduced to the rest of the class. Typically, these introductions include unnecessary descriptions of the disability, and trite "on the inside he's just like you" comments. Despite good intentions, this can result in further stigmatization. Instead, we suggest approaching these introductions in the context of social justice – talking about how we've treated disabled students historically, what we're trying to do now, and why.

Second, educators can help by including disability history in the curriculum for all students. Too often the only kind of disability education students receive is either a medical description or a lecture on the importance of being nice to disabled people. What we believe is most needed is curriculum that posits disability in the context of a civil rights struggle. Tying it to other historical events like the de-segregation of black students can help create this context.

There is much to be learned for all students by familiarizing them with important historical figures and role models both past and present. Learning about people like Ed Roberts and the Berkley group, Justin Dart, even FDR and Helen Keller (many people don't know that she was a radical activist) is a good place to start. Helping disabled students learn where they are situated historically can help them figure out their place in society. There is pride and strength in knowing your history.

Find Places for Students with Disabilities to Gather

In recent years, educators have paid attention to issues that pertain to students of colour and LGBTQIA+ students, and have created clubs and safe spaces for them to gather. In many post-secondary institutions, disability student service offices are available to disabled students, but this is not usually true of schools.

In these clubs, participation is voluntary, and the groups are largely self-run. Participants determine which issues are relevant. There is, however, a cautionary note. Non-disabled people, despite their good intentions, have an unfortunate way of taking over groups. It's one of the side-effects of identifying as helpers or supporters. Because this idea usually runs under the personal radar (most people don't like to think of themselves as bossy or controlling), supporters aren't always aware they're doing it. To further complicate matters, they often believe that because their intentions are good, it must follow that their actions will be. This isn't always the case.

Groups can be hijacked when non-members create the agenda and police the way the interaction takes place. Even in some groups that have a social justice orientation like People First –non-disabled helpers can wind up taking control. Despite the fact that the rhetoric is about empowerment, power is actually being stolen from the group in the name of assistance. It is condescending to think that non-disabled people can or should "empower" disabled people.

Finally, it is important that disabled people have opportunities to learn about, advocate with, and enjoy the company of others who share their experiences. However, it is critical that we understand the difference between segregated groups and groups of solidarity. Understanding that difference reveals that it's not about a group of people being in the same room, it's about why they are there, what they do when they are there, and how they perceive themselves and each other. Most significantly, it's about who's in charge. In short, the difference between segregation and solidarity can be reduced to a single word:. *Power.* It's about who has the power to determine how people see themselves, what they do together, and who gets to define the issues and the ultimate goal they're working towards.

CHAPTER 11

HELL-BENT ON HELPING: BENEVOLENCE, FRIENDSHIP, AND THE POLITICS OF HELP

Previously published in part in Thousand, J., Villa, R., & Nevin, A. (1994). *Creativity and Collaborative Learning: A Practical Guide to Empowering Students and Teachers.* Baltimore, MD: Paul Brookes. 2nd edition 2017.

This is a revised version with considerable additions in 2018. Reprinted with permission.

Years ago we were asked to facilitate a discussion with a group of disabled teenagers about their experiences with inclusive education. These students were considered success stories in their schools, and the conference organizers thought this would be a wonderful opportunity for these teenagers to share positive experiences with each other. We were chosen as facilitators because Norm is physically disabled (as many of these students were), and it was thought that his presence would foster more openness. No non-disabled people were allowed into the room except a few assistants who were there specifically to help the students communicate.

To our surprise, rather than the lively discussion we'd expected, the students seemed to dutifully recite the platitudes they thought were expected of them. Although they told us they liked being in a regular school, we sensed an undertone of resignation and saw little enthusiasm. We were pretty sure we weren't hearing the whole truth, so we probed a little but to no avail. While the students were polite, they remained vague and even somewhat uncommunicative. Much to our consternation, this unsettling tone persisted for awhile.

The mood shifted abruptly when one student laboriously typed into a little ticker-tape communication device that "kids are real dips when they pretend to care." To our amazement, this comment ignited a tinderbox of suppressed resentment. Suddenly all the kids were volunteering examples of patronization and condescension from their fellow students and even their teachers. "All the kids are nice to me. They say hi and all that, but I don't have any friends."

Another student added, "The kids fake being friends with me just so they look good in front of their teachers."

"They set up these little clubs for all these do-gooders, and they talk to us in baby talk and treat us like little kids or their protégées!"

Almost without exception, these success stories of inclusive education revealed that although the students appreciated the better education they felt they were receiving, they also believed that their social membership in the school was a facade, a public project that bolstered the esteem of teachers and administrators and even their fellow students but that wasn't doing much for them. Needless to say, we were shocked and concerned by these revelations. However, we were not entirely surprised.

The experiences these students described are an insidious and often overlooked expression of devaluation familiar to many disabled people; namely, benevolence, underestimation, and condescension. While segregated education, a lack of accessible housing and transportation, underemployment or no access to employment at all are significant barriers, benevolence is arguably one of the most difficult forms of oppression to overcome, mostly because it appears (and is usually intended) to be kind and supportive.

The idea that benevolence can be oppressive may at first seem puzzling. In our society, as well as in many other societies, benevolence is seen as a good thing, an admirable quality or attribute. However, benevolence without social justice is a bit like a being owned by a kind slave-owner; it still implies a one-up/one-down relationship. Benevolence is founded upon a presumption that some people are capable of bestowing it, and others are simply the lucky recipients. Inherent in acts of benevolence is an often unacknowledged assumption of inferiority in the receiver. Unfortunately, not only do the recipients pay for this kind of benevolence with their dignity and self-respect, but also there is an ever-present expectation of gratitude.

In this revised chapter we examine how, despite the best of intentions, many efforts to include disabled people do not live up to the promise of inclusion. We suggest that understanding the dynamics of both benevolence and help can assist us to move toward genuine acceptance, authentic relationships and mutual benefit. In addition to significant additions to this chapter that include vignettes and stories, we have expanded the discussion beyond the venue of school to include both students and adults with disabilities.

Benevolence and the Politics of Help

The move toward cooperative and inclusive education is part of a larger move away from social oppression for individuals with disabilities. It is part of a groundswell movement of social reform that holds as a central tenet the belief that all children and adults, including those with disabilities, are capable of learning and contributing to their classrooms and communities.

Students formerly educated in separate schools or segregated classrooms are appearing in increasing numbers in neighbourhood schools and regular classrooms. Across North America, we are coming to recognize that full participation in communities and schools should be the right of all individuals and that segregation on the basis of physical, intellectual, or cultural differences is fundamentally wrong.

This is the first generation of children with and without disabilities to grow up and be educated together. Consequently, within inclusive education we have come to entertain a cheerful optimism that this generation will be different from those of the past. We are hopeful that greater contact between children will begin to break down the barriers of misunderstanding and dispel the myths that have created society's response to disability.

At first glance, this change might seem to be taking place. Individuals with disabilities are more visible and increasingly involved in community life. If we believed that greater proximity led to greater acceptance, it could be argued that we are successfully participating in the creation of a new social order. Unfortunately, this is only partly true. Instead, we are finding that increased visibility and presence alone do not necessarily ensure that those with disabilities are fully respected and included.

True inclusion is dependent on the development of meaningful and reciprocal relationships between those with and without disabilities. As classrooms and communities become increasingly diverse, new strategies are being developed to ensure that the new students and community members are more than simply present. Friendship circles, school clubs, and special buddy systems have been implemented as formalized attempts to foster interaction and develop relationships.

While increased interaction may result from such efforts, friendship often remains elusive. Disabled children may have successful buddy systems during school hours and still be isolated and friendless after three o'clock. The same is true for adults who receive support from service agencies. People without disabilities may be helpful and involved, but a reciprocal relationship upon which genuine friendship is based does not always develop. The difficult and often frustrating question is then: What are the barriers impeding the development of friendship, and how can we move past them?

Friendship and Help

At the beginning of the twenty-first century, the most significant barriers preventing individuals with labels of disability from fully participating in schools and communities are still attitudinal. Specifically, our society still perceives those with disabilities as perpetual recipients of help. Descriptors like *less fortunate* and *needy*, telethons and tear-jerker journalism—sometimes sarcastically referred to by members of the disability rights community as "inspiration porn" (Young, 2012) —all continue to perpetuate this view.

Unfortunately, there is still a distressing tendency in some schools and even some agencies providing support to disabled adults to base their interactions on these broader societal misperceptions, despite a sincere desire to end the isolation experienced by so many. Friendship clubs and buddy systems based on stereotypical beliefs risk perpetuating prejudices and myths and even exacerbating the problem. It is critical, then, to regularly and carefully examine the nature of the interaction we facilitate and the attitudes that inform it.

Obviously, it is essential that both children and adults have opportunities to interact. Formalized friendship and support circles may be effective ways to build relationships. However, an overemphasis on the helper/helpee relationship can easily skew the delicate balance of giving and receiving that is the precursor of true friendship. We believe that this was the case for the students mentioned above. The prevalence of benevolence and patronization instead of authentic friendship was underscored yet again in another inclusive education conference.

> Four third-grade children from a local elementary school have come to speak to a room full of adults. They've been invited, with their teacher, to talk about friendship. Actually, three of them are there to talk about their friendship with the fourth child. Children in third grade make friends all the time. We ask ourselves, "What could possibly be unusual enough about this situation to bring these children here today?"

What's unusual is soon apparent. Three of the four children in the room can speak; one of them can't. Three of the four children in the room can walk; one of them can't. The three walking, talking children are here to tell us about their relationship with the boy in the wheelchair.

Adults in the room begin to smile as the first classmate talks. Approving nods accompany the child's words, "He's different on the outside, but inside he's just like me."

The conversation whirls around the boy in the wheelchair as he scans the room, looks at his communication board, and sometimes watches his classmates.

"We take turns being his buddy," offers one young girl "Everyone has a turn."

As the children talk and answer questions, it is interesting to watch the interplay between the subject of the discussion and the girl to his left. She has one arm around his shoulders and in the other hand holds a large towel. She wipes his mouth repeatedly. At one point, he appears to lose patience and struggles a bit. One hand jerks forward. The girl seizes his hand forcibly and holds it still. He makes a noise of clear irritation and attempts to pull his hand free.

His classmate smiles fondly at him, continuing to restrain his hand, and wipes his mouth again.

We look at each other, and one of us says, "Professional caregivers are not born; they are made. And this is how that happens."

Is there anything wrong here? Not much, we might say. A nine-year-old who in other times or other places might have been attending segregated classes or not going to school at all and a group of nice third-graders together are learning a few lessons about difference and similarity.

We might even agree with comments made by audience members. We heard the boy's three classmates being called "the hope for tomorrow" and "exceptional kids."All over the room, adults were beaming. After all, this relatively new phenomenon seems to hold some hope for an end to discrimination and distance between those who have disabilities and those who do not.

However, as the presentation continued, it became increasingly apparent that although both adults and children thought they were talking about friendship, much of the discussion taking place was really about help. There was undeniable warmth between the children, but most of the comments and nonverbal interactions reflected a helper/helpee relationship, not a reciprocal friendship.

We were uneasy as we observed these interactions, but we weren't entirely sure why. What was it about how these children were relating to one another that seemed problematic?

One of the perks of the presentations and training we do is that we are afforded the luxury of travelling the world and talking to groups of disabled people, teachers, human service workers, and parents. One of the questions we often ask yields interesting and sometimes disquieting information. "How are things going in terms of inclusion and community involvement? What's working, and what's difficult?"

For years the answers we got seemed to merely skate on the surface. "Things are going well," we were most often told, and most of the stories we heard foregrounded positive experiences. However, over time we began to hear faint tremors of concern. People seemed reluctant to voice these concerns, almost as if voicing them would be treasonous or mean that in some way they had failed. It felt as though there was a secret that everybody knew, but nobody wanted to talk about. Gradually, though, with some gentle prodding, people became more forthcoming and willing to talk about their concerns. "Well," some would tentatively admit, "inclusion during school hours is going well. But after school the phone doesn't ring, and she never gets invited to birthday parties or play dates."

Support staff would echo the same concerns as they applied to adults. "I do my best to facilitate community involvement and the development of relationships outside the service system. But it seems like it all fizzles out if I'm not there to keep supporting it."

These comments were worrisome, since most of us understand that inclusion isn't just about a few hours in a day but must be a broader enterprise. We began to wonder what was inhibiting the development of the authentic and reciprocal relationships all these well-meaning people were trying so hard to facilitate.

What's Getting in the Way?

When initially attempting to foster relationships between children with disabilities and their non-disabled classmates, it is common practice to have children help the new student. Such help may take the form of physical care, keeping company during breaks, or schoolwork assistance. Help-giving contact can reduce an initial sense of strangeness or fear, and can, if carefully done, lay the groundwork for friendship. As we began to think more deeply about what we'd been hearing, namely that genuine friendship remained elusive for many children and adults with disabilities, we began to suspect that oddly enough it might have something to do with help.

Needless to say, this was not good news. After all, we all need help. Clearly there is or should be nothing wrong with help; friends often help each other. Furthermore, few of us aspire to a society of total independence or what might be more accurately called self-sufficiency; we more often talk about the value of interdependence. So if help was a problematic inhibitor to relationship development, what did that mean, and how could that be overcome?

The more we thought about it, the more we realized that it probably wasn't help itself that was getting in the way; it was more about the *way in which help was being offered*. What we were seeing and hearing was a form of help that subtly but powerfully posited the helper as competent and the helpee as needy. To further exacerbate this problem, many of the structures that well-meaning teachers and others had devised to support relationship development seemed predicated on help, emphasizing one-sided helping relationships over reciprocal peer contact. We recognized that this was what we'd seen in the vignette above.

What many in inclusive education and the community living movement have been slow to recognize is that help in and of itself is not and can never be the basis of friendship. Overemphasizing the helper/helpee aspect of a relationship can create barriers that preclude equitable interaction. Unless help is reciprocal, the inherent inequity between helper and helpee will inevitably contaminate the authenticity of a relationship.

Friendship is not the same as help. Attempts to include children and adults with disabilities have sometimes blurred this distinction. Friendship clubs are often really assistance clubs. For example, how much time is spent on the logistics of help? "Who can take Jane to the library on Monday?" "Who can help George eat lunch on Friday?" Still more insidious, how much time is spent in bringing George's classmates into a multidisciplinary team system to analyze the effectiveness of his current behaviour management plan?

Professional caretakers, as we noted earlier, are made, not born. How does it happen? Put a third-grade helper next to a third grade helpee. Add a sizable amount of adult approval, and there you have it. Similarly, recruit a well-meaning non-disabled adult to spend time with an adult with a disability without paying attention to the dynamics of the relationship can result in a patronizing interchange where the relationship is considered an act of charity on the part of the non-disabled "friend"

It is not entirely thrilling that kids who take part in friendship circles during school go on to careers in human service and special education. Don't misunderstand. Lots of wonderful people choose these professions. However, an unfortunate result is that lots of children and adults with intellectual and physical disabilities have legions of professional caregivers and helpers but no friends in their lives. We must guard against merely creating another generation of professionals and clients, with the former group seen as perpetually competent and the latter perpetually needy.

But what's a teacher or a support worker to do? To create a helper is relatively easy; to facilitate a friendship is tough. After all, friendship cannot simply be mandated. At best, it seems to be made up of one third proximity and two thirds alchemy!

Perhaps we must begin by acknowledging what should be but is not always obvious. That is, no one has the power to conjure up friendship at will. Maybe that's just as well. Friendship is about choice and chemistry and cannot be readily defined, much less forced. This is precisely its magic. Realizing this, we can acknowledge without any sense of inadequacy that we are not, nor need to be, friendship sorcerers.

However, teachers and others do have some influence over the nature of proximity. To create and foster an environment in which it is possible for friendship to emerge might be a more reasonable goal. In order to achieve this goal, it is essential that we examine the nature of the interactions we facilitate. In particular, we must look closely at the dynamics of help in our classrooms and other spaces, and look not so much at whether people *should* help each other but *how* that help takes place.

The Politics of Help

Let's begin at the beginning and examine what help means to all of us. In most societies today, helping others is viewed as socially admirable. Those of us who are in a so-called privileged position are asked to give to others. We know we should give to our families, communities, and most of all to those less fortunate than ourselves. Yet why are most of us, while perfectly comfortable offering help, decidedly uncomfortable receiving it?

The answer is simultaneously simple and enormously complex. Consider the contrasting perceptions regarding the giving and receiving of help as presented in Table 1. Although our society associates a host of positive attributes to help, these attributes clearly are reserved for the helper.

TABLE 1: CONTRAST BETWEEN OFFERING HELP AND RECEIVING HELP

Personal Dimension	Why We Like Offering Help	Why We Dislike Receiving Help
ABILITY	Affirms capacity	Implies deficiency
VALUE	Affirms worth	Implies burden
POSITION	Affirms superiority	Implies inferiority
OBLIGATION	One is owed	One is obligated
VULNERABILITY	Masks our vulnerability	Reminds us of our vulnerability

When people without disabilities are asked to imagine their lives with a disability, their reactions reveal interesting assumptions about disability, being dependent, and the meaning of quality of life. "I'd lose my autonomy," we hear. "I'd be so helpless," says another person. "I'd be vulnerable, and I wouldn't be able to do things for myself!" These are typical responses. In fact, a close look at the controversial right to die issue reveals a disturbingly clear extrapolation of these sentiments; in today's society, many of us would rather die than lose our independence.

Those who still are able-bodied and young seldom think about these issues, having the luxury of viewing help as something that is ours to offer or withhold at will. Unless we happen to break a bone or become incapacitated with some temporary illness, we don't usually think much about how it feels to be the recipient of help. However, as age and the possible prospect of infirmity approaches, it is not uncommon for the always-uncertain future to be viewed with apprehension if not dread.

Is it the need for help itself that causes us to feel this way, or is it the kind of help we expect to get? Those who have closely examined this issue believe that the problem lies primarily with the lack of self-determination commonly experienced by helpees. It seems that often dignity must be forfeited in order to receive help. The power to decide where and when help should take place, who should help us, and whether in fact help is needed is often stripped away.

People with disabilities sometimes do need help. However, if they are uncomfortable receiving it, as most of us are, they are left in a classic no-win position of either doing without help or enduring the underlying demeaning messages. Furthermore, it is almost impossible to confront the issue directly. If the helper's motives are questioned, the inevitable response is an indignant or sorrowful "I was only trying to help." The unspoken but often implied expectation for gratitude is another complicating factor. Disabled adults who employ care assistants tell us that it is difficult to raise issues of conflict with their helpers for this reason. They worry that if they appear ungrateful, support will either be suspended or stopped, or they will be subject to what is sometimes called "soft retaliation." In other words, the transfer is a bit rougher than usual, the sandwich comes too quickly, or the tone of the interaction is punitive. Consequently, for many people with disabilities, help can be a four-letter word.

In inclusive and cooperative education and indeed in the broader community, we are working toward a time when asking for and receiving help is not considered an admission of inferiority and when being the helper does not imply moral or social superiority. The goal is a future in which the human community learns to merge help with respect. In the interim, it is important to acknowledge that the broader societal perception of help does not yet match this ideal, especially as it relates to individuals with disabilities.

Responses to Diversity:
From Marginalization to Valuing

Conformity and uniformity are highly valued in today's society. In general we are uncomfortable with those who are different. However, rather than admit this, our discomfort is often masked by rationalization. We cover our fears by asserting that our actions toward those with disabilities are for their own good. "It's a dangerous world," we say. "Those who are different must be protected from the potential evils of the world." Then, without any apparent sense of contradiction, we go on to say, "Differences are potentially dangerous. We must protect society from those who are different."

Isolation in the name of safety is a double-lock on the door of community. It effectively prevents those relegated to the outer circle from entering and belonging, while still allowing individuals within to feel that lofty moral imperatives have been well served. We know that good intentions based on unacknowledged fears can result in oppression. Some of the cruelest actions committed by humanity upon its members have been the result of so-called good intentions.

The act of forcible segregation for individuals seen as different is not reserved for those with disabilities alone. Throughout history, dominant cultures have avoided, marginalized, and even aggressed against minority groups. For people with disabilities, avoidance and marginalization usually occur under the auspices of protection. The result is still systematic removal from regular society. Institutionalization and segregation in special schools and work environments have been the means of enforcement.

In the past few decades, more attention has been paid to the injustices and inherent problems created by segregation. As a society we are beginning to examine some of the underlying motives and are finding that our actions lack justification. But even as some of the more blatant forms of marginalization and discrimination are changed or eliminated, other hurdles are raised for people labeled as different.

We have gone on to say, "You can be with us but you must first be like us." In other words, if you can reform, take part in rehabilitation, and reduce the evidence of your disability, look and behave "normally," then you will be allowed back into mainstream society.

Many remedial, behavioural, physical, and compliance-based therapies and life-skills programs have been expressly designed to help minimize the evidence of disability and create an impression of greater "normalcy." The intent is to improve quality of life through increased functioning and skills development. The carrot held up is the promise of future belonging and acceptance. The real message is, "You are not valuable as you are."

Those who work on social justice issues are stripping the mask of good intention from the faces of both marginalization and reform. The hurtful results are made more public; their legitimacy and continued existence are now in question.

Tolerance and Benevolence

There is another response toward individuals who are different. At first glance, it is more appealing and is consequently more difficult to recognize as oppressive. In our society we believe that dealing well with diversity will require tolerance. In fact, we are regularly exhorted to become more tolerant toward others. Many view intolerance as morally reprehensible and wish and work for a truly tolerant society. The intent—to create more acceptance of diversity—can hardly be questioned. Tolerance has seemed, for many, a worthy goal. But if it is the ultimate and only goal, true social justice will never be realized.

If we comply with the demands made by those with disabilities because we fee we "have to", or if our response is merely lukewarm resignation or benign paternalism, we will not create a society in which equity and respect will be afforded to all its members. Simply being tolerated is not necessarily to be valued. Being present does not automatically mean being included. Having an endless parade of well-intentioned helpers is not the same as having a group of friends who value and respect you.

In sum, to move beyond mere tolerance, another response to diversity—that of valuing—must prevail. In a valuing paradigm, diversity is viewed as normal, people are considered of equal worth, relationships are of mutual benefit, and belonging is a central societal theme.

Table 2:Responses to Diversity

MARGINALIZATION	Segregation Avoidance Aggression
REFORM	Rehabilitation Assimilation
TOLERANCE	Resignation Benevolence
VALUING (Diversity as Normal)	Equal Worth Mutual Benefit Belonging

We live in a society that tells us there is only one right way to be. At times all of us feel measured against an unfairly strict standard: white, able-bodied, young, intelligent, successful, attractive, straight, thin, and preferably male. Normalcy is a tight bell-curve, allowing little deviance without societal repercussion. Even those of us who find ourselves encompassed well within the confines of the curve feel pressure to conform to the middle, whereas those who fall outside its range feel that they are seen not only as deviant but also deficient.

It is puzzling that this standard of normalcy includes so few of us. We know that diversity, not uniformity, is the real societal norm. After all, the human community consists of great variety: race, gender, language, colour, religion, ability, and sexual orientation. People of colour make up most of the world's population. Women comprise 51 percent of the global population. Most of the world does not live in a state of affluence. As Michel Foucault (1980) once pointed out, difference is what's really inside the bell curve; normalcy is whatever is left over.

There have always been people with disabilities in society. Social justice for disabled people will come about only as we learn to value diversity and recognize the multiplicity of gifts within the human community. Our strength is our diversity. We need a paradigm shift of the most profound kind, and clearly this paradigm shift will require a change in attitude.

However, the problems inherent in the creation of attitudinal change continue to be difficult for the agents of any social movement. Attitudinal barriers stubbornly defy legislation, do not respond to architectural adaptations, and do not necessarily improve with the application of more money or better programming. They are notoriously slippery, the insidious products of unconscious socialization.

To further complicate things, as any good social reformer with a modicum of honesty will admit, attitudinal barriers don't exist only among those retrogressive oppressors out there, but are just as often within ourselves. In the immortal words of Pogo, "We have met the enemy, and he is us."

Although institutions and other segregated settings continue to exist, we have, to some measure at least, begun to push society beyond blatant forms of oppression like marginalization and reform. On a daily basis we are confronted by our prior assumptions, called upon to question them, and asked to move toward a new awareness that differences do not imply deficiency, that people with disabilities are capable of significant contributions.

Even as we push for structural reforms that provide physical access, equal opportunities, and freedom of choice for disabled people, it remains true that genuine valuing of diversity will require further confrontation with the more subtle forms of discrimination (e.g., tolerance and benevolence) and the courage to examine our own beliefs and practices as part of the process.

From Tolerance to Valuing

How do we move beyond mere tolerance to true valuing of diversity? For many, the struggle is often not in understanding why we should do something but in knowing what we should do next.

Rather than seek answers, perhaps it might be more helpful to begin by developing a new set of questions. We need questions that are broad in scope that will challenge the paradigms both inside and outside the context of inclusive education and service delivery models. What kind of educational system do we want? What kind of supports might be possible? What can schools become? Even more to the point, what kind of society do we want to live in?

Schools and support agencies will be transformed only as we move away from a blinkered "that's the way we've always done it" mindset and begin to focus on creating a community that promotes belonging and acceptance for all and does not rely on competition and stratification to provide its members with a sense of worth. We know that cooperative learning strategies in schools are one way to accomplish this goal. We know that person-centered planning is another way that works for children and adults alike. A further task for teachers in inclusive classrooms and those who provide support for adults is to create the space in which relationships can develop by consciously thinking about and working on the nature of proximity. The following are some practical ideas to assist the process.

Don't Make Friendship a Big Deal

Friendship is wonderful. However, it is not a big deal. If we commend and praise people without disabilities for their interactions with their peers with disabilities (either publicly or in other ways), we inadvertently make friendship a big deal and imply that all people are not created equal. We reinforce the idea that it is morally and socially admirable to "help the handicapped" and thereby may remove the opportunity for equality and reciprocity. Friendships based on a helper/helpee dynamic will, by definition, remain a one-up/one down relationship.

Similarly, facilitating relationships between adults in community settings must be done sensitively and must never be predicated on implied or stated needs. For individuals raised in the era of telethons and fund-raisers, the notion that adults with disabilities can be autonomous and competent remains difficult to fully understand. Support workers in schools and human service agencies can help to gently reframe this misconception, often by moving into the background and letting relationships develop naturally.

Respect Personal Boundaries

Adults are seldom comfortable talking about childhood sexuality, but the truth is children start noticing each other in kindergarten. However, people with disabilities often receive messages that tell them they are asexual, and these messages begin early. Boundaries of touch that would not be crossed between kids without disabilities should never be crossed with their classmates with disabilities.

An unfortunate side effect of tolerant or benevolent interaction is a tendency to treat the different child like a life-sized doll or pet, or a classroom mascot with whom the usual physical boundaries of touch may be violated. We must always ask, "Do the interactions between children in any way compromise the dignity of the individual with the disability?"

This is true for adults as well. After I (Norm) began using a wheelchair, it was astonishing to both of us to see how entitled even perfect strangers seemed in crossing my personal boundaries. People pat my head, my shoulders, and even sometimes other parts of my body. I highly doubt that they would do this with a non-disabled man.

In addition, it is crucial to recognize that disabled people are statistically far more likely to experience sexual, physical, emotional, and financial abuse than non-disabled people. If we do not recognize, respect, and support an individual's physical autonomy, we risk setting them up for abuse. When boundaries are routinely crossed, people learn to disregard them. What looks cute in second grade—full frontal hugs, for example—is not so cute and can be downright dangerous when it happens on the bus with a perfect stranger.

A number of years ago we were invited to an informal discussion at an agency providing support to adults with intellectual disabilities. The group, comprised of individuals with and without disabilities, sat in a large circle. During the course of the conversation, a woman with an intellectual disability got up and began walking around the circle behind the participants. This in and of itself was not a major distraction or in any way problematic. We always hope that people will do the things for themselves that they need to do in order to stay engaged. For some, this involves movement.

As she walked behind us, she began to play with people's hair. Although the people she was touching seemed uncomfortable and nonplussed by the contact, no one said anything. In fact, we observed a number responding with what seemed to be insincere smiles and hand pats. As she continued her walk, she came to us. Norm's hair is quite long, and he wears it in a ponytail. She began stroking his head and flicking his ponytail. Norm turned to her and said, "Please stop."

In a second the atmosphere in the room was electrically charged. Everyone turned to look at Norm. We realized that it was unlikely that anyone had ever confronted this issue with her before. Why not?

It is patronizing to allow incidents like this to take place. Would we allow unwanted touch from a non-disabled person? It's unlikely. Yet this woman's support staff seemed unwilling to say anything. It's as if it would have been unkind to remark on it. And yet how kind is it to be complicit in ignoring something that has problematic ramifications and might even inadvertently set someone up for future abuse? We are not suggesting that helping people learn to respect personal boundaries should be done in a curt or abrupt way. After all, it is often the fault of non-disabled people that these lessons were not learned earlier. We can be gentle and yet firmly assert our right to maintain our own boundaries and in so doing communicate that this right extends to the person we're talking with as well.

Another compelling example we heard came from a psychologist who spends her time helping people with intellectual disabilities who run afoul of the law or have illegal and abusive things done to them. She used a true story to illustrate the problems caused by disregarding the need to help people learn about boundaries.

She was called to a situation where a young man with an intellectual disability had been arrested. He'd been granted a job interview, and when he arrived at the front desk, he promptly dropped his pants and exposed himself to the receptionist. The police were called, and he was charged with indecent exposure and taken away to the police station.

The psychologist emphasized and very much wanted the audience to know that once charges have been laid for this kind of behaviour, they are notoriously difficult to undo. She arrived at the police station determined to do her best for this young man. In the course of trying to figure out why this incident had occurred (he had no history of this sort of behaviour), she learned something that made the incident make sense.

Growing up, this young man's mother had told him how important it was to make a good first impression. One of the things she stressed was personal hygiene and looking "pulled together." Part of this was making sure his shirt was tucked in. One of the best ways to accomplish this, she'd told him, was to tuck his shirt into his underwear. That's what he'd been doing—he'd dropped his pants while trying to tuck his shirt back in.

Even with the best of intentions, teachers and others can do problematic things that undercut autonomy and dignity and even endanger the disabled person. Sometimes, for example, privacy for a disabled person is not considered as important as it should be. We've heard stories of people who use public washrooms and forget to close the door of the stall since their families overlooked this as important. It's easy to see why this might be dangerous or embarrassing in other settings. Consider the following true story.

A number of years ago a woman came up to us after we'd presented a workshop based on what we're talking about in this chapter. "I have to tell you a story because I think it fits with what you were saying," she told us. "When I was teaching an inclusive third-grade class, one of the kids was a little boy with a significant physical disability. He was incontinent, and so his diapers had to be periodically changed." She smiled. "That's when the Pamper Club started," she added proudly.

We looked at her, puzzled. What on earth was a Pamper Club? Then, to our horror, she explained. "We had a section in the back of the classroom with room dividers around it. That's where we changed him. He wore diapers, so that's why we called it the Pamper Club. Children who wanted to could help."

We were shocked and at a loss for words. It was particularly difficult since she was genuinely proud of what she'd done and didn't seem to see any difference between the creation of the Pamper Club and what we'd been speaking about.

Dignity and respect must never be violated under any circumstances. Although this example is drastic, and we hope that very few people would find it acceptable, it's important to note that it *did* happen. We must be alert and vigilant to lesser examples that still may compromise an individual's dignity.

Modelling Behaviour

There is a lot of discussion about how kids learn from each other and how a child's peers are often effective arbiters of social appropriateness. Although this is most certainly true, we must remember that teachers and support staff remain the most powerful modeling agents in the classroom and in the wider community. If interactions between the teacher and the child with the disability and likewise the support staff and the people they are supporting are respectful, the other students and members of the community will take their cues accordingly. There are many components to respectful interaction and good modeling, but one of them is often overlooked. We offer you another story that illustrates some of the finer points.

Many years ago, our friends and colleagues Rosemary Crossley and Anne McDonald wrote a book called *Annie's Coming Out* (1980). It was later made into the film *A Test of Love*. The story is true and follows the relationship between the two women over a period of several decades. Rosemary met Anne when she went to work as a speech therapist in an institution in Melbourne, Australia. Anne, who had cerebral palsy, had been institutionalized as an infant. At age sixteen she weighed a mere forty-eight pounds. This was because she was laid almost prone while she was being fed, with her head and neck at an awkward angle. Many people with cerebral palsy experience an exaggerated gag reflex, and Anne was no exception. This position coupled with the gag reflex made it almost impossible for her to eat. At the time the two met, Anne was severely malnourished. This was only one of the indignities and abuses she'd experienced during her time in the institution. There had been many others, and she'd also witnessed abuse against others who lived there. As we know, trauma for the person who observes abuse can be as intense as it is for the person experiencing it, particularly when the observer is powerless to help and must simply watch.

When Rosemary and Anne met, Anne wasn't able to speak. She had never been offered a viable communication system, which left her both vulnerable and frustrated. That changed when Rosemary arrived and began helping her learn to read and develop a method for communication. One of the first things Anne said when she was able to communicate was, "Get me out of here!" Unfortunately, although Rosemary and her partner, Chris, expressed a willingness to share a home with Anne, her parents did not agree. This precipitated a court challenge, which was ultimately successful. Anne lived with Rosemary and Chris until her untimely death a few years ago. The best part of this story is that during the years they worked and lived together, Anne had a productive and happy life. She was a staunch advocate and activist for other disabled people, particularly when it involved what she maintained was an important civil right: helping nonspeaking people to access communication systems. She was also involved in many leisure pursuits. One of the Facebook posts we remember fondly (and with a bit of alarm) was Anne participating in reverse extreme wheelchair bungee jumping!

The reason we're including this story is because of a very telling remark Anne made that is highly relevant to this discussion. One day Rosemary asked her what she thought was a relatively simple question.

"What is the hardest thing about the way people treat you?"

Anne's response was quick and unequivocal.

"Baby talk!" she said.

Think of Anne's history as we've described it. Removal from her family. Malnutrition, abuse, and no ability to communicate. Boredom and isolation. When we consider all of these things, her response might seem surprising. Baby talk, while admittedly annoying, seems at first to be a pretty innocuous problem. However, her response shouldn't surprise us. For many disabled people, baby talk is the bane of their existence. We experience it all the time. For example, in restaurants I (Emma) am routinely asked what Norm would like to eat, and if the server bothers to ask him, it is often in that high squeaky voice that is usually reserved for poodles, cats, and children under the age of six months. We know disabled people who describe being accosted on the street by well-meaning passersby and subjected to personal questions or suggestions for outlandish cures delivered in that same loud, high, squeaky voice—and most often in a kind of exaggeratedly close proximity that would never happen between two non-disabled people.

We have a dream that is not facetious. If we all work together, we can eradicate baby talk in our lifetime. There's a point of enlightened self-interest in doing so because it isn't just disabled people who experience this irritating patronization. Elderly people do, too. Given that with any luck all of us will be older adults at some point, it behooves us to work to end baby talk before we get there! Modeling respectful interactions is a critical component of truly inclusive practices. Baby talk should never be tolerated.

A child's classmates may provide useful information about one another and why children do the things they do. Sometimes children will see things that remain invisible to adult observers. Students often see and hear things teachers don't. They often have unexpected insights into the very issues that plague us most. For example, a friend of ours was involved in an inclusion project in a junior high school. One of the students he'd been working with seemed to have good relationships with the other students in his class but puzzlingly was consistently isolated and alone in the cafeteria during lunch period. One day, frustrated and at a loss for how to proceed, our friend asked a couple of the other students why they didn't sit with their friend during lunch. One of the students made a face. "It's that thing he eats with!" The disabled student was tube-fed, and his lunch was a bag of pureed food suspended on a pole beside him. "It's gross! Throw a sweater over it or something!" Covering up the pureed food was all it took. From that head-slapping moment on, the student was among his peers in the cafeteria.

Another example is illustrated by a story told to us by our friend Lara. Lara had a daughter named Sylvia, who had a significant disability. Sylvia used a wheelchair, and when she was in the third grade, she was just beginning to use a rudimentary communication board.

Lara had always been a staunch advocate for her daughter's educational rights, so Sylvia was in a regular third-grade class. "They call me the mother from hell," she once told us, "and when I come to school, I can clear the hallways in seconds flat without saying a thing!" For Sylvia's Individualized Educational Program (IEP) that year, Lara pulled out all the stops. She insisted that Sylvia be present for the meeting along with her family, friends, and classmates (something that doesn't always happen – it is much more common for school professionals to have IEP meetings without the student or their supporters). It became the social event of the season, and invitations were at a premium.

One of the children who insisted on an invitation was a boy in Sylvia's class who had the dubious distinction of being one of the school's worst behaviour problems. Given the boy's reputation, Lara had had qualms about the friendship. However, her other children, who also attended Sylvia's school, protested and said, "Mom! He's Sylvia's friend. If it's not broken, don't fix it!" Despite Lara's reservations, she decided to invite him.

They began the IEP by talking about Sylvia's communication. Maybe it would be more accurate to say they were talking about her lack of communication. Ruefully, everyone admitted that she didn't really have much.

Suddenly, from out of the cheap seats, the little boy with the big reputation rose to his feet.

"That's not true, is it, Sylvia?" he said, clearly outraged. Sylvia made a noise that sounded suspiciously like a confirmation.

"Now," he said, "when Sylvia wants to go outside, this is how she tells me. When she wants to come in, this is how I know. If she's hungry, I can tell because she does this" He demonstrated a head movement. "When she's cold, this is what she does." The list went on for a good five minutes. Throughout his speech, Sylvia watched him, occasionally making supportive noises.

The adults in the room, including Sylvia's parents, listened in amazement. "To tell you the truth," Lara told us later, "we had our jaws on our chests. I've got to admit that it was a bit embarrassing to be upstaged so thoroughly by an eight-year-old. You'd swear he knew her better than we did."

Finally, his diatribe concluded, the school's number-one behaviour problem pulled himself up to his full height, looked disdainfully at his silent and gobsmacked audience, and said, "Well, I didn't just come for the juice and cookies, you know!"

There is, of course, a caveat. The risk involved in eliciting input, especially about behavior, may be the development of an increased sense of difference and distance. People with disabilities tell us that it is easier to be ignored than to be patronized or seen as a "class project." By involving students and others without being careful to mitigate this possibility, we can unintentionally transform them from friends into helpers and in so doing perpetuate the one-up/one-down relationship.

We can still get the information we need without compromising the equity of peer relationships by positing the issue as the school's or the community's problem rather than the person's. This way it is us who do not yet have the insight, experience, or information necessary to support the person well, not the person who is in need of fixing. It may emerge that the real issue, one well worth discussing, has more to do with how we might make schools and communities more responsive to all their members.

Reciprocity and Contribution

Although a majority of educators and human service professionals acknowledge that the rights of individuals with disabilities should be respected, there is an ongoing and often distressing debate about whether reciprocity is really possible and what kind of contribution is realistic to expect. We're sometimes asked, "What can a person with a significant disability really bring to a relationship?"

This question reveals more about our own stereotypical views of disability than about the limitations of a disability itself. After all, there is nothing universally true about any disability. Generalizations about "the disabled" will never generate the information necessary to address serious questions about the nature of reciprocity or contribution.

Dembo, Leviton, and Wright (1975) first identified a societal tendency to generalize and make broad inferences about the nature of disability. They called this common phenomenon "disability spread." We used this graphic in an earlier chapter, but it is worth revisiting in this context. Specifically, disability spread is what happens when we extrapolate the characteristics we associate with the notion of disability to the particular individuals we meet. These perceptions are often based on stereotypes and what we think we know about a particular disability. They are expressed in predictable ways. For example: "All people with Down syndrome are happy." "People with cerebral palsy usually have an intellectual disability." In fact, these characteristics may or may not be true of any individual. Figure 3, illustrates this concept.

FIGURE 3: DISABILITY SPREAD

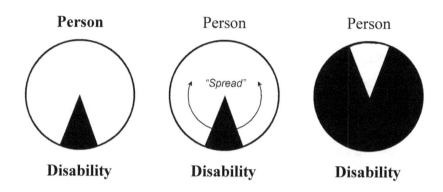

Many inferences and assumptions are made about disability in our society. For example, we are inclined to see people with disabilities as a collection of needs and deficiencies (McKnight, 1977). We are led to evaluate people based on what is missing rather than what is present. When our perceptions are based on stereotypical myths and misperceptions, we will not see a real person with any clarity.

In fact, every individual is a complex collection of components. Each of us has a variety of interests, skills, capacities, and a unique background. We all have different physical characteristics and our own idiosyncratic personalities. In our interactions with others, we want most to be understood and seen for who we are and hope that we will not simply be judged at face value. For individuals who have visible disabilities, being judged at face value is precisely what happens most often. When disability is seen as the largest component of a person, much of what is unique and "human" about them will be obscured. When needs and deficits are what we see, we only see what that person cannot do.

We must also pay attention to opportunities for disabled students and adults to make contributions. Many disabled people describe lives spent being the recipients of help; they are seldom, if ever, asked to make any contribution at all. For most of us, feeling that we are useful and contributing members of society is an important part of our identity. Imagining lives without this sense of involvement would likely make us feel sad and disconnected. Contribution may not always look the way we expect, but it is crucial that we find opportunities to facilitate it.

We heard this compelling story in a workshop years ago from a woman who teaches at a university. She is the parent of an Autistic son. At the time of this story he was about ten years old. One day her husband, who works at the same university, called and asked if he could invite the dean to dinner the next day. She readily agreed and began planning the menu and calculating preparation timelines. At three thirty she planned to prep the vegetables. By four o'clock the roast should be in the oven.

At three on the day of the proposed dinner, her son became upset and within minutes was seriously melting down. She did all the usual things she does to help him regulate, but nothing was helping. Three thirty came and went. No vegetable prep. Four o'clock likewise passed. By four twenty she was beginning to panic. She said, "I did things I *never* do. I put him in his room!" Finally, in desperation, she took him by the shoulders and surprised both herself and her son by saying, "I need your help!" She led him to the kitchen, put a vegetable peeler in his hands, and showed him how to peel potatoes. Instantly, he became calm.

She said, "I learned something that day. In our family, we had never asked our son for any kind of help. I have a bookshelf full of books on behavioral interventions, and not one of them talked about contribution!"

Like many families, hers had a regular Saturday morning chore list. Her son had never been part of it. The next Saturday he was given the task of dusting the furniture. She laughed as she told the story. "Sometimes all the furniture gets dusted; other times one corner of one table gets dusted really, really well. But that's not the point. He's part of this family, and he's making a contribution. That's what's important."

I (Emma) learned much about the subtleties of contribution through my experiences supporting adults with significant physical and intellectual disabilities. Probably the most lasting lesson came from a young woman named Jeanette. We helped Jeanette to leave a provincial institution in British Columbia in the late 1980s when institutions in that province were closing and people were given opportunities to move back into their home communities.

Jeanette had the dubious distinction of being called the most medically fragile person to leave a provincial institution. While this is a strange way to characterize a person, it was true that Jeanette got sick a lot. She required tube feeding and a ventilator, and was often hospitalized for various respiratory illnesses. To exacerbate the situation, Jeanette was unable to speak.

What those of us who knew, cared about, and supported Jeanette saw was a vibrant young woman with an indomitable spirit, a killer smile, and the brightest blue eyes imaginable. She had a sense of humour and was unilaterally loved by her support staff. She'd reconnected with her family and in a very short time had made good friends and was living a good life.

Unfortunately, her health concerns were considerable, and continued to sideline her, since life was often interrupted by hospital stays. It didn't take long before we understood that every time Jeanette entered the hospital, someone who knew and cared about her should be with her. She should never be left alone with only hospital staff because invariably, if we left, upon our return we would find an unauthorized "do not resuscitate" sign posted on her chart or the door. Each and every time we had to argue with the doctors and the nurses to have it removed. Since she was unable to speak, it was simpler to ensure that someone was always with Jeanette in order to forestall those difficult exchanges.

One day a nurse who was caring for Jeanette stopped one of our staff members and said, "I used to think you people had lost your minds. Why in the world were you fighting to keep this woman alive? What on earth is her quality of life, anyway? Why were you insisting on life-saving treatments for her?" (This, despite the fact that the treatments Jeanette received were not heroic or "life-saving"; they were simply the kind of treatments anyone with a respiratory issue might be offered.) "But," she continued, "I'm starting to understand. I see Jeanette with her friends, family, and support staff. She's warm and friendly, and those relationships seem close and genuine. I've even begun to create a relationship with her myself. So I've changed my mind. I think I get it."

John Bradshaw, the television therapist who predated Dr. Phil, once said, "We are less and less a society of human beings and more and more a society of 'human doings.'" This is undeniably underscored every time we attend a social gathering where we are introduced to new people. What's the first question we ask or answer? "So what do you do?" In many Aboriginal cultures, this question is seen as irrelevant. In these cultures the important question is "Who are your relatives?" and "Who is in your community?"

Did Jeanette *do* much? Not really. Her physical limitations precluded much of what the rest of society regards as meaningful contribution. But did Jeanette contribute? Absolutely! Her very presence was a contribution, and the people who knew her understood this. Unfortunately, many people simply looked at her and made assumptions about what she could and could not contribute, and did not believe that what she had to offer was enough.

Notions about quality of life are often based on fear and stereotype, not to mention misuse of the golden rule. People imagine themselves in the position of someone like Jeanette and firmly believe they'd rather be dead than inhabit her body. Those assumptions are not only profoundly dehumanizing and false but also potentially lethal, especially if those who hold these views have decision-making power over life and death. Those "do not resuscitate" signs posted on Jeanette's hospital charts were a stark reminder that such concerns are not hyperbolic but play out in real and dangerous ways.

We will not recognize the diverse contributions of individuals who wear obscuring labels until we move our focus from the disability and look for the complexity, individuality, and contribution we take for granted in ourselves. Only getting to know a person in all their multifaceted individuality can cause the disability to magically shrink and assume its real proportion—only one small facet of who a person is. Only then will we find ourselves able to see and receive the variety and richness of possible gifts.

Merging Respect and Help

Too much help can be a disabling force. One of the biggest challenges teachers face in inclusive classrooms is getting other kids to stop doing everything for the child with a disability. It's often the case in adult services as well. Support staff jump in and do everything while the people they support sit on the sidelines, bored and watching. Too much help, even when enthusiastically given, is fundamentally disempowering. Help should always be "natural and situation-rooted" (Wright, 1983, p. 311), and it should be what subjects of a fascinating study on help and disability termed "necessary help" (Ladieu, Hanfmann, & Dembo, 1947, in Wright, 1983, p. 310).

Help outside the context of choice and self-determination is disrespectful. We all want to feel necessary. However, when our desire to feel needed is at the expense of someone else's sense of competence and autonomy, we commit a lasting act of injustice. People with disabilities literally spend lifetimes struggling to be heard. We must learn to listen. As Marsha Saxton (1985) wrote,

> All of those people trying so hard to help me... All of them hoping for me to ... do well, all wanting to be kind and useful, all feeling how important helping me was. Yet never did anyone of them ask me what it was like for me. They never asked me what I wanted for myself. They never asked me if I wanted their help... I do not feel entirely grateful. I feel, instead, a remote anger stored beneath my coping pattern of complacent understanding. People do the best they can to help in meaningful ways, I know. I just wish all the disabled children [sic] would say to their

helpers: "Before you do anything else, just listen to me."
(pp. 133–134)

We must listen to both the verbal and nonverbal messages expressed by someone who may or may not want our help. We must use this information to guide our actions and increase our sensitivity. It doesn't sound like much, but the ramifications are enormous. It is often during times that we are hell-bent on helping that we listen least well. We all know stories about people with visual impairments being forcibly escorted over crosswalks by well-meaning pedestrians, of people in nursing homes being fed when they are not hungry, of what the participants in the Dembo study aptly called "unexpected attacks" of help (Ladieu, Hanfmann, & Dembo, 1947, in Wright, 1983, p. 309).

As a physically disabled person, "attacks of help" happen to me (Norm) all the time. Sometimes they are innocuous or merely irritating; sometimes they are more significant. Consider the following examples.

> I was presenting a conference that was held in a major hotel in Denver, Colorado. For the week I attended, I'd gotten to know the hotel maid as we passed each other in the hallway and when she came to clean the room. On the last night of the conference the organizers were taking all the speakers out to dinner. I'd planned the evening carefully so that in the morning when I was scheduled to leave early for the airport I wouldn't need to rush.
>
> I have a particular way of packing my bag so that my shirts don't get creased. I fold them and then create a packet of shirts that I can peel off one at a time as I need them. Before I left for dinner, I refolded my shirts and laid them on the bed, ready to put in my suitcase the next morning in preparation for my next speaking engagement. When I returned after dinner, I saw that the maid had been in my room, turning down the bed and leaving the ubiquitous little chocolate on my pillow. However, to my horror, I realized that she'd also gone a step further and hung up every one of my shirts!

I imagine that she probably felt a little closer to God through this altruistic act, but I can tell you that I also said something linking her to God when I got in and saw what she'd done. I daresay the meaning was slightly different.

But that wasn't the most infuriating example.

We were on our way home on the last day of a grueling road trip. Our travels had us connecting flights at O'Hare Airport in Chicago. It was a Friday afternoon. If you've never traveled through Chicago airport on a Friday afternoon, you should count yourself lucky. Chicago is what is called a hub city in the airline industry. This means that thousands of people who live in the west and work in the east must pass through O'Hare on their way home, and thousands of people who live in the east and work in the west have to do the same. We call it a 'Mardi Gras of road warriors.'

If you want to travel between B and C concourses, you must pass through a tunnel. This tunnel is flanked on either side by four huge escalators. Nowadays I use a wheelchair in the airport, and we manage to bypass the treacherous escalators by way of the elevator. However, at that time, I was still walking. Both of us were pulling roll-aboard suitcases, our briefcases slung over them. We were about halfway down the escalator, with about 868 impatient, weary, and slightly inebriated road warriors behind us, when a book in my briefcase fell onto the escalator step in front of me.

Normally this would not be a problem. I have a standard operating procedure when things like this happen. The best thing to do is simply leave the book on the escalator, step off to one side at the bottom, and wait for a break in the crowd to retrieve it.

However, this was not to be. There was a man at the bottom of the escalator who spotted the book and waved up at me. 'Don't worry, son,' he called. (I could live to the ripe old age of ninety, and they'll still be calling me son.) 'I'll get your book!'

I immediately recognized the problem. In order to retrieve my book, he was going to block my exit. In order to successfully step off the escalator, I needed a ten foot landing strip, and I immediately recognized that he was going to block my exit. I had one of those existential moments of impending horror where the world goes into slow motion. 'No, please, sir!' I yelled. 'Just leave the book!'

However, this man was undeterred. I have a theory that he had a secret lifelong dream to be a Shriner, and this was his opportunity to help the handicapped, and no one was going to stop him! He had what we call like to call "goodwill glaucoma." As predicted, he stepped in front of me and, in the process of reaching for the book, tripped me. I fell spread-eagle in front of the escalator, and my suitcase rolled over me, pinning me to the ground. Now the 868 road warriors and Emma were doing a Michael Jackson moonwalk backward up the escalator in an attempt to avoid tripping over me. They were annoyed at me because I fell, I was annoyed at the good Samaritan because he tripped me, and he was annoyed at me because I wasn't grateful.

Then, as I was picking myself up and dusting myself off, he leaned down and said, "You know, you really should use the elevator." I was speechless with fury. I could see the headlines of the Chicago Tribune the next day: Disabled Activist Stabs CEO with Button Hook."

Respectful help is always about asking the person if they need the help we're offering. It's a simple thing to do. Even if a person doesn't speak, or has trouble answering the question, it's still important to try. And in this context, one of the most helpful things teachers and others can do is to assist a disabled person to learn to initiate the support they need. If the person hasn't had a lot of experience doing this, it may take some time. It's important to continue to ask, "How can I help you?" If the person says they don't know, it sometimes helps to ask, "What would you say if you did know?" This question allows the person to speculate and reduces the pressure to have the right answer. If they still don't respond, be a waiter. "OK, I could do this, or this, or this." Initiating the support they need is probably the most important life skill a disabled person can learn. It will serve them well all through life.

Empathy and Social Justice

Most children are acutely conscious of what is fair and what is not. It isn't usually difficult to appeal to a child's sense of justice. Furthermore, powerlessness and social stigma are not the sole experiences of individuals with disabilities. Children, by virtue of their status in society, generally understand what it feels like to be without influence. They know how it feels to be silenced, to be disregarded, and to have decisions that concern them made arbitrarily and regularly by others.

We have downplayed and underutilized these experiences, thinking that white, middle-class, able-bodied children don't experience oppression and won't understand. In fact, most children experience rejection, isolation, and a sense of powerlessness at some time. Whether these are children of colour or children who must learn English as a second language; whether they are the children who dress differently, eat different foods, or have ethnically "different" last names; or children who just don't seem to fit somehow, there is a kernel of commonality in these experiences. Memories of bullying or exclusion are powerful and often still startlingly present and accessible for many of us even into adulthood.

Too often, in discussions of social justice between educators and children and among non-disabled adults, the issues are portrayed as "theirs." We show people what institutional life looks like, we talk about the negative effects of segregation, and we ask them to think about how it feels to be teased because you have a disability. As mentioned in a later chapter, we even subject them to simulated situations or role-plays that supposedly allow participants to feel, for example, what it's like to be blind by wearing a blindfold for an hour or so. Unfortunately, the unintentional result is often more distance and an even greater sense of fundamental otherness. At best, this approach fosters sympathy, and at worst, a guilty relief: "Thank heavens it's not me." We haven't always done the best job in introducing people who are seen as newcomers to schools and community in the most effective way.

We must take care not to inadvertently reinforce the notion that individuals with disabilities are objects of pity. Equitable relationships cannot be built on a foundation of pity. Instead, we must build on the shared experiences and the shared stories between us to create a sense of empathy, a sense of "I know what you mean." This does not disregard our different experiences. It is certainly true that having a disability and being an immigrant are not completely comparable experiences. Likewise, being left out of games on the playground and being the victim of racist behaviour is not the same. However, where experiences do intersect, we have an opportunity to build connection and understanding that may extrapolate to other situations in unexpected ways.

We have understood the need to teach black history in our schools, and increasingly we are teaching Aboriginal and other histories as part of the curriculum. We have recognized the need to provide narratives and even role models so that children can see themselves represented in the greater societal story. What we have not yet done is provide students with access to disability history. Teaching disability history is another way we can foster pride and inclusion and celebrate our unique experiences and backgrounds. The disability history is a rich one, full of stories both positive and negative that would likely interest and engage all of our students. Many people reach adulthood without ever having contact with powerful disabled role models or any awareness of these histories. As a result, a culture of shame persists, especially among individuals with intellectual disabilities. This can be countered by foregrounding stories of competence and power, introducing them to activists, encouraging membership in advocacy groups like People First, and encouraging pride.

Social justice is an important aspect of education. The development of empathy and shared understanding between individuals of diverse backgrounds and abilities is critical if our world is to survive into the next century. We need young people who will work together to address the issues of inequity and injustice that still face us.

This chapter was initially included in a book primarily devoted to cooperative learning within heterogeneous schools. Some people wondered why the epilogue we wrote focused almost exclusively on inclusive education. There's good reason for that. We believe that individuals with intellectual and physical disabilities may well prove to be the proverbial canaries in the experimental coal mines of education. These are the people who will teach us most about the nature of help, friendship, respect, and truly relevant support. In this revised chapter, we have discussed how these issues impact adults with disabilities and their support staff as well, since the issues have huge overlap. Through our interactions with individuals who have disabilities, both our schools and the larger community stand to learn valuable lessons that will lead us to greater appreciation of diversity in all its forms. The creation of a better world is dependent on our collective ability to learn these lessons well.

PART 3

INTERSECTIONS, IDEAS, AND INNOVATION

CHAPTER 12

CHESS, ARTIFICIAL INTELLIGENCE, DISABILITY, AND INNOVATION

Disability is not "a brave struggle" or "courage in the face of adversity"…disability is an art. It's an ingenious way to live.

Neil Marcus

As our friends and relatives will tell you, we live in an apartment dominated by the presence of chess sets. Due to an early interest in chess, Norm began collecting them as a teenager, and this obsession has continued to the present day. Soon after we met I (Emma) also became involved in bolstering this collection. Over the years we have acquired dozens of them. Twelve sets are on display and at least as many are stored away for lack of space.

The chess sets and boards we own and display on bookcases and tables are a beautiful and dramatic backdrop to our lives. They are also powerful symbolic reminders. While many associate chess with war and overt competition, we associate it with problem solving, strategy, observation, and patience. We have both learned many important lessons from the study and practice of chess that have benefited our lives in unusual ways. Norm is the real chess player in our duo. He studies and plays pretty much on a daily basis and has participated in chess clubs and tournaments. For me, the love of chess is certainly about the game itself, which I find fascinating, but also highly aesthetic. I love the symmetrical and linear construction of the checkered boards and the incredible intricacy and diversity of the pieces. They are works of art.

We are also fascinated by the history of chess. It is one of the oldest games in the world and has been played cross-culturally for centuries. Many historians believe it originated in India more than 1500 years ago; a few believe it had its roots in China. After its inception, the game swiftly moved westward. Although there have been changes—pieces named and renamed and allowable moves for the pieces negotiated and renegotiated—it has remained relatively unchanged for most of its history. Conventions were developed that chess players from all over the world continue to study, memorize, and utilize. It has been suggested that the number of possible moves in chess is infinite, with some suggesting that by the second move, 702,084 moves are possible; by the third, 9 million; by the fourth, 318 million. Nevertheless, with the exception of a few brilliant virtuosos, chess players continue to rely on the standard conventions for opening, middle, and end-game strategies. These strategies are steeped in tradition, and most chess players will tell you that if you have any hope for improvement, you must study, memorize, and follow them.

That is, until the advent of online chess engines and in particular an artificial intelligence engine called Alpha Zero. Alpha Zero has disrupted taken-for-granted ideas and led accomplished chess players to question all their assumptions. It has shaken the chess world to its very foundations. But more about that later.

In this essay, we will explore how chess has informed our understanding of what it means to innovate, and we will look specifically at the relationship between chess, disability, and creativity.

Norm: How Chess Got Me Included
in a Regular School

For me, the love of chess began early. My father taught me the game at the age of eight or nine, and I was quickly hooked. I immediately began poring over chess books and puzzles, and at night I would put myself to sleep by staring at a magnetized chess board hanging on my bedroom wall and mentally solving chess problems. Chess became an obsession. My father was quite competitive and as a result never condescended by allowing me to win. He would not concede a game unless it was fairly won. Much to his frustration, by age ten I was regularly winning our games. Luckily for me there was a vibrant and serious chess club at Sunny View Public School, the segregated school I attended until grade seven. Our science teacher, an avid chess player, would often play out and demonstrate famous games by chess Grand Masters Capablanca and Lasker during lunch to a rapt audience of disabled chess-master wannabes. As a result of his coaching, my father's encouragement, and my membership in the chess club, by the time I entered a regular junior high school, I was already a fairly strong chess player for my age.

Although I didn't recognize it at the time, there was more happening on the chess board than simply the game. Chess was training me to build and strengthen my frustration threshold, and when I look back on it, I realize that it was helping me to develop the skills and mind-set necessary to manage life with a disability. I was learning to think ahead, plan for contingencies, and consider my options not just laterally but sometimes even in three dimensions! "If they move here, where will I move?"

In grade seven, as I mentioned in Chapter 1, I successfully argued my way into a regular junior high school. In some ways I attribute my ability to convince the school to accept me to what I learned from playing chess. Let me explain.

In most respects, I predate inclusive education and even its precursors, mainstreaming and integration. Very few, if any regular schools were accepting disabled students when I was thirteen, and Ledbury Park

Junior High School in Toronto was no exception. However, I was determined to transfer out of the segregated school to a regular school in my own neighbourhood. In the very rare instances where disabled students had been able to move from a segregated school to a regular school, the procedure was standard. A representative of the segregated school would be sent to meet with an administrator of the receiving school. In my case, the representative of the segregated school told my mother, "If anyone will be able to convince the school to accept Norman, it will be Norman himself." So a meeting was set up between Mr. Bremner, the assistant principal of Ledbury Park, and me. As a representative of the school district, Mr. Bremner held the power to decide whether I could attend his school. I prepared rigorously for the interview since I knew he would be skeptical that I could manage both the physical and curricular challenges of a large urban junior high school. Meeting with Mr. Bremner felt strangely like walking into a chess tournament. In much the same way that I might have considered the possible opening moves of my opponents on the chess board, I carefully considered all of his possible objections.

As expected, Mr. Bremner began by laying out his concerns one at a time. How would I deal with math class? How would I manage industrial arts? What about physical education? Was I able to negotiate the stairs? I countered each one of his objections with a preplanned move of my own, explaining in detail how I would deal with the issues he foresaw. At the end of the interview, concerned but convinced, he reluctantly agreed that I could attend Ledbury Park. "But for God's sake," he added, "don't fall!"

What I'd learned from chess that I was able to apply in this interview was how to think ahead, plan strategically, deal with frustration, and stay observant, aware, and patient even in the face of significant roadblocks. In chess, your opponent is always throwing out problems that you have to solve. It's essential that you consider the problem carefully before responding, and when you do respond, to be sure that you have looked at all your available options and picked the best one. There's a quote from chess Grand Master Stanley Kubric that states this perfectly:

> You sit at the board and suddenly your heart leaps. What chess teaches you is that you must sit there calmly and think about whether it's a good idea and whether there are other better ideas (https://www.brainyquote.com/quotes/stanley_kubrick_115201).

Once I was allowed into Ledbury Park, navigating the new school was a formidable challenge. Not only was it a larger and less accessible school with a different demographic, but it was also fraught with social rules the other kids seemed instinctively to understand that I had to frantically decode. Rather than panicking, I once again relied on chess strategy. What's the best way to deal with the situation? As each new problem presented itself, I had to carefully consider it and look for the best solution. The process was the same whether it was a logistical problem, such as figuring out how to do calculus on a typewriter, or a social problem like trying to figure out the best way to make people comfortable with my disability and ensure that they could understand my speech.

Given that I couldn't write, one of the first problems I had to solve concerned note-taking in class. As I considered my options, I developed what are called candidate moves in chess. This means looking at the number of viable options before choosing a course of action. I thought about typing my notes, dictating them into a tape recorder, or asking my teachers for a copy of their notes. Each one of these turned out to be an unplayable move. Typing was too slow and disturbed the class. Taping the lecture meant I had to listen to it all over again at home and then arduously type out the notes. I quickly discovered that this was prohibitively time consuming and inefficient. As for the teacher's notes, they proved nonexistent, far too brief, or completely unintelligible. So, once again, in the language of chess, none of my candidate moves were viable. What I needed was a new and original option. After concentrating on this problem for several days, the solution arrived almost unbidden into my mind. I identified the student in each class who took the most copious notes and supplied them with a piece of carbon paper. I could sit back, fully take in the lecture, and leave with a comprehensive set of notes. Problem solved!

During my first year of university, I wrote a book outlining the many workarounds and hacks I'd developed to manage school effectively. Many of these are outdated and would be considered unnecessary today with the development of accessibility aids like computers, screen-readers, iPads, and other AAC devices. Many of the more modern schools we visit today are also required to have ramps and elevators and accessible washrooms. However, the mind-set that allowed me to stay creative in the face of the many hurdles I encountered at school remains the way I approach problems today. Luckily, through my experience with chess, I'd developed confidence in my ability to solve problems. It had become part of my identity and was a source of pride.

Would I have learned this approach without chess? I'm not sure.

Norm: Life Hacks and Lessons Learned

During junior high school, I became a member of the Ledbury Park Chess Club (and in doing so arguably identified myself as a certified nerd). One of the lessons I learned came from an unexpected source. One day, on a mission to collect some piece of audiovisual equipment for a class, I ventured into a small room at the end of a long hallway where all of the equipment was stored. The room was the size of a closet and jam-packed with reel-to-reel and cassette tape recorders, film strip machines, sixteen-millimetre projectors, and a multitude of other now-extinct devices. The person who controlled this room, signing equipment in and out and making any needed repairs, was a man named Mr. Csia. Upon entering, I noticed a chess board set up on a small table in the corner. I asked what I immediately realized was probably a silly question. "Do you play chess?" Mr. Csia smiled and nodded. I asked if we could play. He pulled the table out and said, "You play white."

I have to sheepishly admit that I came into the room with typical teenage arrogance, assuming that my successful experience in school chess clubs and tournaments would make these games slam dunks. I was very quickly disabused of this notion. Every game went the same way. My opponent, the unassuming Mr. Csia, would make a move and then nonchalantly return to whatever task he was working on. The moves he made seemed to require little of his attention, never mind reflection, and he would invariably, easily, and decisively win every game. One game led to the next, and soon I was playing Mr. Csia every lunch, recess, and even after school, all with the same disappointing result.

One day, in frustration over another potential loss, I conceded a game I presumed I could not win. Rather than accepting my resignation, Mr. Csia offered to pivot the board and play my pieces. I readily agreed to play what I was sure was a winning position. Almost effortlessly, he worked from my inferior position and promptly won the game. In response to my bewilderment and obvious frustration, he said, "Norm, you must learn to manage your discouragement. Your major opponent is not the person on the other side of the board. It's the voice inside your head telling you what's possible or not possible."

In the decades since Mr. Csia offered this advice, I have called on his wisdom many times in my daily life while thinking about how to overcome seemingly insoluble problems; in our work as activists dealing with bureaucratic roadblocks, and on many other occasions. Emma and I often quote Mr. Csia to each other.

What I learned later (that Mr. Csia had never said) explained the effortless wins. The modest technician had been the Czech Republic's junior chess champion.

Emma: Chess and Disability and Rehabilitation

Most disabled people spend a significant part of their lives involved in rehabilitation and remediation programs. These programs are typically developed and implemented by well-meaning non-disabled professionals and are often based on the idea that the less disabled a person is, the better their quality of life will be. Most non-disabled people (and even some disabled people) don't question the logic of this idea; it seems obvious. However, trying to make disabled people do things in the usual ways, from the tasks of daily living to solving more complex cognitive procedures, is often like trying to pound proverbial square pegs into round holes. This is arguably a somewhat violent description of therapy, but the sad fact is that many disabled people will describe their experiences in exactly this way. Superimposing conventional strategies onto unconventional bodies and minds is at best a mismatch and at worst a painful and often visceral reminder that they will never measure up. When non disabled people approach problem solving from this vantage point—trying to make disabled people behave in normative ways—they miss opportunities for innovation. They create artificial constraints based on existing conventions that may prevent the development of more useful and creative responses.

Unfortunately, many non-disabled professionals are like conventional chess players: they rely on long-established approaches they believe are tried and true. When confronted with seemingly insoluble problems, many seem to believe that the solution is to do the same thing, only at greater intensity. In other words, if three repetitions of an exercise haven't delivered the desired results, maybe ten will. If twenty hours of Applied Behaviour Analysis (ABA) hasn't resulted in behavioural change, maybe forty hours will. If the Reti opening in chess wasn't successful, maybe the English will be.

In addition, when non-disabled professionals design programs and implements to assist disabled people to function more effectively, they unfortunately often miss the mark. For example, many rehabilitation specialists still work diligently to help improve functioning within the context of normally expected child development milestones. It seems obvious. Help a child move through developmental stages quickly, and they will develop new skills that build on the previous ones.

This is often a mistake. I ruefully admit here that I have fallen into this trap. It took me several years after meeting Norm to admit that during my initial training and practicum as a preschool teacher I made and imposed a device called a button board on my poor unsuspecting students. A button board, in case you didn't know, is a piece of wood with two pieces of cloth stapled onto its back. One side has buttons, and the other has button holes. When the two pieces are wrapped around to the front of the board, presto! It becomes a device often used in occupational therapy rooms to help people with poor fine motor control learn to do up buttons. Seems like a low cost and effective tool for accomplishing this important task, doesn't it?

When I first met Norm, he told me a story that fundamentally changed my view of this apparently innocuous and supposedly useful tool. Norm described the button board as an instrument of torture. He told me that he'd been subjected to it for years in the occupational therapy room. Torture, I thought? Really? Wasn't that just a wee bit overstated? Well, once I heard the story I had to concede that maybe it wasn't. I had to admit that he had a point when he wryly suggested that it was one of the only activities where he was actually punished for succeeding. How? When all the buttons on one board were successfully done up, the occupational therapist would present him with another board, this time with smaller buttons.

One day, as Norm tells it, he was walking around the therapy room and spotted a small device hanging on the wall. "What's that?" he innocently asked. The therapist replied, "Why, that's a button hook."

"How does it work?" he asked.

She explained, "Well, you put it through the button hole, snag the button, and then pull it back out. Just like that, your buttons are done up."

"Can I try it?" he asked.

"Of course," she replied.

Within seconds he'd done up all of his buttons. "Good for you!" the therapist gushed.

He turned to her in anger and said, "Good for me? If something like this exists, why on earth have I been forced to use the button board for years?"

The answer, of course, is that manually doing up buttons is something a child of his age is expected to learn, and it is presumed that learning to do up buttons in the usual way will help a child to pass expected milestones and will lead to better fine motor control and, further, help them fit in with their non-disabled peers. These are ideas that educators, therapists, support staff and parents - like conventional chess players - have been memorized and rarely question.

Being disabled and managing the obstacles of life, whether doing up buttons, learning complicated social rules, or navigating through an often inaccessible world, requires a great deal of innovation and lateral thinking. Most people with disabilities become master innovators, because when you live in a world that isn't set up for you, you have to be. Disabled people learn innovation through experimentation, study, practice, self-knowledge, and sometimes even osmosis in ways that non-disabled people never have to. For most non-disabled people, innovation seems almost optional, because most things are set up to accommodate them. As a result, many never learn to be as creative as they might wish to be. On the other hand, navigating the world with a disability is much like navigating a chess board; moves must be carefully planned, and ease of movement is never taken for granted. Innovation is the most critical skill.

These are skills that often develop early. For example, when our son Evan was very small, even before we knew he was hard of hearing, he was already developing ways to learn language and interact successfully with his world. For example, he primarily gravitated to men. It was only when I learned about his hearing disability that I understood why he sometimes seemed to prefer the company of men and I was able to stop taking it personally. When I saw the banana graph of his hearing, I quickly understood that he heard best in the lower registers. He also positioned himself where he could see faces directly, and without even being conscious of it, taught himself to read lips.

This is just one small example of the many ways disabled people learn to cope with what are often unfriendly and difficult circumstances. In our apartment we have many small adaptations that allow Norm to navigate easily. For example, we tie string to doorknobs so he can pull the doors closed, since it's impossible for someone in a wheelchair to shut the door behind them in awkwardly small spaces. Because our washroom is not entirely accessible, we switched the door from an inward-opening trajectory to one that opens outward. For me, the adaptations I require have more to do with sensory issues. We have few overhead lights in our apartment, and those we have we seldom use. I also use lap pillows and weighted pads or blankets and wear blue-tinted glasses when it gets too bright outside or when I have to be in environments with fluorescent lights.

As a result of living in a world not designed to accommodate difference, disabled people become master innovators. Unfortunately, those without disabilities, because they don't have to, are often much less creative than they might believe. This would not be a problem if it weren't for one thing; it is generally left to non-disabled therapists, teachers, support staff and parents to develop the innovations that disabled people need. We will return to this idea in a subsequent chapter.

Am I implying that disabled people are the only creative and innovative people on the planet? If we return to the button board and the ingenious button hook, you might argue that the inventor of the button hook, (one Elias Howe, otherwise known for his more famous invention, the sewing machine) was a non-disabled person, and he was still creative. It's important to acknowledge (and is probably glaringly obvious) that yes, in fact, there are many non-disabled inventors, and we are grateful to Elias Howe for his useful invention. In making a claim for disabled ingenuity, we don't intend to discount anyone who isn't disabled, but simply to point out that what is often optional for non-disabled people is critical for those with disabilities.

Howe developed the button hook primarily to help non-disabled folks do up their buttoned shoes. What we wonder (but don't know) is who the first person to notice its utility for disabled people might have been. It's entirely possible that it was a disabled person. The point here is not whether Elias Howe was or wasn't disabled and was creative nonetheless; it is that relying on conventional strategies is often a colossal waste of time. All Norm's years in the occupational therapy room did not change his fine motor control one bit. All this wasted time could instead have been spent learning much more useful things (like chess openings, for example). We often joke that if participation in more interesting and important pursuits had been superseded by the need to master fine motor control tasks, we might still be waiting on the discoveries made by the late Stephen Hawkins.

Extending the Chess Metaphor: Enter Alpha Zero

Now permit us a few minutes of chess geekiness before we go back to looking at disability in the context of chess.

Over the past few years, a variety of computer chess playing engines like Stockfish, Rybka, Houdini, and Komodo have been developed and used to calculate almost infinite variations on the many standard ways chess has been played by humans over the centuries. Although these engines have proved formidable in their ability to outplay the Grand Masters, they too have now been surpassed by an artificial intelligence (AI) algorithm system developed in 2017 by DeepMind called Alpha Zero.

Unlike some of the other engines, Alpha Zero was programmed without access to any human approaches to playing chess; it was not exposed to conventional openings, middle and end game principles and strategies, or any chess books or puzzles. The way Alpha Zero learned chess was by playing millions of games with itself over a short period of time and forming rules and strategies based solely on its own successes and failures. Within twenty-four hours it was winning games against human Chess Masters and all the other major engines mentioned above.

Observers are often astounded at the decisions Alpha Zero makes. When prediction programs and international Chess Masters analyze its games move by move and try to predict which moves it will make next, they often fail. This AI engine consistently wins games by relying on non-traditional strategies like aggressive pawn marches and seemingly unnecessary and illogical sacrifices of major pieces. Alpha Zero does not utilize the numeric value system taken for granted in the chess world. Typically, pawns are counted with a value of one, knights and bishops as three, rooks as five, and queens as nine. The ever so egalitarian Alpha Zero does not appear to regard a pawn as having less value than a rook or a queen. Therefore, it often makes what human chess players feel are outlandish moves, like those huge sacrifices or counterintuitive pawn configurations. Grand Masters note that the program also rejects standard notions about the need for material gain in favour of space, mobility, and activity. Its games are dynamic, unexpected, and highly creative.

At the risk of anthropomorphizing the engine, it seems that Alpha Zero plays chess like a gleeful and precocious preschooler, and delights in confounding convention by taking over the board through quick action. It rapidly claims space and moves its pieces all over the board while its opponents, relying on traditional openings, have barely had time to develop their pieces. It thereby maximizes its own mobility while simultaneously constraining and minimizing the potential for its opponent to mobilize.

Demis Hassabis, one of the developers of the engine and a chess player himself, calls Alpha Zero's way of playing alien and completely counterintuitive. He equates it to chess from another dimension. Others note that precisely because the engine is self-taught, it is largely unconstrained by conventional strategies.

What Alpha Zero has done is question and then discard more than 1500 years of commonly accepted chess principles. In the process it has opened up a plethora of new ideas about how chess can be played. But beyond reinventing chess, does Alpha Zero offer us new ways to think about other aspects of life? With its creators, we believe it does.

Whatever fears you may harbour about the rapid development of artificial intelligence (and there are many legitimate concerns), there may also be lessons to be learned from engines like Alpha Zero. Alpha Zero reminds us that despite our trust in previous conventions and wisdom, we have not yet figured out everything that is possible. There is always something beyond our understanding, and there are many alternative ways to both conceptualize and act on those possibilities. But before we can do this, we must free ourselves of our tendency to do things the way we've always done them.

What Do Disabled People and Alpha Zero Have In Common?

Being disabled means having to constantly search out new and unusual ways to accomplish what needs to be done. This translates into a process of scanning the horizon for potential hacks that will save time and energy. Time and energy that can then be devoted to more important pursuits.

We are going to be a bit controversial and suggest that perhaps when it comes to creating innovative strategies to assist disabled people, most non-disabled people are like conventional chess engines with all the tried and true openings, middle and end games. But perhaps disabled people are more like Alpha Zero. Disabled people remind us that life is far more than just functioning, it is about actually living, and finding ways to live in environments that are often difficult and confusing. As one person anonymously suggested "if necessity is the mother of invention, then disability is its grandmother!"

When we talk about chess – and Alpha Zero – as metaphors for managing life with a disability, people sometimes interpret what we're saying (and even us!) as somehow heroic. They presume that we are super-imposing an optimistic chess metaphor onto what is often viewed as a tragic and limiting medical condition. We believe that this misses the essential point. As Neil Marcus points out in the opening quote, disability is not about bravery and tenacity. It is much more about trial and error, innovation and even artistry. A chess metaphor also allows us to tentatively reframe the experience of disability and provide a counterpoint to some of the commonly held narratives of what it means to be disabled.

In making this argument, we do not in any way wish to minimize the very real challenges and issues faced by disabled people or the equally real constraints placed upon them by people, institutions and policies. These are indeed formidable obstacles. We also do not want to suggest that an individualistic approach is what's needed. Disabled people are regularly exhorted to pull themselves up by their boot straps and this is neither helpful nor realistic. Disabled people are also often defined by their non-disabled counterparts as worthy of admiration for their "spunk" and "determination." This is the stuff of which bad stereotypes are made and is also not helpful (Young, 2012.)

However, what is fascinating to us is that many of our disabled friends and colleagues also describe life with a disability not so much as a "brave struggle" or "ongoing hardship", but as a series of circumstances – and yes, frustrations – that require problem solving and innovation. The home of our friends Catherine Frazee and Patricia Seeley in Nova Scotia is a structural monument to innovation. Catherine and Pat have ingeniously configured the inside of their home to accommodate Catherine's significant physical disability. Outside they have found ways to work with a steep hillside garden overlooking the Bay of Fundy to create something at once beautiful, magical and completely accessible. We (and they) understand that this is not something always available to those with lesser means. However, it does not take away from the fact that there is much to be learned about innovation, creativity and lateral thinking from disabled people.

We like the metaphor of chess. And we are intrigued by the extended metaphor that Alpha Zero offers. Metaphors are active agents that help us to create a sense of what is real and true.

What happens if we entertain the idea that it is equally or even more valid to say that "the experience of disability is fundamentally a problem-solving process analogous to solving a series of chess problems" rather than saying that "disability is a medical condition that prevents people from participating fully in community life"? What happens if we begin to question the way the non-disabled public – and most particularly, health professionals – have superimposed a medical metaphor onto disability? Which metaphor is most accurate – chess and problem solving or medicine and rehabilitation?

What chess and Alpha Zero remind us is never to underestimate or overlook the sideways solution and to always look for alternative ways to solve problems. Never settle for the first option – look for better moves. Chess – and most specifically, Alpha Zero - remind us that innovation delivers what convention, rehabilitation and remediation promise.

CHAPTER 13

MY YEAR WITH "FRANKENKNEE" (AND WHY SIMULATION EXERCISES DON'T WORK)

Emma

Sometimes people say you can learn a lot about what it's like to be disabled when, for example, you break a limb. I've heard people go as far as to say that after an accident that left them with impaired mobility for a little while, they now know what it means to be disabled. These ideas are the basis for a lot of misguided simulation and sensitivity exercises where people are blindfolded to ostensibly get a sense of what it means to be blind or someone spends the day in a wheelchair trying to understand the barriers wheelchair users face. Apparently, if you believe this premise, it's possible to extrapolate from these experiences in order to get inside the lived experience of a disabled person. I'd like to challenge that view in this essay.

When I call these exercises misguided it's because, well, that's what they are. Despite their popularity, they don't actually work. The truth is that you can't get a real sense of what it's like to be disabled from spending a day with your hands tied behind your back or not being allowed to talk. It's a simplistic idea, and it leads to simplistic assumptions.

What never gets discussed in those workshops and during those exercises is that disability is not so much about struggling against limitations as it is about innovation and improvisation. There are a million little hacks and tricks that disabled people use to navigate the world. These workarounds are so individualized and fine-tuned that they are impossible to replicate through some simplistic simulation. It would be impossible for a non-disabled workshop leader or participant without disabilities to figure out all the ingenious ways that disabled people use to manage on a daily basis. It would likewise be tough for a disabled person to facilitate such an enterprise, since everyone is different, and what works for one person will probably not work for another, even if you have the same disability! So don't believe the disabled workshop facilitators, either.

But perhaps most importantly, focusing on the inconvenience of any particular limitation in an attempt to foster understanding and empathy overlooks the biggest impact of disability, something that has little to do with physical or cognitive limitations. The biggest barrier disabled people face is systemic discrimination. Sitting in a wheelchair for a day or walking around a room blindfolded will not introduce you to the sense of discouragement disabled people experience when underestimated in job interviews, denied educational opportunities, excluded from participating in policy-making that should rightly involve them, and encountering impediments to the ability to manoeuvre through the community. In fact, in the well-intentioned process of trying to replicate disability through simplistic simulation exercises, you may inadvertently be contributing to that systemic discrimination.

How? Well, another reason these exercises are problematic is that what is learned is often not what is intended. Instead of instilling a sense of empathy and connection, they often induce a visceral sense of dread. While it is true that participants will on some level feel that they've had an eye-opening experience and say things like, "Wow, I had no idea our community was so inaccessible," or "I can't believe how tired I get when I have to work this hard to communicate," underneath those seemingly insightful comments there's often something else going on. They are secretly relieved when the blindfolds come off, and they get to stand up out of that wheelchair or resume using their voices. "Thank god it's not me." What those simulations most often do is confirm already existing stereotypes.

I am not physically disabled. However, last year I fell and broke my kneecap quite catastrophically. It was literally broken into four equal parts. I required surgery, hardware, and a leg brace and was given strict instructions on what I could and could not do. Almost a year later, I had more surgery to remove the hardware holding my knee together as it healed and also to repair my meniscus and debride the area around the patella. My friend Leah affectionately renamed my knee "Frankenknee" due especially to the strange scarring caused by the incisions and the application of dozens of staples. For quite awhile it indeed looked eerily as though I had been sewn together by Dr. Frankenstein!

During the course of both recoveries, I learned some things about inconvenience and limited mobility. But did I learn anything that would give me insight into what physically disabled people like my husband experience? Not at all. For one thing, I was always aware that my situation was temporary and fixable. However, I did learn some things that might be relevant in the context of this discussion.

When I broke my leg, I didn't so much learn what it was like to *have* a disability; what I learned was how to *manage* with a physical limitation. Disability, if you like, was transformed into a verb rather than a noun. I also came to realize that for many years I'd been in a process of apprenticeship about how to manage. I'd been learning from the very best mentors, those who are so seldom asked for their perspectives: disabled people themselves.

As I mentioned in Chapter one, I've been hanging around people with physical and developmental disabilities my whole life. My husband is disabled, as are most of my closest friends. So when I first broke my leg and realized that I'd be spending a lot of time navigating the world in some pretty awkward ways, it probably isn't surprising that it didn't faze me much.

People were shocked and horrified at my injury, but strangely, I was not (this was helped by the fact that I have a puzzlingly high pain threshold). Rather than asking "Why me?" I kept thinking, "Well, why not me?" After all, limited mobility is something Norm and I work around all the time. Yes, it was awkward and difficult at times, but we also shared quite a few laughs as we tried to navigate our apartment using two different (and sometimes colliding) mobility devices. There is a pragmatism I see in many of the disabled people I know that I was able to borrow and appreciate. Rather than bemoan my situation, I recognized very quickly that I needed to start thinking creatively and figure out how to manoeuvre. My next thought was, "OK, now what?" And just like that, I was able to draw on what I'd learned over the years.

It actually went much further than that. It had to do with the way I thought about my newly limited ability to get around easily. When my father lost mobility in his later years, he used a cane and often terrified us with his lack of balance and series of close calls. He adamantly refused to use a walker even though it would probably have afforded him greater security. His son-in-law (Norm), whom he adored, used both a walker and a wheelchair, but for some reason my dad felt that if he did, it would be demeaning and stigmatizing. It was puzzling to us.

I had no such qualms. Norm's walker, a battered and much-used member of the family we'd affectionately named Silver, turned out to be my salvation in those early weeks post-surgery. I was grateful that we'd never gotten rid of that clunky old thing after Norm started using the wheelchair exclusively. Given that I lack the physical coordination to use crutches, the walker was the perfect solution. And because I have known so many proud disabled people, I didn't think much about the stigma my father couldn't abide—being seen in public using a walker. (Although I did come to recognize that even among injured people, there is a hierarchy. It would seem that crutches are more socially valued than walkers. Who knew?)

It was through my association with disabled people and solidarity with this community that I could metaphorically thumb my nose at society's ridiculous assumption that walking independently is an accurate indicator of competence and value. Using a walker was pragmatic. If your body needs a mechanical extension or you need a cognitive workaround, use it.

But here's the other thing I learned, and I learned it from my physically disabled friends. Trust your body. Listen to your body.

I learned this one the hard way. I should probably have understood it sooner. As a lifelong active person, someone who not only loves but craves activity, when I injured myself I believed what everyone said about rehabilitation and embraced it enthusiastically. Work it hard. Push to regain what you've lost! My surgeon recommended it. My physiotherapist mandated it. Everything in me agreed. My husband, on the other hand, did not. He worried that I was pushing too hard.

Undeterred, I persisted. Initially, this was a good thing. My surgeon saw me as a rock-star patient. I'd regained almost all my range of motion within a few weeks. So, being me, I surmised that more was better. I upped my time on the recumbent exercise bike and doubled my time on the Pilates reformer. I walked. I stretched. I rowed. I did squats. Until I couldn't.

Suddenly I was doubled over in pain from a bout of bursitis underneath my kneecap. It was unclear whether I'd done this to myself or it was a case of iatrogenesis, since the physio-terrorists (um…therapists) had done something excruciating called "cupping" to my poor atrophying hamstring muscle a couple of days before. My surgeon speculated it might have been the cupping since the bursitis showed up exactly where the hamstring met the patella. Apparently my poor body was valiantly trying to accommodate all the activity and simply couldn't keep up. I was confused. "But I'm doing all the right things!" I thought. A foray online to research the consequences of overuse (something I didn't really want to know about) yielded a sobering answer. Rest, these fitness gurus said, is just as important as activity. I should have known.

My disabled friends understand this much better than I do. Whether it's a physical or a cognitive issue, there's a lot of discussion about how hard we push ourselves and whether we should. In disability culture, the amount of energy it takes to do the things that need to be done is something called spoon theory. Spoon theory was first conceived by Christine Miserando in 2003 when she used a handful of spoons to illustrate the units of energy it takes to accomplish a task. The more spoons are removed, she explained, the less available energy there will be. This is a reality that disabled people deal with all the time. How much energy do you expend before it becomes debilitating? How far do you push your body or brain?

When I first heard of spoon theory, it made a lot of sense to me. As an Autistic person, I get how much energy I expend in social situations and in managing executive function issues. And living with Norm, I've understood it in terms of physical disability. I see how hard he works to manage daily tasks and fine motor issues like typing and email and managing the minutia of daily living and personal care. I just never understood it in terms of my almost-always-cooperative physical body. Like many Autistic people, activity has always been my go-to for self-regulation and the management of anxiety. Now, for the first time, I had to figure out how to do those things without movement—or at least without as much movement. It was only as I came to understand the need to slow things down that I really understood the screen saver my husband has always used as a reminder to move slowly and avoid rushing. His screen saver is a huge smiling tortoise, and it's a symbol that reminds him to question society's addiction to relentlessly hectic activity.

During the course of recovery, I engaged in a lot of self-talk, but it was self-talk grounded in conversation and relationship with others. I needed the visual image of that tortoise and the wisdom of my disabled peers to manage my panic and the Armageddon narratives that filled my head when I thought of the need to—gasp—slow down and recover. I'm lucky. I have those role models who helped me put it all into perspective.

So that's what I mean when I say that what can be learned about disability will not be found in a sympathetic, "Oh, it must be so hard for you" mind-set or a clumsy attempt to generate insight through imitation. Instead, it will be found by appreciating the wisdom and experience of disabled people; a perspective that is largely overlooked and unappreciated.

My sister, who is on a wait list for knee replacement, told me that there are support and educational groups led by people who have experienced this surgery. The workshop facilitators talk about what to expect and help participants think about how they will manage post-surgery—what kind of help they might expect to need and how to organize their living spaces. This makes logical sense. There's wisdom and useful information to be imparted that could potentially be very helpful. But I still find it interesting that this happens routinely in groups of non-disabled people talking primarily to each other but seldom elsewhere. Disabled people, again, are so seldom asked to share their wisdom and experience.

Am I suggesting that the role disabled people should take in the world is simply to provide some kind of pretty life lesson for the non-disabled? Heaven forbid. Does this mean I'm minimizing the real difficulties disabled people face? Of course not. I do not discount those difficulties. I am not trying to romanticize disability or place anyone on a pedestal or nominate them as candidates for sainthood. What I am suggesting instead is that our disabled citizens are an untapped resource in understanding alternative and innovative ways to live and move through the world.

Disabled people can provide a powerful counterpoint to commonly held narratives about what it means to be disabled. It isn't just the pragmatics; it's also countering prevalent assumptions and misconceptions. There are many problematic things that non-disabled people assume about disability that go beyond mere underestimation that are important to clear up. These misconceptions have the capacity to fuel big decisions, and the consequences of believing them can be dire. For example, when non-disabled people believe that disability is a fate worse than death, that idea can influence the response to larger public issues like health care and euthanasia. When non-disabled people believe that disabled people cannot and do not contribute to society, that can have implications for whether support is seen as deserved or merely a favour to be granted.

What can we do to counter this kind of fear-based thinking and the actions that flow from it? For starters, we can listen to disabled people. Who better to counter these false premises than disabled people themselves? We can also engage with each other in real ways with the understanding that we have much to learn about what it means to be human, all the many ways to be human, and what it means to remain human in a world that too often dehumanizes some of its members. And we can ditch the simulation exercises.

There's an analogy Norm's often used that I particularly like. Goes like this: when we are born, it's like we're born onto a race track. From the moment we take our first breath, we have to start running. At every stage of development, we are compared to our peers. Who walked first, who said the first word, who gets the best grades, who has the best job or makes the most money. No matter where we are, there are always people ahead of us that we are trying to catch up to, and people behind us who are trying to overtake us.

However, when you're disabled, as Norm says, you're also born onto that race track, but within minutes the referee blows the whistle, disqualifies you and escorts you onto the bleachers. "From there", he says, "I sit down, get myself a coke, sit back and watch all you non-disabled people run around and around the race track. I have the overwhelming urge to yell 'guys, there's no finish line!'"

Think about this. If there are no people sitting in the bleachers to provide that kind of social commentary, how will the rest of us ever know we're on the race track?

I've learned more about lateral thinking from disabled people than all the lateral thinking specialists in the world could have taught me.

CHAPTER 14

COUNSELLING, SUPPORT GROUPS, CHRONIC SORROW, AND THE MYTH OF CATHARSIS

My (Norm's) master's thesis topic was about how healthy families deal with the birth of a disabled child. My research led me to clinical literature that, as a disabled person, left me feeling insulted and devalued. Specifically, this literature foregrounded something called "chronic sorrow."

In recent years, I (Emma) have noticed a proliferation of self-help books, blogs and online websites that claim to offer support to the families and caregivers of Autistic and otherwise disabled children and adults. Many of these similarly have as their focus the idea that it is a foregone conclusion that parenting disabled children will lead to pervasive sadness and hardship, and that the best way to cope with these feelings is through a process of catharsis. Although Norm's research took place in the 1980's, it is clear that the notion of "chronic sorrow" persists.

In this essay, we will challenge the notion that the birth of a disabled child will necessarily result in the experience of chronic sorrow and we will also challenge the idea that the best way to work through difficult emotions is through catharsis.

Chronic Sorrow

Parents are often encouraged by doctors, social workers, and sometimes even family and friends to attend counselling following the birth of a disabled child. Counselling can be a helpful way to process the experience and build resilience as the family adjusts to new challenges. However, the kind of counselling they receive is critical to the outcome. If a counsellor operates unaware of the biases they themselves may hold about disability, those views can easily be communicated to their clients. In the aftermath of diagnosis, parents who take part in counselling may be particularly vulnerable to taking on those biases.

Some of these biases come implicitly from broader societal perceptions and an overall dread of disability, but some are explicitly underscored and entrenched in counselling literature. For example, for many years counsellors were told to expect that the parents of disabled or sick children would almost certainly experience chronic sorrow (Olshansky, 1962). These researchers theorized that chronic sorrow was an inevitable and natural response to having a disabled child, since such a birth was unquestionably a tragedy. Inherent in this belief was a taken-for-granted assumption that life with a disability (and likewise, life spent parenting a disabled child) would be one of ongoing hardship and sadness.

The idea that chronic sorrow was not only an understandable response to the birth of a disabled child but was also inevitable led many counsellors to believe that their primary role was to encourage parents to actively grieve their changed circumstances. From this position, it wasn't a far stretch to suggest that it was even psychologically healthy to mourn the death of the hypothetical perfect child they'd hoped for. These ideas gave rise to a plethora of journal articles and books on this topic (Ellis, 1989; Bristor, 1984; Karg Academy, 2019).

The idea of chronic sorrow and grieving has always incited a vigorous debate in our minds. We understand that acknowledging painful emotions is sometimes critical in coping with a difficult life situation. We also know that when people have feelings... well, they have feelings. It's useless to try to convince a person not to have the feelings they have. In this sense, acknowledging the presence of grief and even chronic sorrow seems to make sense.

At the same time, we cannot help railing against well-intentioned non-disabled clinicians who indirectly endorse that, because of the disability, the birth of a disabled child is an occasion for sorrow rather than celebration. The implication is that disabled children are damaged goods or poor facsimiles of non disabled children—and therefore less valuable. As we mentioned earlier, a friend, celebrating the birth of a beautiful daughter with Down syndrome, told us about the horror and utter disbelief she felt at receiving cards of condolence instead of congratulation.

Counselling

There is no doubt that therapists who believed in the notion of chronic sorrow have had the best of intentions in encouraging their clients to come to terms with grief. After all, there is still a widespread idea that unacknowledged grief will eat away at a person and result in depression or worse. In this context, helping parents learn to manage episodic or even ongoing sadness makes perfect sense. Further, it seemed rooted in support and empathy. But are these assumptions necessarily true?

While most counsellors are committed to providing their clients with the nonjudgmental space to process feelings, some go further and encourage venting as an appropriate way to overcome difficult emotions. Though no self-respecting therapist would ever call what they are aiming for venting, many still do support the notion that catharsis, or getting the painful feelings out, is the best way to manage them. Admittedly, giving birth to a disabled child can provoke difficult emotions; after all, many parents will have had little or no experience with disability and may still be reeling from dire warnings and dismal prognoses from medical practitioners. Some report feelings of guilt "Was it something I did?", and many report feeling out of their depth and overwhelmed by their new responsibilities. Counselling can be a helpful way to process these feelings and find a positive way forward. However, is it possible that encouraging parents to repeatedly express emotions like sadness, fear, and anger may in fact be counterproductive? Rather than clearing the space to move forward, perhaps encouraging the repeated exploration of negative feelings may actually reinforce them. In this way, chronic sorrow may prove to be a self-fulfilling prophecy.

Support Groups

In recent years with the advent of the internet, we began to see a proliferation of blogs and Facebook pages that claim to offer a grassroots way for the parents and caregivers of disabled children and adults to share stories and give each other much-needed information and support. Some do precisely that and offer a counterpoint to the negative and stereotypical societal attitudes that families of disabled people often face. Both internet-based and in-person positive support groups can provide a welcome oasis in which parents can share experiences in a non-competitive, supportive environment.

However, there are other groups that are questionable in both intent and result. Some of these so-called support pages and groups provide little more than a forum for a downward spiral of histrionic complaints and horror stories. Worse, many actually encourage wholesale venting and the unsavoury practice of over sharing the difficult moments of parenting and support through graphic accounts, pictures, and even videos showing their disabled children during their most humiliating moments, including meltdowns and even difficult bathroom situations. When it is suggested that such accounts violate a child's right to privacy and dignity, members claim that "honest" sharing is an important practice that helps them get through life feeling understood and less alone. Perhaps the most egregious example of this kind of sharing is a video made by the fund-raising group Autism Speaks featuring

Alison Singer, the parent of an autistic daughter. In this video, Singer describes the urge to drive herself and her Autistic daughter off the side of the George Washington Bridge. She recounts the story to the camera in front of her daughter, who is repeatedly seen trying to hug her mother, and tells the filmmaker that she resisted the urge only because she also had another non-disabled child to think of.

Being understood and feeling less alone are certainly important. Parenting any child - disabled or not - can be an isolating experience. Having a group of empathetic peers can help parents of disabled children build the resilience they need in order to navigate an ableist world and advocate with and for their children. Upon reading some of these accounts, though, we were deeply concerned that some of these spaces were not as benign and helpful as they were reputed to be. Was it possible, we wondered, that rather than providing help and support, they were actually accomplishing the exact opposite—reinforcing attitudes of resentment, fear, and martyrdom? Further, were they perpetuating dangerous stereotypes and problematic ideas about disability? We have seen disturbing patterns in some online discussions where parents aren't so much supportive as engaged in a strange game of one-upmanship. Far too often the conversation is a variation on "You think that's bad? Wait until you hear what my kid did!"

As mentioned, many of the authors and contributors to these blogs and Facebook pages claim they are dedicated to providing safe spaces for parents to discuss the nitty gritty challenges of parenting a disabled child. As we will see later in this essay, if the focus is on the expression of negative feelings, they will prove not only unhelpful but also dangerous. In addition, we can't help but worry that seeing and hearing themselves described in negative and demeaning ways will be potentially hurtful, alienating, and even traumatizing for the children and adults who might later see what was written about them. As we all know, nothing on the internet ever disappears.

Understanding the dynamic of emotional contagion is important in this context. Humans are hard wired to influence each other. In other words, we have a tendency to try to make each other feel the way we are feeling. In blogs and support groups that highlight misfortune and difficulty, these feelings can be contagious; intensified rather than alleviated. Those groups that focus on cure and eradication can be equally problematic. For example, many of the nonstandard treatments touted as cures for autism are questionable at best and downright dangerous at worst. Bleach enemas, severely restricted diets, and other quack cures have endangered and sometimes even killed their recipients. In addition, the unfounded and thoroughly disproven belief that vaccination causes autism continues to persist in these forums. Purveyors of these cures capitalize on a globalized anxiety and fear of disability.

What both support groups and counselling have in common seems to be the notion that catharsis is not only helpful but also necessary. But is it? In order to unpack the issue, let's start by looking at the origins of catharsis.

A Brief History of Catharsis

Where did the idea that venting is a helpful way of dealing with stress come from? Perhaps we need look no further than the ancient Greeks—Aristotle in particular. Through the development of the theatre of tragedy, Aristotle believed that by evoking pity and terror in the audience, something called "purgation" would occur. In other words, the audience would be effectively purged of their negative feelings and emerge post-theatre renewed and ready to engage with the world productively. This was later called *katharsis*, from the Greek. The purpose of catharsis according to Aristotle was to rid the individual of personal stress and presumably return them to a state of homeostasis.

Catharsis made its entrance into psychotherapy with Sigmund Freud and his contemporary Josef Breuer, who first began using hypnosis as a way to release buried feelings in a process called abreaction (Breuer, 1895). They believed that repressing strong feelings was counterproductive and unhealthy and that stored feelings were the origin of mental health problems as well as physical ailments. They further hypothesized that repressed feelings would pressurize and poison the person, and they must be released if both physical and mental health was to be restored.

Breuer and Freud used catharsis to bring forward memories supposedly stored in the unconscious. In modern mainstream usage, catharsis describes pivotal moments when a difficult feeling is acknowledged and thereby released. This process, even in common vernacular, is widely seen as a healthy response. We are often told that we need to blow off steam or get it out of our systems and even re-experience negative feelings in order to move past them. This notion is largely unquestioned and often appears in mainstream self-help literature. It is also entrenched in some religious practices. For example, the Catholic Church continues to use confession as a form of catharsis and in some instances still engages in rites of exorcism.

While Freud later reconsidered some of these ideas, catharsis is still one of the foundational ideas in psychotherapy and indeed in many other forms of therapy. Practitioners of psychodrama, primal therapy, Reichian therapy, rational emotive behavioural therapy, and bio-energetic and emotion-focused therapy have all at one time or another placed a focus on the role of catharsis in counselling. While some therapies like primal therapy have fallen out of favour in recent years, counsellors trained in emotion-focused therapy continue to believe that catharsis is the best way to relieve personal distress. The American Psychological Association concurs and noted in 2007 that "the greater the expression, the greater the relief."

Does Catharsis Deliver on its Promise?

Is it true that catharsis is the best way to overcome stress, sadness, fear, and anger? In recent years, its use in counselling has been called into question. Jemmer (2006) believed that emotive sharing can result in re-traumatization and what he called "re-learning" of the traumatic event. Bushman (2002) did not believe that catharsis was as helpful as people automatically believed, and Carol Tavris, in her book *Anger, the Misunderstood Emotion* (1980), held that revisiting powerful emotions like anger over and over again only served to reinforce and crystallize them. She noted that despite the widespread belief in the cathartic experience, the purgative effect did not seem to happen for most people. In fact, angry people who were encouraged to vent their anger often became even angrier!

An example of what these researchers warned against occurred immediately after the tragic events of 9/11 (Shalev, 2009). Counsellors were surprised and appalled that standard and approved debriefing approaches that valued catharsis were not only unhelpful but also proved counterproductive and even damaging. Approaches that encouraged sufferers of PTSD and trauma to "relive" the moment in order to move forward did not deliver on that promise. Instead, people were re-traumatized. As counsellors began to question these approaches, other ideas based on supporting resilience emerged. For example, in the aftermath of the Pacific Ocean tsunami in Samoa, narrative therapists Kiwi Tamasese and Charles Waldegrave suggested that helping people find the things they needed to rebuild their lives and re-engage with their communities was a much more effective way to help them overcome trauma and loss than encouraging them to emotionally relive it (Personal communication, 2012).

Counselling and Self-Help in an Ableist and Individualistic Society

Clinicians and self-help purveyors often defend a grief-oriented approach to counselling and support by maintaining what we have already stated, namely that some parents need a place to openly express the disappointment and frustration at having a disabled child. To this end they argue that when hearing these stories, listeners need to put their own values aside and simply act as nonjudgmental witnesses of the parents' experience. However, perhaps we need to ask ourselves whether counselling and self-help based on unconditional supportive listening will really provoke change, or whether it will simply lead to fatalistic resignation and worse, an escalation of negative feelings.

The unquestioned assumption that cathartic experiences will result in acceptance does not acknowledge that these feelings do not occur in a vacuum but instead originate in a society that already holds a catastrophic view of disability to which none of us are immune. These views are a by-product of a larger and dominant bias that still posits disabled people as substandard. Validating feelings of hopelessness without providing a robust alternative view doesn't prompt a move beyond these biases.

Clinicians working in the areas of domestic violence, racial/aboriginal identity, and sexual and gender orientation have long held that it is vital for individuals of marginalized groups to recognize their experience of devaluation in the context of pervasive societal biases (McCarthy, 1982; Lego & Thompson, 2008; Bieschke, Perez,& DeBord, 2007). They recognize that to simply acknowledge feelings without helping to position those experiences in a social and political context is tantamount to blaming the victim. Counsellors working with battered women understand that an important part of their work includes helping women learn about and resist the power dynamics inherent in a patriarchal society. Similarly, LGBTQIA+ youth are counselled on how to feel proud and normal in a homophobic society. The focus in groups like these is on helping people to become aware of and actively resist powerful societal narratives that posit them as broken, deficient, and "less than."

Unfortunately, it would seem that a social justice orientation has not yet arrived in many of the places where parents of disabled children receive counselling or go for support. Compared to the counselling and support that goes on for other marginalized groups, a grief-oriented approach seems outdated and politically obtuse. So why does it persist? We believe it is largely because the majority of people still see disability through a medicalized or pity-based lens. Unfortunately, there has been very little overlap between traditional counselling and current thinking from the field of disability studies and disability activist groups. When disability continues to be viewed through a medical lens without a corresponding political and social analysis, it leads many to see the problem as tragedy and lack of service rather than injustice and societal prejudice. Many see the goal as either cure or awareness; few ever consider that the real goal could be pride.

The Consequences of a Belief

What happens when disability is seen as a tragedy, burden, and inconvenience? What are the consequences of holding negative views of disability that go largely uncontested in both the larger society and in a counselling context?

Unfortunately, the devaluation of disabled children is reinforced and exacerbated by claims that the presence of a disabled child in a family often results in increased alcoholism, higher divorce rates, and in some cases, even domestic violence. These beliefs are often still cited today as unquestionably true, and in the middle of the last century were often used as justification for institutionalizing a disabled child. "You can go on to have other [read: non-disabled] children," parents were told. "Put your child somewhere where they can be with their own kind, and get on with your lives before they are destroyed."

Let's look at the claim that parents of disabled children are more likely to divorce. There remains a persistent belief among both clinicians and the general public that couples with disabled children experience a higher divorce rate. Whether this is actually true is debatable and contested through a growing body of literature on healthy families of disabled children (Kunc, 1987; Sobsey, 2004). Nonetheless, the belief persists and has serious ramifications that should not be underestimated.

Consider this: generic divorce/separation literature points out that children often blame themselves for their parents' divorce. Counsellors urge divorcing couples to take specific pains to reassure their children that they are not at fault for the separation or else risk inflicting permanent psychological damage. That is, unless those children happen to be disabled. Then the issue becomes murkier. Do we really believe that children are not at fault for a divorce, or do we believe that *some* children are not at fault, while others are?

Isn't there a double standard here? If we entertain the idea that the stresses of parenting disabled children may be the cause for divorce, what are the consequences of that belief? Where then is the concern for the psychological welfare of these children? Is it assumed that simply because they are disabled, they wouldn't be aware of what's being said? As far as we've been able to see, this issue doesn't even arise as a concern in the literature. We've often wondered what a family therapist would do if a disabled child blamed themselves for their parents' divorce. How would the counsellor reassure the child that the divorce wasn't his or her fault if they actually believed that disability *was* a causal agent? If a counsellor endorses the idea that marital discord after the birth of a disabled child is to be expected, how can they reconcile this with the opposing view that children should be reassured of their blamelessness?

It's difficult for any of us to work against our own convictions. No matter how impartial and neutral a counsellor might believe themselves to be, it is inevitable that what they believe will leak into the conversation. Perhaps some assume that what these children hear won't hurt them or that they won't understand, given their disabilities. However, as most of us know, children are very perceptive when it comes to reading the emotional state of their parents, and disabled kids are no exception. Blaming a divorce, alcoholism, or domestic violence on a child's disability is not only simplistic scapegoating but also unfair and dangerous.

Grieving the "Death" of the Perfect Child

What is not widely known is that much of the professional literature on chronic sorrow is directly derived from literature dealing with death—specifically, parent reactions to the death of a child (Kubler-Ross, 1969; Pearse, 1977). This disturbing conflation of disability and death, with all its unsettling ramifications, remained uncontested for many years. It was only when disability rights advocates began to protest the notion that their births were something to mourn that this prevalent view was brought into question.

Advocates pointed to the blatant biases inherent in the idea of chronic sorrow and expressed outrage that rather than helping parents contest these biases and develop a more balanced view of disability, proponents could be encouraging the development of even more deeply entrenched stereotypical notions. Rather than counselling for resilience and helping families develop strategies for coping in a world not set up for disabled people, these activists worried that parents were being led to an increasingly negative view of disability.

It makes sense that a compassionate counsellor or support group facilitator would want to help alleviate the pain that families experience in any way possible. As we've already discussed, many of the books and blogs they read suggest that parents should be assisted to verbally express painful feelings, up to and including any secret wish they might harbour that their disabled child would just die. Again, the theory is that as a parent overtly acknowledges these private thoughts and works through the guilt they induce, they will move toward an acceptance of their circumstances, which is arguably the goal of good counselling and support.

But does this approach actually accomplish what counsellors and parents might hope for? Is admitting a wish for the death of a disabled child really a healthy cathartic expression that automatically leads to acceptance? Further, are there dangers and unintended consequences inherent in this approach? Let's look at some very real and troubling consequences of such a view.

Parents are rightfully held responsible for the care of their children. In this context, if the parent of a non-disabled child openly expressed a wish that their child would die, it would almost certainly result in such a huge cry of social outrage that it would reverberate all the way onto *The Jerry Springer Show*. It is likely that the child in this scenario would be apprehended and taken into protective care. But do the rules change for families of disabled children? When these parents openly state, whether in a blog post or a counselling session, that they wish their disabled child would die, it is not always seen as irresponsible, or a flight into selfishness, but is instead seen as a sign of emotional honesty. Counsellors who would normally register alarm at such a confession and immediately report a disclosure like this might now override any concern and give precedence to the parents' feelings.

As benign and supportive as it may feel to the counsellor or the participants in a self-help blog or group, the unquestioned consequences of this practice can be lethal and cause real hurt. Unfortunately, there are many ways to hurt a child. The pain a child might experience by knowing consciously or unconsciously that they are not fully valued constitutes one kind of pain. But there are times when the hurt a child might experience is life-threatening. There are far too many instances where parents actualize the wish that their child would die and kill their disabled children. We wonder how many of those deaths were inadvertently aided and even encouraged by the supposedly benign validation of painful feelings.

Look, for example, at the famous case of Tracy Latimer, a twelve-year-old girl with cerebral palsy from Saskatchewan who was murdered by her father in 1994. After initially denying any involvement in her murder, he finally confessed, claiming his actions were an act of mercy. In the months that followed Tracy's murder, professionals and the general public did not blame Latimer for his homicidal action but instead suggested that a lack of family support and the stresses of caring for and raising a disabled child were responsible. They also believed his contention that Tracy's was a life of unrelenting pain, even though this was highly contested by others who knew her.

In the minds of many, this rationale seemed to mitigate the horror of his action and provide a reasonable justification for this homicide. It was distressing to the disability community that the huge outpouring of public sympathy that followed Tracy's death was not for her but instead centred on her father. Most people believed Latimer's contention that Tracy had been put out of her so-called misery as an act of love. The ensuing groundswell of public support subtly implied permission, and in the months that followed Tracy's death, there was an unprecedented rash of child killings by other parents and caregivers.

During the same period, Susan Smith, the mother of two little boys, Michael and Alexander, drowned them by driving her car into a lake. The public response to these murders stood in sharp contrast to the murder of Tracy Latimer. The public called for a severe sentence for Smith, and indeed she was prosecuted to the full extent of the law, receiving a life sentence. It took a long time for the courts to find Latimer guilty, and even then, his ten-year sentence was far less than Smith's. Today he is petitioning the court for a pardon and continues to garner significant public support.

Why the difference in response from both the public and the judicial system? What was the difference between Michael, Alexander, and Tracy? The obvious and appalling answer is the presence of disability. Tracy Latimer had a significant physical disability. Smith's children were non-disabled.

Many of the murders of disabled children that followed Tracy Latimer went either unprosecuted or under prosecuted. One of the worst examples was that of six-year-old Charles Blais, an Autistic child whose mother drowned him in the bathtub. After her acquittal, she lived in a halfway house for a year and then astonishingly went on to become the spokesperson and fund-raiser for Autism Canada!

Twelve-year-old Issy Stapleton's mother regularly posted her resentment about raising an Autistic daughter in her blog. Far from helping her work through feelings, the validation she received from parents who read her blog resulted in increasingly vitriolic posts with increasing accounts of distressingly personal information about Issy. It appeared that venting accomplished exactly what Carol Tavris warned us about: it did not reduce negative feelings but instead crystallized and intensified them. Stapleton tried to kill herself and her daughter by locking them into a van with a lit barbecue. She was unsuccessful, and fortunately Issy survived, but it is unclear what damage was done due to the gases she ingested. Unfortunately, others are not so lucky.

Every year on March 1, all over the world, organizations like the Autistic Self-Advocacy Network (ASAN) and other groups of disabled people hold a day of mourning and candlelight vigils for disabled children and adults murdered by parents and caregivers. We light candles, bring flowers, and read out the names. The list of names is distressingly long—into the high hundreds over the period of less than two decades. Dick Sobsey, one of the most prominent researchers on violence, murder, and disability, has pointed out that the stated rationale for many of these murders is love (1994). Perpetrators profess to have loved their children so much that they simply had to put them out of their so-called misery. While it is horrifying to consider, it is important to note that the modus operandi for many of these killers is not generally benign. Feeding your child bleach, leaving them to starve in closets or empty fridges, drowning or suffocating them, or stabbing them to death does not seem a merciful way for anyone to die. These are only a few of the ways in which parents and caregivers have killed the people they claimed to love and were supposed to care for and protect.

When we look at the smug reports from countries like Belgium, Denmark, and Iceland claiming to have almost "eradicated" Down syndrome prebirth and the blatant ableism in the work of some bioethicists like Peter Singer, the idea of a benevolent genocide is not so far-fetched.

We raise these issues even though they are difficult to write, read, and talk about because they are important. If we do not confront the ableism that allows these murders to be justified by law courts, the media, and the general public, we risk becoming a society of murder apologists. If we continue to validate the difficulties parents face by urging them to continue to vent, we reinforce the dangerous stereotypes already out in society. By engaging in moral relativism and claiming that no one can judge or exhorting us to walk a mile in someone else's shoes before we condemn their actions, we inadvertently condone these atrocious acts. Disabled people, rightly, are terrified of the consequences of this kind of rhetoric.

What Can We Do Differently?

We believe it is past time to move beyond concepts like chronic sorrow and grieving the death of the "perfect child" (as if non-disabled children are perfect) and understand the dangers inherent in this approach. Does this mean that parents should be shamed or discounted for their feelings? Not at all. What it does mean is that we need to finally come to see disability in a political and social justice context.

As the late Michael White (2011), a narrative therapist from Australia, pointed out, "It is never a matter of whether or not we bring politics into the therapy room, but whether or not we are *prepared to acknowledge the existence of these politics*, and the degree to which we are prepared to be complicit in the reproduction of these politics" (p. 49). White goes on to say that "it is impossible to assume that the therapeutic context is sacrosanct…apart from the culture at large." Therapists, White points out, are attracted to the idea that their actions will change lives, and their training encourages this ethic of control. "This is not a context in which therapists can presume a position of neutrality, a context in which therapists can hold out a claim to a space that is free of the relations of power and of the biases associated with their location in the social world" (p. 63).

Counsellors, self-help group facilitators, blog and internet writers all share a responsibility for ensuring not just the well-being of parents and caregivers, but equally for their disabled family members. The responsibility is grave. Fostering resilience and actively interrogating and countering negative societal biases should be the goal of any helping relationship. Fortunately, there are counsellors and support groups and internet writers that are beginning to challenge the idea that disability is synonymous with tragedy. Consider the following examples.

The Washington Father's Group

Some years ago we were invited to speak to a group of fathers of disabled children. Much to our amusement, although it was ostensibly a men-only group, I (Emma) was welcomed as an honorary father. What immediately struck us was the anomaly of this group. We have seen support groups for mothers of disabled children but very few that focus on the parenting issues faced by men. We found this a hopeful development.

James May, the founder of the group, had been counselling fathers of disabled children in his general practice for some time before he began to wonder if developing a peer support group would prove helpful. The men he'd been counselling were enthusiastic, and soon others began to join. Members told us that this group was a helpful way for fathers to gather together, share experiences and expertise, and support one another through difficult times. May developed a series of ground rules for the group. One of the most interesting was designed to eliminate any one-upmanship or social stratification among members. They were not allowed to tell each other what they did for a living or talk about their work lives. They were there as equals.

We spoke to the group about the right to be disabled and that disabled people are not broken or in need of fixing. This generated a roomful of nods and enthusiastic responses. As the interchange moved from presentation to discussion, these ideas were forefront in the responses of the group. Men, we were told, often seem to struggle with the desire to fix their disabled offspring. "It's what we are socialized to do," they said. "We're supposed to fix things. We immediately recognized that the disability wasn't something we could fix, and it was frustrating. We didn't know what to do."

"Where does that urge come from?" they asked each other. "Why do we feel like we aren't being useful or productive unless we're busy fixing what we believe is broken?" By deconstructing societal messages like the need to always be in control of every situation, they described themselves feeling freer and more able to accept and enjoy their changed circumstances. Not surprisingly, many reported that their partners were appreciative of this change! They described improved relationships with their disabled children as well. "Now that I've let go of the idea that I need to change my son," one father said, "I am enjoying my child for exactly who he is. We're finding ways to connect and have fun. The things we do are different from what I'd envisioned. He can't play baseball or other sports like I'd always imagined, but the things we do together are just as good. I've learned to be more accepting in general. I think I was way more judgmental toward others than I'd imagined, and giving that up has improved my life in lots of ways."

Parenting Autistic Children with Love and Acceptance (PACLA)

PACLA is an online group of Autistic and non-autistic moderators dedicated to countering negative societal attitudes towards autistic people and supporting parents to accept their children exactly as they are. This is primarily accomplished by foregrounding and amplifying the voices of Autistic adults. Its motto is "Change the world, not your autistic child." PACLA brings forward issues of social justice and actively challenges the prevailing notion that autism is a fate worse than death and that parenting an Autistic child is a close second. Its approach is unapologetically radical, with a blog and a series of memes that actively question existing stereotypes about autism.

Respectfully Connected

Respectfully Connected is another blog featuring stories and op-ed pieces by Autistic women who are also parents of Autistic children. Their message is neurodivergent/autism-positive and posits autism firmly in a social justice context.

There are other websites and blogs that offer ideas and resources for parents; too many to mention here. One of the best and well worth perusing is "30 Days of Autism" by Leah Kelley. This blog has links to many, many others. https://30daysofautism.blog/

CHAPTER 15

THE *I AM AUTISM* COMMERCIAL AND THE COMPONENTS OF A GOOD MAGIC TRICK

"What the eyes see and the ears hear, the mind believes."

Harry Houdini

As you might have guessed, both of us have an abiding interest in disability issues. What you might not know is that when we're not out there trying to change the world, we enjoy watching videos that feature magicians and hypnotists. We happily engage in the willing suspension of disbelief, and although we try to decode and demystify the tricks, we are also delighted when we are fooled.

A good magic trick is based on misdirection and contains at least four essential components.

- Expectation
- Intention
- Repetition
- Force

In this essay we will look at how some fund-raisers for disability organizations employ these four components to misdirect and thereby manipulate the public into parting with their money. We'll contend that misdirection is accomplished by providing the audience with a singular view of disability while simultaneously and deliberately obscuring alternative interpretations. Further, we'll maintain that far from being positive or even neutral, these singular and skewed interpretations negatively affect disabled people. The way disabled people are portrayed takes the eyes of the unsuspecting public away from the real issues of disability—and disabled people themselves—and focuses them on what the fund-raisers want us to see. We'll use an example of a commercial produced by Autism Speaks[1]called *I Am Autism* (2009) to prove the point.

Misdirection; Expectation, Intention, Repetition, and Force

Before we talk specifically about fund-raisers and how they operate, let's look at a few of the ways magicians influence us into seeing and believing something other than what's actually happening. Misdirection is widely considered the hallmark of magic illusion, and the four components—expectation, intention, repetition, and force—are the means by which misdirection takes place. For the purpose of this discussion, we will look at each of them separately even though you will see that they are inextricably intertwined.

---

[1] "Autism Speaksis an large international charity founded in 2005. It is seen as a hate group by many Autistic people and those who love and support them due to its role in actively promoting stigmatizing and ableist attitudes through fear-based fund-raising and awareness campaigns that add to the oppression of Autistic people. In response, Boycott Autism Speaks was founded in 2013 to push back against Autism Speaks's branding of *awareness* and practices that exclude the voices of Autistic people, take resources from community-based services, spend less than 4 percent of the money raised on services for Autistic people and their families, and instead spend millions of dollars in search of a cure or prevention of autism" (Kelley, 2019, p 13.)

Misdirection

Magician Henry Hay (1972) tells us that misdirection is essentially a manipulation of interest that causes us to look in the direction the magician wants us to look. Magicians use eye gaze, body position, conversation, and often a well-placed joke to divert the audience's attention away from where the trick is actually taking place. Cognitive psychologists and magicians studying the art of misdirection concur that *where we're looking* is less important than *what we're paying attention to*.

Misdirection is a process of reframing and influencing perception. Teller (of the famed Penn and Teller duo) says there is actually a bit more to it than simply diverting the audience's attention. In his famous animated ball and hoop trick, the ball moves about as if it were an independent living thing. In fact, Teller manipulates it with a very thin string invisible to the audience. Many audience members, despite the fact that they can't see the string, are still inclined to believe that there is one. When Teller makes the ball jump repeatedly back and forth through the hoop, we are led to doubt our assumptions. It seems implausible that the ball could move through the hoop if it were attached to a string, so now the audience begins to doubt there is a string involved. Of course the hoop itself is rigged to make the trick possible. Teller uses this example to show that misdirection often relies on a second illusion that proves the validity of the first.

Expectation

In order to accomplish misdirection, magicians rely on our expectations; in other words, they cleverly exploit the fact that we are inclined to see what we expect to see, and we look for familiar patterns. Most of us process the world based on our expectations and generally filter out the rest. This phenomenon is understandable, since we wouldn't be able to cope if we had to take everything in at once. However, it's important to recognize that this tendency can create tunnel vision and often prevents us from noticing extraneous but important information. Consider the following example.

In a famous Harvard University experiment some years ago, researchers Christopher Chabris and Daniel Simons (2009) graphically illustrated how human beings are susceptible to the effects of what these researchers call selective attention. Participants in their study were showed a short black-and-white film clip of six people, three in black shirts and three in white, tossing a basketball back and forth. They were asked to count the number of times the ball was passed between the three people wearing the white shirts. During the course of the clip, a person in a gorilla suit walks into the middle of the group, stops in the centre of the frame, pounds on their chest, and then exits on the other side. In the experimental setting, Chabris and Simons found that over half of those watching did not see the gorilla. They called the experiment the Invisible Gorilla and used it to point out how selective attention operates. We see what we pay attention to. In this case we are focused on counting the number of passes made by the white team, causing us to overlook the gorilla. The video clip became a YouTube sensation and has been used (including by us) worldwide with similar results.

Intention

Audiences commonly report "seeing" ghost images of coins or balls tossed into the air even as the magician adroitly palms them with the other hand or removes them in some other way. In many instances the trick is almost laughably obvious, but audiences miss it simply because they expect to see these items where they think they have been thrown. One of the ways magicians accomplish this subterfuge is by leading our eyes to follow their body movements and eye gaze in a particular direction. They understand that we will be inclined to make a cognitive leap and infer from those movements what the next ones will be. Another way they ensure that the audience is following the movement is by telling us exactly what they are doing, step by step. "I am now reaching for this coin." Consider the following example.

At the Magic of Consciousness Symposium in Las Vegas in 2007, Teller advised the audience to watch carefully for intent. He said, "The intention is what's deceiving… The best way to conceal secret stuff is to make the intention so overpowering that people will follow that instead of the sleight of hand." In an illusion involving a red ball and a wand, Teller showed this audience of neuroscientists how clearly signalling what he intends to do will cause them to look in the direction he wants them to look. He demonstrated by deliberately standing some distance away from a small table positioned on his right, which required him to make an exaggerated reach. With his right hand, he picked up a red ball from the table. He showed the audience the ball and then appeared to toss it from his right hand into his left (which was raised in the air and perfectly still). What he actually did was squish the ball, which, unbeknown to the audience, was made of foam rubber, and kept it hidden in his right hand.

Continuing the illusion, Teller made another sweeping reach back to the table with his right hand (which contained the squished foam ball). Without allowing the audience to see the ball, he picked up a wand sitting on the table and flourished it dramatically in the direction of his left hand, telling them that the ball would now disappear. In the final "Ta-Daa" moment, Teller opened his left hand, and as promised, it was empty. The audience believed they'd seen him toss the ball from his right to his left hand. Although the ball seemed to magically disappear from his left hand, in fact it was never there.

In this simple trick, Teller used body movement and eye gaze to signal intention. Expectation and an assumption of intent caused the audience to follow his reach with their eyes and thereby miss the trick entirely. In this way Teller capitalized on our tendency to infer from one movement what the next one will be.

Repetition

You may have noticed that many magicians use language borrowed from the field of hypnosis. It is the language of suggestion and repetition, and there are certain rules both hypnotists and magicians follow in order to build trust and gain maximum influence. Because audience members know that the magician will be trying to fool them, they are always on the lookout for subterfuge. And because magicians understand this, they take considerable pains to counter the viewer's suspicions. Repetition is critical to this process, since the more you hear something the more likely you are to believe it.

Milton Erickson (1976), arguably the father of hypnotherapy, once said that the focus on repetition in hypnosis is a form of confirmation, a number of little demonstrations that lead the unsuspecting participant to increasingly believe in the hypnotist's credibility. For example, if a skilled hypnotist puts a person into a deep trance, they might offer a posthypnotic suggestion, saying, "It will be difficult to open your eyes." To the participant's surprise, upon waking, they find that this is true. Feeling their eyes glued shut leads the person to take a step closer to believing in the power of the hypnotist. Once that first step has been taken, the hypnotist is able to make a slightly more outrageous suggestion without being questioned. They might say, for example, "You will now forget the number four." The participant is now indeed likely to forget the number four simply because the inability to open their eyes has begun to convince them that the hypnotist is credible. Repetition begins the process of persuasion and trust-building. It's a step-by-step enterprise that doesn't happen all at once.

Magicians, like hypnotists, use this strategy of controlled repetition to build the trust necessary for persuasion. If you listen carefully to the patter most engage in during a sleight of hand trick, you'll notice that they not only tell the audience what they are doing but also continually stress that the participant is not being coerced in any way. Comments like, "You've shuffled the cards and chosen the one you want, and you can see that I haven't touched them. Do you want to shuffle again?" are commonly repeated phrases in the set-up for the trick. In this way, the magician subtly overrides any sense the participant may have that they've been unduly influenced and replaces it with the idea that whatever they are doing is completely of their own volition. The operational principle here is that if we are repeatedly told that we have been given a choice, we tend to believe we have acted freely. The illusion of free choice is an essential part of any trick, and like the hypnotist, the magician relies on repetition to make it work.

Force

Another common technique magicians employ is called a force. A force is essentially the hidden manipulation of cards or objects to produce a result predetermined by the magician. Once again, the participant is carefully led to believe that their choices are made freely and are uninfluenced by the magician, but in fact they are being led to make the choice the magician wants them to make.

Here's an example of a simple card trick anyone can perform that illustrates how the force is used by the magician to secure a predetermined outcome. In this trick, the magician deals three columns of seven cards each face up on the table and asks the participant to choose any card they wish. The participant shouldn't point or say which card it is, just mentally note it. Once the card is chosen, the magician will ask the participant to identify which column their card is in and then places the selected column in the middle of the two other columns. He or she will then gather up the cards, deliberately ensuring that the selected column remains in the middle. The magician deals the same twenty-one cards in three columns face up and once again asks the spectator to identify the column that contains their chosen card. This process is repeated three times. At the end of the third round, the column with the selected card is once again placed in the middle of the other two columns. Through a process of mathematical reduction, the magician knows that the spectator's card will always be the fourth card down in the middle row, making it the eleventh card in the deck. To the astonishment of the participant (assuming they've never seen the trick before), the magician unerringly picks the correct card and reveals it with a flourish. The participant believes that in each round they have given the magician only a vague idea of where the card is (the column but not the specific location), but by the third round the magician has narrowed the card from one in seven, to one in three, to one in one. The magician doesn't need to know what the card is; only that it will always be the eleventh card. The force is embedded in the trick.

In some instances the magician accomplishes a force by using a combination of language and eye contact to punctuate a pivotal moment in the trick. The magician knows that deliberately and dramatically stopping the trick just before the reveal and speaking directly to the participant will inevitably elicit a moment of eye contact, effectively taking attention away from the cards. They are then effectively able to use this brief second of inattention to confuse the participant long enough to forget what they were looking at. When the magician resumes the trick and reveals the forced card, to the astonishment of the participant, it's the card they chose. It seems random but in fact is entirely forced.

Misdirection, Expectation, Intention, Repetition, Force... and Disability Fund-Raising

Now let's pull this all together and answer the question that might be arising in your mind: What the heck has any of this got to do with disability fund-raisers? Let us explain.

In order to unpack the way fund-raisers use the components of a good magic trick to solicit donations for their organizations, let's use a hypothetical example. Imagine for a moment that there are four cards laid out on the table. Each one represents an experience or a perception of disability. Imagine that these four cards are labelled as follows:

- DISABILITY AS TRAGEDY
- LACK OF EDUCATION AND EMPLOYMENT OPPORTUNITIES
- LACK OF SUPPORTS
- SOCIAL DEVALUATION AND PREJUDICE

The fund-raiser, like a magician, wants to force the potential donor's choice to a particular card they have preselected. Let's assume the one they want you to pick is the first card, "Disability as Tragedy." Now let's look at a concrete and real example of how this choice was forced and how misdirection was employed by a fund-raising organization to accomplish its goals.

A Horror-Able Commercial

In 2009, the organization Autism Speaks (AS) made a video commercial called *I Am Autism* with filmmaker Alfonso Cuaron and AS board member Billy Mann. The film was loosely based on the 1948 March of Dimes short film about polio called *Taming the Crippler*. Both films were created to assist the sponsoring organizations in their fund-raising attempts.

AS is a formidable fund-raiser, generating millions of dollars worldwide through annual campaigns like "Light It Up Blue," "Learn the Signs," walkathons, and other events. When it comes to convincing people to part with their money, it is highly skilled. It has carefully cultivated important corporate sponsors and has thereby gained considerable influence and public credibility, dominating the conversation around autism and successfully foregrounding autism as a dire and frightening public health issue. As part of its "Light It Up Blue" awareness campaign, places like the United Nations, the Empire State Building, the White House, and even Niagara Falls are lit with blue lights every year on April 2. Big businesses like Home Depot sell blue light bulbs during April and donate the proceeds to AS.

The tactics used by AS are the same tried and true approaches historically employed by other fund-raisers like telethons, showing disabled people as tragic, pitiful, and needy. Conversely, their families are portrayed as long-suffering and burdened, brave, inspirational, and admirable. In the tradition of earlier fund-raisers, AS also explicitly utilizes tactics of fear, as we will see shortly.

As we consider the following example, remember that misdirection is the process of manipulating an audience's ideas or perceptions toward a particular conclusion. Also bear in mind that we are inclined to infer from one movement where the next one will be; we tend to focus on what we're led to focus on and filter out the rest; and the more we hear something, the more likely we are to believe it. Through the skilful use of these tactics, public perception is forced. We are given only one preselected view of what it means to be autistic. These are not new approaches, but as we will see, the level of intensity employed in the 2009 *I Am Autism* commercial is almost unprecedented.

I Am Autism

The commercial is approximately four minutes long and is split into two parts. Each segment consists of a montage of video clips showing autistic children and their families involved in various activities. Each of the two sections has a separate and different voice-over narration and features a different musical background.

In the first half of the commercial, a series of autistic children are shown in a variety of solitary activities. The viewer notes a number of unusual behaviours generally associated with autism: hand flapping, averted eye gaze, and repetitive motions. The most striking aspect of the initial segment is the voice-over. The video begins in complete silence, showing a blurry image of a child standing by himself in a dark forest. Gradually, an ominous chord progression (usually associated with horror films) fills the silence. Seconds later, a quietly menacing deep and somewhat distorted male voice purporting to be "the voice of autism" tells the viewer that autism is an epidemic with the insidious motive of destroying the lives of families and individuals. As the video progresses, more children are shown, each of them alone, each of them engaged in what seems to be unusual behaviour. The threatening voice continues monotonously, and a sense of horror takes hold of the viewer. The voice talks about the stress, embarrassment, pain, and suffering "he" inflicts on families. Autism, we are told, respects no person and, further, "knows where you live" and is "coming for you." "I will fight," the voice continues, "to take away your hope. I am still winning, and you are scared, and you should be. You ignored me, and this is a mistake."

Abruptly the tone changes and the commercial flips to the second two-minute clip, this time with an upbeat musical score and a series of male and female voices offering what seems to be a more positive message overlaid onto the same photographic montage used earlier. Through the magic of video, family members now pop into the frames, surrounding the formerly solitary children in protective stances. The voiceovers are pithy and have a defiant tone. They appear to challenge the "voice of autism" by speaking of love and commitment. They call themselves "a community of warriors" and cry out, "You think that because my child lives behind a wall, I am not afraid to knock it down?"

At first glance this seems to be the perfect rebuttal and counterpoint to the first segment. What could possibly be wrong with a group of family members fiercely defending their autistic children? However, a closer look at this part of the commercial reveals that the message hasn't really changed at all. While the first segment is unabashedly oppressive, negative, and menacing, the second, despite its positive appearance, actually evokes just as much fear and trepidation. It's just differently presented. This time the message is muddled; the audience experiences a confusing mix of admiration and dread. Admiration for the brave and heroic families who are doing Herculean things "normal" families could never do and the unexamined dread of disability itself. The message, although couched in the language of love and care, reinforces the same ideas we have been led to accept in the first part of the commercial. There is nothing positive about autism, and it must be eradicated *at all costs*. It is, in fact, posited explicitly as a war that must be battled at great emotional, physical, and financial expense. The disingenuous message, again couched in the language of love and care, is still one that foregrounds the stress and strife of living with and caring for an autistic family member.

One of the most insidious and powerful ploys of this commercial is the deliberate separation of autism from Autistic people themselves. In the first half of the commercial, autism is portrayed as a disembodied and malevolent force lurking at the edges of the community, waiting to strike and create havoc in unsuspecting lives. In this way, AS uses a Frankenstein trope, relying on fear and dread to influence perception. In the second half, families continue the same trope by threatening to beat back the dreaded ogre of autism like pitchfork- and torch-bearing villagers. These powerful archetypes operate below the level of consciousness but are profoundly influential. That their use is both offensive and frightening to Autistic people should not be a surprise.

These are not accidental tactics. They are deliberate and considered; the maker of the commercial fully understands the evocative power of these archetypes. It knows that if you didn't feel sorry for Autistic children and their families and dread the possibility that this misfortune might befall you or yours before watching this commercial, you most certainly will now. It also understands that if you know someone with an autistic family member, you will now be inclined to donate. Which is, of course, the point.

Like any effective magic trick, AS has relied on misdirection and its component parts to achieve its goals. How? From a series of possible choices, this commercial effectively forces us to select the "Disability as Tragedy" card by showing us images and providing us with dialogue that underscores this idea. As Houdini noted in the quote at the top of this chapter, "What the eyes see and the ears hear, the mind believes." Our focus is drawn away from any contradictory information, and like a magician, AS has exploited the fact that we look for familiar patterns and tend to overlook or discount alternative information.

Unfortunately, the familiar patterns we are reinforced to accept are based on pre-existing and taken-for-granted stereotypes about disability that are already rampantly held in our society. Many people believe disability of any sort to be a tragedy, and in this current climate, autism is seen as the epitome of that tragedy. AS has long promoted and cultivated the idea that autism is an epidemic and a fate worse than death, with some even claiming it is worse than cancer (Alan, 2008). When founder Suzanne Wright met with the Pope several years before her death to discuss the aims of AS, she actually compared autistic people to lepers. If we accept these ideas as true, we will not be inclined to look for or listen to disconfirming information or accounts, even when they are raised by actually Autistic people protesting the way they have been represented (https:// autisticadvocacy.org/ wp-content/ uploads/ 2017/ 04/ AutismSpeaksFlyer_color_2017.pdf).

Fund-Raising, Misdirection, and the Consequences of Falling for the Trick

Let's go back to the notion of the magic trick and its components in order to unpack how this commercial (and other fund-raising attempts that operate on a similar principle) actually works. We must first begin by asking ourselves if there other perspectives and alternate narratives we are being forced to overlook. The answer is surprisingly simple. When we dutifully pick the "Disability as Tragedy" card that has been preselected for us and focus on its attendant messages, we have been cleverly and effectively misdirected away from the real issues that face disabled people: poverty; lack of service and support; unavailable or inaccessible housing and transportation; lack of medical, educational, and employment opportunities; and exclusion from policy making. We are being directed away from the social issues and onto sexier and more exciting issues like the potential for cure and eradication.

As mentioned, wholesale descriptions of disabled people as tragic figures and the necessary recipients of charity have long-lasting consequences. These stereotypes are difficult for people to extricate themselves from. Disability groups have been protesting the way they are portrayed by fund-raising groups for decades. We must ask ourselves: What's the concern, and why are so many disabled people ungrateful for the supportive efforts of seemingly well-meaning groups and organizations?

In order to understand these objections, we begin by noting that these portrayals are far from neutral. They perpetuate negative stereotypes that have real and highly problematic consequences. For example, when Autistic people are posited as part of an epidemic, as lacking in empathy, as locked into their own little worlds, as dangers to themselves and society, as drains on the public purse and even as frightening aliens, the consequence of reinforcing these stereotypes overrides any possible good that such funding might bring. More than a few former poster children of the telethons that were common in the second half of the twentieth century and the first decade or so of the twenty-first century are retrospectively furious at having been used as cheap inspiration to evoke maudlin pity or to create unwarranted fear of disability in the minds of the general public. Many Autistic people were likewise outraged at the *I Am Autism* commercial when it first aired and subsequently called for a wholesale boycott of the organization that continues today.

Autistic people worry that portrayals like these contribute to a eugenics mind-set, where the idea that autism can and in fact *should* be eradicated can easily be interpreted as a call for the eradication of autistic people themselves. Hyperbolic? Not according to those researching the agenda of organizations like AS. In its relentless (and so far fruitless) search for a genetic explanation, funded through campaigns like "Light It Up Blue", the thinly-veiled endgame is eradication prebirth. Should the research actually uncover a genetic link, it is decidedly not hyperbolic to assume it may result in the same situation for Autistic people that is happening globally for people with Down syndrome: a wholesale campaign to ensure that they are no longer born.

Clearly, these concerns represent potentially catastrophic consequences for Autistic and otherwise disabled people that must not be underestimated. There are also other consequences that at first glance may appear mundane and merely irritating but are actually much more damaging and hurtful than we might think. For example, many of our visibly disabled friends describe discomfort and outrage at being accosted by perfect strangers on the street—people who appear to have no compunction about loudly expressing their pity and sorrow at the terrible fate that they believe disability implies. Some go further and seem to feel entitled to offer unsolicited help, cures, and advice; whether religious interventions, herbs, diets, strange cures, or "helpful" attitudinal platitudes. Some will gush with exaggerated admiration. "You do so well!" they chirp, while the second half of the sentence hangs uncomfortably in the air: "for someone in such a pitiful state." It is likewise not uncommon for Autistic children (and even adults) struggling in the throes of overwhelm to be accosted by angry passersby who suggest that the best way to deal with the situation is corporal punishment. "I'd never let my kid get away with that kind of behaviour! She's just a spoiled brat!" These examples may seem innocuous, but they are not. They are highly distressing and reveal that the legacy of telethons and fund-raisers have left a lasting impression in the public mind. There's an assumption that life with a disability is nothing but unmitigated hardship and sorrow and that every disabled person is not only pathetic and deserving of pity – and sometimes harsh censure - but also in desperate need of a cure.

Consider this wickedly pointed example of how difficult it is to counter these views once they have taken hold in the public mind. Disabled British comedian Lawrence Clark conceptualized and acted out a sketch called "The Best Fake Charity Collection Bucket" after someone unexpectedly gave him unsolicited money while he was sitting at a bus stop during a trip to South Africa. Puzzled by the interchange, he began to wonder what it would take to make people stop seeing him as a potential charity case. Clark, who has Cerebral Palsy and is a wheelchair user, decided to test the issue by situating himself on a busy sidewalk in London holding a series of conspicuous red donation buckets. The first one read, "Pay off my mortgage." Dutifully, passersby dropped money into the bucket despite Clark's best efforts to prevent them from doing so.

"You really don't want to pay off my mortgage," he told them, going on to say that the whole thing was a rip-off. Undeterred, passersby continued to drop coins into the bucket. Clark upped the ante repeatedly by changing signs on the buckets. "This is a scam, sucker,""I am not a charity case," and "Kill the puppies" are only a few. Astonishingly, even the last one engendered donations! Clark repeatedly told potential donors that he didn't actually want their money. Even when he added that he could go to jail for perpetrating a scam, well-meaning pedestrians relentlessly continued to put money into the bucket. They were going to be charitable, damn it, and nothing was going to stop them! Throughout the sketch, people encroached on Clark's personal space, sometimes asking personal questions about his disability, openly patronizing him, and at times almost wrestling with him in their attempts to access the buckets.

While the sketch is hilarious, it is also painful to watch. It points to the fact that many people were able to override the words they were seeing on the red buckets and what they were hearing directly from Clark himself and instead focused exclusively on his visible disability and wheelchair. Again it illustrates that *what you see* is not as important as *what you pay attention to.* This skit is a stark example of the long-term consequences of expectation as a component of misdirection. Once again, decades of telethons and fund-raising pitches have done their job. Clark remains obscured behind the mask of tragedy, and nothing he can say or do seems to have any effect in changing public perception.

These attitudes, carefully cultivated by fund-raisers, reinforce and crystallize already existent stereotypes about disability. Even worse, they influence people who may actually have the capacity to help improve the lives of disabled people. For example, we have no way of knowing how many potential employers have watched these commercials and telethons, internalized their messages, and thus had negative biases reinforced that make them hesitant to hire a disabled person. Also, consider how many people provide donations when asked and leave feeling that they have done their civic duty. When they are subsequently asked to consider hiring a disabled person or to join in the fight for improved services and supports, how many of them are inclined to think, "I've already given to these people. What more do they want?"

Do the ends justify the means? Are the promises that your money will provide prebirth screening, therapies, prosthetics, operations, and even a possible cure as benign and altruistic as they seem? Since all of these interventions cost a great deal, not to mention the high salaries of those employed in these organizations, they are anxious to secure your donations. Perhaps the better questions are these: What are the costs of the kind of portrayals that fund-raisers like AS rely on, and can disabled people afford them?

The Best Person to Decode a Magician's Trick is Another Magician

So how do we inoculate ourselves against the seduction of the force? How do we resist our tendency to rely on previous expectations, our unthinking interpretation of intent, and the hypnotic influence of repetitive messages? Perhaps it would help if we learned to look at fund-raising as if we were magicians watching other magicians. A magician knows that misdirection will inevitably be part of the trick and stays alert and observant. While the magician on stage leads the audience to look in one direction, the skilled practitioner will remember to look elsewhere for what isn't being emphasized—for what is being obscured.

Houdini was famously annoyed at and not duped by spiritualists and the deceptive tricks employed during séances and other demonstrations popular during his lifetime. He understood that many of these spiritualists were using common mentalist and mechanical trickery and made it a point to debunk them and show the gullible public exactly how the deception was done.

More recently, the Amazing Randy has exposed how supposed psychics use mentalist techniques to convince audiences to believe that they are talking with departed loved ones or hearing prophecies from beyond death. In a recent documentary, a British magician-hypnotist showed how faith healers use well-known hypnotic techniques of rapid induction to convince people that faith healing is real. Many large churches rely on televised faith healing demonstrations to elicit funds, and they manage to bring in massive amounts of money by creating the illusion of cure. It is big business, but what the unsuspecting public doesn't get to see is that most of these "cures" rely on suggestion and are short-lived. Ethical magicians understand that there are people who do not hesitate to exploit a gullible general public, and it makes them angry. Magicians develop their craft for fun; they are not trying to delude or persuade us out of our money. Ethical magicians encourage us to remain skeptical so that we will not be deceived by unscrupulous people.

In this context, let's go back again to the *I Am Autism* commercial for a moment. How exactly did the creators of the video manage to "force" us to look in a particular and predetermined direction while they accomplished their clever fund-raising sleight of hand? Well, once again, like many magic tricks, it's simpler than it looks. Just direct the public to look at a disabled body or a person who doesn't move or act in conventional ways; invoke a little admiration for their long-suffering families; add a dollop of guilt; stir in some dread, pity, and fear; and presto! Your eyes have been taken away from the actual person and the issues that affect them, and you have been directed to pay attention only to what AS wants you to see.

Now take a moment, like a magician watching another magician, and watch what happens if you remove your attention away from the narrative of the commercial. Turn off the sound, and focus instead on the Autistic people you see in the visuals. If you look carefully, you may be able to catch the illusion and debunk the magician. It's the same as if you were watching a card trick and muted the sound, or watched the Invisible Gorilla clip without being told to count the number of passes made by the white team. Not having access to the dialogue or the instructions you have been given means you are free from distraction, expectation, intention, and force, which enables you to become more observant.

If you can distance yourself from the forced and repeated messages of disaster, gloom, and horror in the *I Am Autism* commercial, you will see something interesting. In the midst of all the rhetoric, carefully orchestrated to present autism as synonymous with unmitigated calamity, you will see a little boy jumping on a trampoline and flapping his hands. If the narrative is what you are paying attention to, you will be influenced to interpret what you are seeing as a terrible aberrance, a child engaging in incomprehensible, weird, and antisocial behaviour. You will see dysfunction because that's exactly what the fund-raisers have led you to see. However, ask an Autistic adult what they see, and they will tell you that his body language clearly shows that he is, well, happy. The terrible dialogue overlaid onto this child is at odds with his expression of delight. It's not the only disconnect. The other children in the video montage are not necessarily tragic or unhappy at all. In fact, they are simply engaged in neutral activities.

Remember, it isn't so much what you see that will influence how you think. It's how your attention has been directed.

What we'd suggest we do when confronted by the rhetoric of organizations like AS is simply what everyone tries to do while watching a magic trick: avoid being fooled. If we can develop the same healthy skepticism toward fund-raising ploys that we use with our friend who pulls out a deck of cards and disingenuously asks us to "Pick a card, any card," we may be able to avoid inadvertently participating in a practice that "others" disabled people in damaging ways. No amount of funding will make up for the reputational damage to actually Autistic people that campaigns like the *I Am Autism* commercial have wreaked.

Does this mean that we never donate to anything? Does it mean that all fund-raising campaigns are bad? Not necessarily. Perhaps we would do well to remember what Michel Foucault once said: "My point is not that everything is bad, but that everything is dangerous, which is not exactly the same as bad. If everything is dangerous, then we will always have something to do" (1983a p.231-232).

What's important here is not whether to participate in fund raising but that we become aware of and sensitized to the messages contained in the pitch and the potential effect that pitch may have on real disabled people. We never want to collude with organizations that perpetuate negative stereotypes. We never want to place our hopes for cure over the supports and services real disabled people need. We want to be sure our money goes where we intend it to and not into the pockets of those who would exploit disability for their own ends. The end never justifies the means.

CHAPTER 16

BEING REALISTIC ISN'T REALISTIC

Norm

When you're disabled, non-disabled people often have presumptions about what is and isn't realistic for you. Unfortunately, the things they deem unrealistic are often the very things that are the most fun. Early on in my life I realized that if I simply did what the professionals wanted, my life would become little more than a boring and mundane existence. Anything that appeared to pose even the slightest amount of risk was discouraged. I recognized that if I wanted to lead an enjoyable life, I would have to ignore what all the well-meaning non-disabled professionals were telling me about what was and wasn't realistic.

Let me offer you an example. When I was fifteen years old, most people thought it was entirely unrealistic to even consider the possibility that I could learn to drive. No one was being mean or intentionally trying to hold me back; they were operating on the assumption that they were offering pragmatic advice that would ensure my safety and the safety of others.

Despite all the dire warnings, when I turned sixteen, I managed to convince my parents to let me try. The biggest worry was whether I would have fast enough reflexes to respond in an emergency situation. This was important to me too, so I took a reflex test at the driving centre. I learned that the normal reflex time for a non-disabled driver is anywhere from 0.21 to 0.23 seconds. My time was between 0.23 and 0.25, well under the Ministry of Transport's acceptable limit of 0.3. I began driving with my parents and then took lessons and got my license at age sixteen. The people who were concerned about my reflexes simply lacked the necessary information. I am uncomfortably aware that if those people had been in a position of power and able to decide whether I should or shouldn't have been allowed to drive, I might never have been given the opportunity, despite having the ability. That's a sobering thought.

So here's the embarrassing part. Despite my opposition to all the presumptions about what was and wasn't realistic in my life, I fell into the same trap when my friend Jim, who had hemiplegic cerebral palsy and was paralyzed on the right side of his body, also decided he wanted learn to drive. My immediate response was horror. I told Jim I didn't think it would be realistic and asked him what I thought was a critically important question. "When you have to stop in a hurry, you have to be able to hit the brake in an instant. You can barely move your right foot! How are you going to slam on the brakes when some kid runs out in front of you?"

Just like all the well-meaning non-disabled people who had proclaimed what wasn't realistic for me, I thought I was acting in Jim's best interests (not to mention the best interests of those hypothetical kids running out into traffic). Luckily, Jim didn't listen to me. Undaunted, he went on to take driving lessons. One day about six months later, he drove up to my house in his own car. I ran out, panicked, and said, "Jim! What are you doing driving?" He smiled and calmly pointed underneath the dashboard. I immediately saw that he had installed an additional accelerator on the left side of the brake where a clutch would normally be. With this simple adaptation and a spinner on the left side of the steering wheel, he could drive the car exclusively using the left side of his body.

When I realized I had fallen into the same trap of presuming that something was unrealistic for someone else, I got furious at myself. And when I get furious at myself, I tend to think. I started to wonder what it is that causes us immediately and reflexively to jump to the idea that something isn't realistic.

Let's think about the word itself. When we say something isn't *realistic*, what do we really mean? What are we actually trying to say? My guess is that in the vast majority of instances, what teachers, support workers, social workers, and even parents are saying is, "I don't have a clue how you could do that!" Saying, "I don't know how," is completely understandable, reasonable, legitimate, and probably quite true. The problem, however—and the source of injustice to disabled people—is that when we use the phrase *not realistic*, we transform "I don't know how" into "It's impossible."

Once we decide something is impossible, we not only stop looking for solutions but also often compound the problem by taking another huge leap and definitively declaring that our assessments are correct. Having made this declaration, many of us will now go to great lengths to defend the validity of our views rather than staying open for disconfirming information. Consider the following historical example of this all-to-human dynamic.

Herman Moll

In the early part of the eighteenth century, one of the most prominent and respected cartographers of the day was Dutch mapmaker Herman Moll. Explorers relied on Moll's maps of the world as they ventured into unknown territories like the Americas and Africa. For the most part, Moll's maps were incredibly accurate—with one glaring exception.

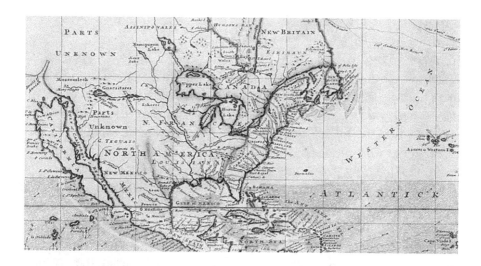

As the map shows, Herman Moll believed that the territory now called California was an island. With Moll's map firmly in hand, explorers would arrive on the west coast of the continent expecting to make a long portage across the island to its east coast. Much to their consternation, no matter how far they portaged, they never reached the opposite shore shown on the map. Over the years many explorers returned to the Netherlands and pointed out to Moll that California was not an island. Despite what they said, Moll staunchly insisted that his maps were accurate and the accounts of the explorers were wrong. He never recanted in all the years before his death in 1732.

The vital lesson that can be learned from Moll's stubbornness is that we can become so attached to the maps in our minds that we will continue to assert their veracity to the death, despite any and all information to the contrary. Although the explorers were likely inconvenienced by having to carry their boats for miles, they weren't stopped by Moll's miscalculations and ultimately continued their trek across America. However, when decisions are made that constrain the choices available for disabled people, the consequences may in fact stop all exploration and go beyond mere inconvenience to severely limiting their choices and, ultimately, even their lives.

Think Like Houdini

In trying to figure out how to live my life and go on to do things that many people considered unrealistic, I had to find ways to circumvent their opinions and do what I wanted to do despite their concerns. In the process I adopted a role model: Harry Houdini. I loved Houdini precisely because he delighted in figuring out how to do what everyone else thought was impossible. Houdini began his public career travelling around to different towns advertising his act with posters proclaiming that "nothing could hold him down" and inviting audiences to observe his "death-defying mystery." In one of his most famous acts, Houdini would ask local police to lock him up with an array of chains and locks. Once this was accomplished, he asked them to assure the audience that he was completely immobilized. Then, with a flourish, they would throw a sheet over him, and in a matter of minutes Houdini would emerge, astonishingly freed of all the locks and chains.

In response to the audience's amazement, Houdini would say, "That was easy. Let's make it harder." And he would! In a subsequent performance, he would submerge himself in a large metal milk can. The top would be locked in place. Within a couple of minutes Houdini would burst out of the can. But he didn't stop there. Again, he would say, "Let's make it harder!"

In his most famous, daring, and difficult performance, the self-proclaimed Master of Mystery would arrive on stage locked entirely in chains and then have himself submerged head first into a glass tank of cold water. He offered a $1000 reward (big money in his day) to anyone able to prove that it was possible to breathe while upside down in the tank—a tank that promotional posters of the day described as "a water-filled torture cell." A curtain was draped over the tank, and once again, to the amazement of his audience, Houdini would free himself within minutes.

I have often wondered what might have happened if Houdini had been the executive director of a service agency or the principal of a school. Confronted by the claim that inclusion was impossible, or that the goals, aspirations, and desires of a disabled person were not realistic, I envision Houdini smiling and saying, "Oh yeah? Just watch."

We Live in a Qwerty World

Trying to emulate the ingenuity of Houdini may seem like a formidable if not impossible undertaking for most of us. But maybe it's not as hard as it looks. Unfortunately, what often gets in the way is what might accurately be called our collective habits of inefficiency. One of the best examples of how we get stuck in our own tendency to do what we've always done is to look at how we use computers and word processors.

In 1868, Christopher Latham Sholes invented the typewriter, and ten years later in 1878, with the assistance of Amos Densmore, he patented what is now known as the qwerty keyboard (named after the first six letters on the upper left side of the keyboard). Initially, Sholes organized the letters in familiar alphabetic order but very quickly realized that this arrangement wasn't practical since the construction of the typewriter keys—elevated on long posts—made them vulnerable to jamming when the typist typed too quickly. He rearranged the keys in the qwerty formation specifically so that the letters we use most commonly would be typed by the weakest fingers on the least dominant hand (the left hand, for most people), and the typist would be forced to slow down.

Today's word processors do not have the same problem with jammed keys, so there is no longer any need for typists to be artificially slowed down. One would think that in the intervening years someone might have corrected this antiquated solution to an obsolete problem and created a keyboard that maximized typing speed instead.

In fact, someone did. In 1936, August Dvorak, a professor of engineering at the University of Washington, with his brother-in-law William Dealy, invented and patented what is now known as the Dvorak keyboard. This keyboard was created with the express intention of making the typists' job easier and helping them to increase speed. Dvorak placed the keys so that the letters most often used were under or closest to the strongest fingers on the right hand (the dominant hand for the majority of people). Puzzlingly, Dvorak's invention didn't take hold, and today most of us (except a few elite speed typists) still use the qwerty keyboard. Speculation about why Dvorak's invention wasn't successful suggests that perhaps it was because the qwerty keyboard was there first or he wasn't terribly good at promotion. The fact that we have stayed with the qwerty keyboard probably reveals more about our tendency to slavishly rely on what we already know than anything else. For most of us, the qwerty key configuration is hardwired into our body memory. Many of us can type quickly without even looking at the keys. Is it the fastest and most efficient way to type? Arguably not. But it's what we take for granted.

Autocorrect

Years ago, with the first release of Microsoft Word, I discovered the autocorrect feature. These days, autocorrect is often a huge frustration for people texting on their phones as it will often replace words with incomprehensible (and sometimes hilarious) substitutions. It can still be quite helpful in word processing as it automatically corrects, for example, misspelled or incomplete words like *teh* to *the*. When I first saw the autocorrect feature, I was delighted to find that it was customizable. That is, I could program the words I commonly misspelled and substitute the correctly spelled words. Because autocorrect is a simple text replacement function, I quickly realized that not only could it correct misspelled words, it could also expand abbreviations. So, for example, I programmed it to replace NK with Norman Kunc. With a little experimentation, I figured out how I could replace NKADD with my name and complete address. From there I was able to make a code of abbreviations for a whole host of words and phrases I commonly use. Given my poor fine motor control, and the arduousness of typing one letter at a time, this feature made answering emails and doing other word processing tasks much easier and faster!

I once described this feature in a keynote address as a way to explore the idea of innovation. At the back of the audience, a man stood up and shouted, "Oh my god! You don't know what this means to me! I work for the National Association of Hydrocephalus and Spina Bifida. Do you know how many times I type out that phrase in a day? You've just shown me how I can reproduce it with just a few letters!"

As part of her job as a human resources professional, our daughter Erinn took part in a training program designed to help minimize inefficiency and improve flexibility and responsiveness in the workplace. Participants were asked to look at their work processes (and even the physical layout of their work stations) in detail and try to identify where they experienced the most frustration—where the bottlenecks were and whether there were unnecessary steps that could be eliminated to improve flow. She described a particular instance where she stood in the doorway of the room where they stored paper and other office supplies. She suddenly realized the inefficiency of how these supplies were arranged. Reorganizing them made future forays into the paper closet faster and easier. At the end of the process, Erinn reported a feeling of relief and told us that what she realized was how much low-grade aggravation there is in continuing to wrestle with issues that could easily be changed by simply rethinking them. But first, she pointed out, you have to notice. Unfortunately, many of us don't notice the habits of our inefficiency.

Coffee and Kraft Dinner

Over the years I, like many disabled people, have developed many tricks that enable me to efficiently accomplish the tasks I want to accomplish. Sometimes I find myself smiling at the inefficiency of many non-disabled people. As we have written earlier, most non-disabled people don't have to search for ingenious solutions to ordinary problems since they are generally able to manage quite well without them. But sometimes even non-disabled people can learn a thing or two from those of us with disabilities.

An example of how we fall prey to the habits of inefficiency is the way that non-disabled people usually make coffee. I love to watch this process. Non-disabled people typically take the carafe out of the coffeemaker, fill it with water from the tap, and then pour the water into the reservoir. Finally, they place the carafe back on the heating element and flip the switch to turn the coffeemaker on. Because I can't pour water from the carafe into the coffeemaker without either spillage or breakage, once again I had to approach this task with Houdini in mind. The first time I was confronted with this problem, I spent a few minutes of lateral contemplation until the solution became apparent. It was surprisingly simple. I put the coffeemaker next to the sink and filled the reservoir with the sink sprayer. Mission accomplished! These days I've perfected the process. I make a single cup of coffee in a single coffeemaker, and the hot liquid goes straight into my cup on my desk. In the years I've been telling this story, I have received numerous emails from non-disabled people who have actually thanked me and said they are now filling their own coffeemakers with the sink sprayer!

Another example of having to think like Houdini in a small but important way arose when I first lived on my own and had to learn to cook my own dinners. Like many men, I started with simple, familiar meals like Kraft dinner (mac and cheese). Straining the macaroni from a pot of boiling water posed a difficult (and potentially dangerous) problem, given my issues with fine motor control and spasticity. I could envision myself getting seriously scalded when I had to remove the pot of boiling water from the stove, carry it to the sink, and drain the pasta.

In therapy, the mantra is "If at first you don't succeed, try, try again." I could envision this task in therapeutic sequence. Initial try—oops! First-degree burns. Next try—oops! Second-degree burns. Not too practical and downright painful. My mantra has evolved into something a little different from the conventional wisdom: "If at first you don't succeed…try another way!" I've decided that determination is only for those who lack creativity. So with Houdini in mind, I tried to rethink the usual process for cooking macaroni and cheese. I began by laying out all the kitchen utensils that were commonly used—and some that weren't. After a few minutes, the solution jumped into my mind. I placed the uncooked macaroni in the kitchen strainer and then placed the strainer into the pot of water. When the macaroni was cooked, I lifted the strainer out, and the boiling water stayed safely on the stove where it couldn't hurt me. The same process worked for boiling eggs. I sometimes fantasized Houdini hovering over my shoulder and saying, "Hmm. Not bad."

Thinking like Houdini allows us to adopt a mind-set of curiosity, where we question what we think is realistic and our own habits of inefficiency, and look for alternate solutions instead of reverting to the most obvious ones.

Innovation Delivers What Rehabilitation Promises

Throughout my life the idea that other people were best able to determine what was realistic for me was often used as the justification for endless therapy and rehabilitation. I'm sure that what these well-meaning therapists hoped and intended was that by helping me to minimize my disability, I would be able to avoid disappointment, stay safe, and accomplish more. However, no matter how much occupational therapy I might have done, I would never have been able to successfully pour boiling water.

In response to the pervasive tendency of non-disabled people to limit my activities and the activities of other disabled people in the name of improved functioning and safety, I have learned to counter ideas of what is and isn't realistic with my own assertion. Namely, *innovation delivers what rehabilitation promises.*

Emma: The Problem with Innovation

Long ago I learned never to try to second guess Norm by either creating or purchasing adaptive devices for him. In my day I've enthusiastically come home with backpacks, kitchen utensils, cups, and a whole host of other useless things. Too often I have been humiliatingly wrong in my well-intentioned guesses, putting him in the awkward position of having to tactfully thank me and then refuse my gifts. Luckily, the embarrassment has been at least somewhat mitigated because Norm has done the same with me. Many of his great ideas and the adaptations he's suggested for me over the years have been less than useful as well.

When individuals who are non-disabled (or even those who have different disabilities from the person they're adapting for) try to second guess what a person needs without asking them first, they can make some really silly, sometimes expensive, and often unnecessary mistakes. For example, many years ago, when the Americans with Disabilities Act (ADA) was first proposed in the United States, corporations were panicked and furious. In a letter to the editor of the *New York Times*, the CEO of a large corporation complained about the exorbitant cost of lowering the drinking fountains in all his company's locations, claiming that the ADA was likely going to bankrupt corporate America. The next day a disabled person wrote back to the *Times* and innocently asked what kind of paper cup dispenser would cost hundreds of thousands of dollars to install.

In the late 1980s, I attended a train-the-trainer session for a disability awareness and job development workshop called Windmills (Pimentel, n.d.). The instructor was Richard Pimentel, a prominent disability rights activist who had played an instrumental role in the creation of the ADA and was a founding member of Milt Wright and Associates, an organization committed to providing job development training to prospective employers all over North America. Pimentel's clients included many Fortune 500 corporations, and he'd even presented Windmills training at the Pentagon. At that time his fee was close to $3000 per day plus expenses. During the era of employment equity and affirmative action policies, he was often asked to consult with employers about customized employment, creating accommodations, and developing adaptations for disabled workers. During the course of the training I attended, he told a story that has stuck with me as a telling example of how the assumptions of non-disabled people can prove not only ineffective but also unnecessarily expensive.

Pimentel described being hired by a Fortune 500 corporation during a period of change they called "right sizing" (which all of us correctly understand as a corporate euphemism for laying people off). He was asked to consult on the creation of an adaptive device for an employee who'd had his left arm amputated. This employee had been hired under employment equity laws which at that time meant that he could not legally be laid off. His bosses wanted to expand his job duties to include filing but could not figure out how this normally two-handed task could be accomplished by a person with only one.

Once they'd explained the situation, Mr. Pimentel asked if he might take a moment to meet with the employee. This puzzled the corporate heads, but they agreed. After finding the man, Pimentel asked him what he thought was an appropriately logical question.

"The big boys upstairs want you to do some filing. Have you ever done any?" The man said he did filing at home all the time. "So how do you do it?" Pimentel asked.

The man grabbed a ruler and pulled open the file drawer with his right hand. He rifled through the files, and once he'd located the file he was after, he jammed the ruler in between that file and the one immediately behind it. The ruler functioned as an impromptu placeholder, allowing him to retrieve the file he wanted with his right hand. Once he'd taken out or added a file, he simply pulled out the ruler and closed the file drawer, again with his right hand.

"May I borrow that?" Pimentel asked. The man shrugged and handed him the ruler. Upstairs, Pimentel plunked the ruler on the table where the corporate heads were still sitting awaiting his return. "Here is your adaptive device," he said dramatically. Richard joked that that was the easiest $3000 he'd ever made. But it is not an anomaly.

The moral of this story is obvious. Ask the person. It's amazing how seldom this actually happens.

This point cannot be overstressed. I will stress it again with yet another, perhaps more mundane example that I sometimes use in presentations. I ask audience members to imagine for a moment that they are Norman's teacher or occupational therapist and that their goal is to help him learn to use the computer. Given his poor fine motor control, the first task is to pick an appropriate keyboard. At this point I typically pause and ask Norm to raise his hands above his head where the audience can see them. I then ask what they notice about his hands. Generally, there will be some laughter and someone will say, "They're huge!"

And they are huge. I emphasize the point by placing my own hands on his to demonstrate scale. My hands are roughly half the size of his, and this usually elicits even more amazed laughter. From there it's an easy set-up to ask the audience to speculate on what kind of a keyboard might be best; invariably someone will enthusiastically shout, "A big one!" At this point I take perverse delight in showing them just how wrong they are. I pull out a small device Norm uses when we're travelling. It's approximately eight by four inches. I tell them that what they wouldn't know unless they asked Norm or watched him type is that the way in which he uses this keyboard is by bracing his hands on either side of it and typing with forefingers and thumbs. This makes a smaller keyboard much more practical as his thumbs can easily reach the middle keys.

These stories illustrate what happens when non-disabled people try to solve accessibility problems for disabled people without input. There are essentially two problems here. First, and perhaps most important, non disabled people generally (and often mistakenly) presume that it is their responsibility to solve these problems. The second issue is that non-disabled people haven't had the experience of solving such problems and are thus are often ill equipped to do it.

When confronted with a problem that seems to require an adaptation of some sort, many non-disabled parents, teachers, and support staff simply forge ahead thinking they have an adequate understanding of the problem and how to solve it. In far too many instances even the problem itself hasn't been well defined. Einstein reportedly once said that if he had sixty minutes to solve one of the world's biggest problems, he would spend the first fifty-nine identifying what the problem actually was. My guess is he would likely have used those fifty-nine minutes primarily to consult with the people who were the most affected by the problem and knew the most about it. Unfortunately, this kind of consultation happens far too rarely for disabled people. Many of us make assumptions about what other people need (as I did with Norm in the early days of our relationship) and seldom ask for their opinions. We go on to make decisions based on what we think would work *for us*. Perhaps this is an example of a time when a variation on the golden rule - namely giving people the adaptations you think would work for you - is ineffective and even a waste of time.

Many of the adaptations disabled people use are just as counterintuitive to non-disabled people as Norm's keyboard is to those audiences. Like the ruler, many of them are surprisingly low-tech and MacGyvered together with bits and pieces collected from what's available and close at hand. For example, conventional button hooks are expensive. Norm makes them out of coat hangers and packing tape. Many of these ingenious solutions just don't occur to non-disabled people. However, this should not pose a daunting problem; all we have to do is turn to the expertise of the people who will use those devices. When in doubt, ask the person!

Dangerous Assumptions

The tendency to make assumptions about what disabled people need and how best to support them without seeking their input has consequences that can go far beyond the mere imposition of unworkable physical adaptations. Decisions we make based on what we believe is possible (realistic) for someone can have serious and life-limiting consequences, sometimes even preventing people from following their dreams and aspirations. Aside from the obvious underestimation and the underutilization of the disabled person's capacities and self-awareness, our doubts about what's possible can have another unintended and tragic consequence. They can be contagious and even result in the person we're supporting coming to doubt their own abilities and giving up on their dreams.

Consider the following stories in this context.

Evelyn Glennie

Evelyn Glennie is a world-famous percussionist. We've had the privilege of hearing her play live, and her finesse, musicality, and finely tuned sense of rhythm never cease to amaze us. What Glennie seldom discloses, since she considers it largely irrelevant, is that she is Deaf. People are often astonished to learn this, and I confess to being surprised myself, even though my Deaf friends have explained how sound travels through objects like walls and the floor into the body as vibrations. Understanding this, I can easily imagine Evelyn Glennie playing, for example, the tympani drums because of their deep and resonant sound. When I hear the tympani, I can feel their vibration move through the floor and the chair I'm sitting on to thrum deep in my chest, so it isn't hard for me to imagine Ms. Glennie experiencing the same. However, what *is* difficult for me to understand is how she manages to "hear "the myriad of the other softer and more delicately toned instruments she plays—marimbas, xylophones, cymbals, and vibes.

Some years ago we watched a documentary that showed Evelyn Glennie walking around her studio in Scotland with a pair of drumsticks in her hand. She lightly tapped a series of cymbals, and each time commented on which of them had either too much or not enough "sizzle."Again, I get how she might hear tympani. As a hearing person, I don't understand how she knows which cymbal has too much or too little sizzle. The fact remains that despite any skepticism I or other hearing people might feel at the idea of a profoundly Deaf person going on to become an international musical sensation, that is exactly what Ms. Glennie has done.

Danny Delcambre

Danny Delcambre is a chef. If you happen to be a foodie, you might be impressed to learn that he studied under world-famous New Orleans chef Paul Prudhomme. For years Delcambre owned and operated a restaurant in Seattle called the Ragin' Cajun. Many dignitaries and famous people ate there. Looking at Danny Delcambre you would not know that he, like Evelyn Glennie, is also Deaf. Further, you would not know that he is also legally blind. As a hearing, seeing person, it's difficult for me to imagine how he has managed to safely navigate a hectic industrial kitchen environment to run and oversee a thriving restaurant. However, despite my incomprehension, that is precisely what he's done.

I have often felt, upon thinking about Ms. Glennie and Mr. Delcambre, that it is a really good thing I was not in charge of either of their transition planning committees when they were leaving school and deciding what to do with their lives. I'm not sure I would have had the confidence or imagination necessary to support them in what I would have assumed would be their highly implausible chosen fields.

Many disabled people have careers that seem unlikely. For example, when Norm was entering university, he thought he might like to be a teacher. He was rejected as a candidate for teacher training because the gatekeepers of the school of education believed that his speech impediment would prevent him from being an effective teacher. It is ironic to note that he has spent the last thirty plus years giving keynote addresses, in-service presentations, and workshops—primarily to audiences of educators. As another example, we once employed a bookkeeper with numerical dyslexia. Katie told us that the way she dealt with her tendency to invert sevens, sixes, and nines was much the same way that you or I might navigate an icy sidewalk. We'd likely think carefully about where we put our feet in the same way that Katie thinks carefully about where those numbers belong. I can report that she was an exceptionally skilled bookkeeper. I once told her story in a presentation, and afterward a woman came up and said, "I'm a bookkeeper too, and I'm also dyslexic with numbers. The way I manage is by turning the books upside down."

At this point, perhaps you are thinking, "Well, that's all fine and good for exceptionally talented people like Evelyn Glennie and Danny Delcambre and Norman Kunc and those bookkeepers. But what about ordinary people like us or people with intellectual disabilities?" Consider the following.

Our friend and colleague the late Judith Snow was a woman with significant disabilities. In fact, she needed assistance to do most of the day-to-day tasks in her life. As a result Judith was a skilled lateral thinker. Her ability to move about and do the things she wanted to do depended on it. She told us this story.

Judith was asked to facilitate a transition planning meeting for a young man with an intellectual disability we'll call James. The first question she asked him—it's an important question that sometimes gets overlooked was: "What would you like to do when you leave school?"

James didn't hesitate. He said, "I want to be an astronaut." Several people in the room blanched at this revelation, and I suspect I might have too had I been present. After all, there are only a handful of astronauts in the world, and most of them have multiple PhDs. What would be the odds of this young man with an intellectual disability having any reasonable expectation of joining them?

If I were confronted with a declaration like this, in Judith's position it's likely that I would have tried to muster my best supportive social skills and said something like, "That's great!" followed immediately by the next question: "And what else...?" I'd be desperately hoping that there was a more realistic "what else" that we could fall back on. After all, as I assume is true for all of you reading this, nobody wants to be the person to rain on someone else's parade and dash their dearest aspirations.

As a woman with a significant disability, Judith didn't do what I might have done. She was undeterred because she'd learned long ago not to make the assumptions I'd likely have been making. She asked James, "So what would you need to know in order to become an astronaut?"

James said, "I guess I'd need to know some things about spaceships and some things about outer space." After some conversation, the group decided that a good place to start to learn these things was at the local planetarium, so they planned a visit.

They arrived at the planetarium a few minutes early, and while they were waiting for the show to begin, they struck up a conversation with the director. After James explained why they were there, the director said, "Hmm. I am looking for a volunteer usher, and it could work into a paying job. Are you interested?"

To make a long story shorter, if you'd visited the Toronto planetarium some years ago before it unfortunately closed, you'd have seen James. He was one of the staff members who all wore NASA space suits. He was responsible for explaining the program and showing patrons to their seats. He loved his job and proved very good at it.

In hearing this story, I really hope you aren't thinking, "Aw, that's great. The young man with an intellectual disability thinks he's an astronaut." No! James knew he wasn't an astronaut, and he said, "I still want to be an astronaut, but right now this is really cool." Would any of this have happened if Judith hadn't been there to forestall the objections and skepticism of the other committee members? It's unlikely.

As with Evelyn and Danny, I am glad I wasn't James's transition planning person. Once again, I worry that I would have lacked the imagination to support him in his dreams. In fact I might have quickly brushed his dream away and tried to focus him on an alternate course that seemed more realistic. This would have been a tragic mistake.

Think Like Socrates

Like Norm, I also have a role model. He's probably not someone you'd expect; he isn't a well-known performer, presenter, author, or public figure. In fact, I've never even met the man. I only know him by reputation, hearsay, and through the written words of others, since he never actually wrote anything down himself. To the best of my knowledge, computers weren't even around in 429 BC.

Who is this mystery man? My role model is Socrates. Surprised? Let me explain. In order to do so, I will have to do a brief synopsis of what Plato claimed Socrates did. I'm sure scholars of Plato's Republic and the Socratic dialogue will cringe as I do Socrates what is likely a great disservice, but here goes.

As you probably know, Socrates was a Greek philosopher. When he engaged his contemporaries in debate, he did so through what later (not surprisingly) was called the Socratic method. He would walk around the Agora (market) and engage people in discussions about truth, government, and other important topics. Socrates would pose questions like "What is justice?," "What is knowledge?," or "What is truth?" These are important philosophical questions that we still struggle to define today.

Socrates would send the debaters away to wrestle with these big questions. Sometimes the process of crafting a definition would take days. When they returned, having arrived at consensus and satisfied with their definition, Socrates would listen to their arguments intently. He would then engage in a process of asking questions and forcing them to define their terms—particularly their ethical terms of reference. After they were finished, he would say, "I don't think so, and here's why" and begin to systematically undermine each of their arguments.

I've always had a visual image of those poor adversaries of Socrates, lying on the floor like demoralized puddles once he was through repudiating their hard-won theories. Then I imagine them doing what I would probably have done—standing up, putting their hands on their hips, and saying, "OK, then. If you're so smart, what is justice? What is truth?" Apparently, that's exactly what they did.

Socrates would respond to these challenges with the same answer. I've always imagined him shrugging his shoulders as he replied.

"I don't know," he'd say. Then he would add the crucial second part of that sentence. *"But at least I know that I don't know."*

Socrates believed that the only infallible thing was fallibility. To know that we don't know is crucial if we want to avoid doing harm. "Do no harm" is the Hippocratic Oath doctors must swear to, and perhaps any of us who carry power or influence in someone else's life should be required to take it too. I believe that Socrates' response is probably as good as it ever gets for any of us. We often don't know what's best or even possible for someone else. As long as we can acknowledge that we don't know and stay genuinely curious and open, and as long as we ask people what they want and listen seriously to their responses, we will be unlikely to do harm.

Making assumptions not only often leads us to faulty conclusions but also can tragically limit what's possible for another person. People with disabilities are often vulnerable to the arrogant assumptions made by others on their behalf. As mentioned, these are the moments when the notion of the golden rule—in this case attempting to walk a mile in someone else's shoes—has some serious problems. What we believe would be good for us is not always what's good for someone else. If we can proceed on the assumption that we do not have all the information, we can find the innovative solutions we need.

Two Dogs

We have heard a story that supposedly comes from the Lakota Sioux people. It goes like this: an elder was speaking to a group of his people. He said, "Inside each of us are two dogs, Happy and Mean. They're always fighting. I have a question for you. Which dog do you think will win?" He sent his people away to debate and consider.

The next day the group gathered together again. They hadn't returned with a single answer and were in fact quite divided. Some people thought Happy would win, whereas others thought this assessment was naive and that Mean would win. When they'd finished offering the elder their contradictory rationales, the elder said, "You're both wrong. The dog who will win is the dog you feed the most."

In the context of this book and the arguments we've made here, allow me to make an extrapolation of this little story. In this case, the names of the dogs are changed. They are Possibility and Not Realistic. In the end, the moral is the same. The dog you feed the most will be the dog that wins.

A CREDO FOR SUPPORT

Background:

In 1995, we were asked to write a short chapter with advice for people newly entering the field of human services. Unfortunately, we didn't pay attention to the deadline, and when we realized it was fast approaching, we embarked on a coffee-fueled and panicked process to get something out to the editors of the anthology. Lacking the time we needed to craft considered paragraphs, we resorted to a series of bullet points – don't do this, do that. In the months that followed its initial publication, we turned it into a short video we titled "A Credo for Support."

Over the years this video has been used as a vehicle for staff training and translated into seven languages, and – much to our surprise - won several media awards. Some years ago it was transformed into a spoken version by the People First organization in San Luis Obispo in California. You can find these videos on Youtube if you'd like to view them. We particularly recommend the People First version.

A note to our younger audiences. You'll find a reference to the late comedian Jerry Lewis that is less than flattering. Many younger people don't know that Jerry Lewis ran the Labor Day Muscular Dystrophy Telethon for many years, and was notoriously patronizing to the disabled people who appeared on it over the years. Some disabled people who had been poster children for his telethons later formed a group called "Jerry's Orphans" to protest the telethons and the demeaning messages they promoted. To make matters worse, in many of the comedic roles Lewis played in movies like *The Nutty Professor*, he often imitated people with physical and/or intellectual disabilities.

We've been told by many people that the Credo for Support has provided some pivotal moments of learning and dialogue. We thought it would be a fitting conclusion.

Throughout history,
people with physical and mental disabilities
have been abandoned at birth,
banished from society,
used as court jesters,
drowned and burned during The Inquisition,
gassed in Nazi Germany,
and still continue to be segregated, institutionalized,
tortured in the name of behaviour management,
abused, raped, euthanized, and murdered.

Now, for the first time, people with disabilities
are taking their rightful place as fully contributing citizens.

The danger is that we will respond with remediation and benevolence
rather than equity and respect.

And so, we offer you

A Credo for Support

Do Not see my disability as the problem.
Recognize that my disability is an attribute.

Do Not see my disability as a deficit.
It is you who see me as deviant and helpless.

Do Not try to fix me because I am not broken.
Support me. I can make my contribution to the community in my way.

Do Not see me as your client. I am your fellow citizen.
See me as your neighbour. Remember, none of us can be self-sufficient.

Do Not try to modify my behaviour.
Be still & listen. What you define as inappropriate
may be my attempt to communicate with you in the only way I can.

Do Not try to change me, you have no right.
Help me learn what I want to know.

Do Not hide your uncertainty behind "professional" distance.
Be a person who listens, and does not take my
struggle away from me by trying to make it all better.

Do Not use theories and strategies on me.
Be with me. And when we struggle
with each other, let that give rise to self-reflection.

Do Not try to control me. I have a right to my power as a person.
What you call non-compliance or manipulation may
actually be the only way I can exert some control over my life.

Do Not teach me to be obedient, submissive, and polite.
I need to feel entitled to say No if I am to protect myself.

Do Not be charitable towards me.
The last thing the world needs is another Jerry Lewis.
Be my ally against those who exploit me for their own gratification.

Do Not try to be my friend. I deserve more than that.
Get to know me. We may become friends.

Do Not help me, even if it does make you feel good.
Ask me if I need your help. Let me show you how you can best assist me.

Do Not admire me. A desire to live a full life does not warrant adoration.
Respect me, for respect presumes equity.

Do Not tell, correct, and lead.
Listen, Support, and Follow.

Do Not work on me.
Work with me.

Dedicated to the memory of Tracy Latimer

1995 © Norman Kunc and Emma Van der Klift

REFERENCES

Alan, M. (2008). *I Wish My Kids Had Cancer: A family suriving the autism epidemic. https://www.amazon.com/ Wish-Kids-Had-Cancer-Surviving/dp/1606720708*

Allen, B. (2005). Foucault's nominalism. In S. Tremaine, Ed. *Foucault and the Government of Disability* (pp. 93–107).Ann Arbor, MI: The University of Michigan Press.

American Psychological association. (2007). Dictionary of Psychology. Washington: DC. Author: Vandenbos. G.

Autism Speaks. (2009). https://www.youtube.com/ watch?v=9UgLnWJFGHQ

Bessier, A. (1988). *Flying Without Wings,* New York, NY: Bantam.

Bieschke, K., Perez, R., &DeBord. K. (2007). Eds. *Handbook of Counseling and Psycholtherapy with Lesbian, Gay, Bisexual and Transgender Clients.*Washington, DC: American Psychological Association.

Bushman, B. J. (2002). Does venting anger feed or extinguish the flame? Catharsis, rumination, distraction, anger and aggressive responding. *Journal of Personality and Social Psychology Bulletin,28*(6): 724–731.

Bristor, M. (1984). The birth of a handicapped child: Awholistic model for grieving. *Family Relations, 33*: 25–32)

Carter Long, L. (2015).#SaytheWord: The power of language for disability identity.*Disabled Spectator.* Retrieved fromhttps:// disabledspectator.com/saytheword-power-language-disability

Casey, A., Hill,J.,& Goodyear, V. (2014). PE doesn't stand for physical education, it stands for public embarrassment: Voicing experiences and proffering solutions to girls'disengagement in physical education. In S. Sanders, S. Flory, & A. Tischler (Eds.), *Sociocultural Issues in Physical Education: Case Studies for Teachers*(pp. 37–53). London, UK: Rowman & Littlefield.

CBC. (2018). Miracle child. *The Passionate Eye.* Retrieved from https://www.cbc.ca/passionateeye/features/the-boy-born-without-a-brain-is-now-a-practical-joker-who-loves-playing-mar

Chabris, C.,& Simons, D. (2009). *The Invisible Gorilla: How our intuitions deceive us.*New York, NY:Crown Publishing Group Random House.Retrieved from http://www.theinvisiblegorilla.com/gorilla_experiment.html

Clark, L. (2011).*Comedian Laurence Clark: The Best Fake Charity Collection Buckets.* Retrieved from https://www.youtube.com/watch?v=_U_byvTzW4w).

Cobb, S. (2013). *Speaking of violence: The politics and poetics of narrative in conflict resolution.* New York: NY: Oxford University Press.

Coren, S. (1993). *The left-hander syndrome: The causes and consequences of left-handedness.* New York: NY: Vintage Books Random House.

Crossley, R., & McDonald, A. (1980). *Annie's coming out.* Victoria, Australia: Penguin.

Davis, L. (1995). *Enforcing normalcy: Disability, deafness and the body.* New York, NY: Verso.

Dembo, T., Leviton, G.L.,& Wright, B. A. (1956). Adjustment to misfortune: A problem of social- psychologicalrehabilitation. *Artificial Limbs 3* (2). 4–62. Reprinted in*Rehabil.Psychol.* 1975, 22, 1–100.)in Wright, B.A. (1983).*Physical disability: A Psychosocial approach.*2nded.New York, NY: Harper and Row.

Dreyfus, H. L. & Rabinow, P. (1983). On the Geneology of Ethics: Overview of Work in Progress. *Michel Foucault: Beyond Structuralism and Hermeneutics.* Afterword. 2nd Ed. Chicago: University of Chicago Press.

Donnellan, A. M. (1984). The Criterion of the Least Dangerous Assumption. *Sage Journals Behavioral Disorders.* Vol. 9 issue: 2. Page(s) 141-150.

Ellis, J. (1989). Grieving for the loss of the perfect child. *Child and Adolescent Social Work Journal, 6* (4): 259–270.

Erickson, M. (1976).*Hypnotic realities: The induction of clinical hypnosis and forms of indirect suggestion.* New York, NY: John Wiley & Sons Inc.

Frank, A. (1995, 2013). *The wounded storyteller: Body, illness, and ethics.* Chicago, IL: University of Chicago Press.

Freud, S.,& Breuer, J. (1885, 2005). *Studies in hysteria.* London, UK: Penguin.

Friere, P. (1970). *Pedagogy of the oppressed.* New York, NY: The Continuum Publishing Company.

Foucault, M. (1980). *Power/knowledge: Selected interviews & other writings 1972–1977.* New York, NY: Pantheon.

Gliedman,J. & Roth, W. (1980). *The unexpected minority:Handicapped children in America.* New York, NY:Carnegie Corporation.

Illich, I., Zola, I.K., McKnight, J., Caplan, J., &Shaikan,H. (1977). *Disabling professions.*London, UK:Marion Boyers.

Jemmer, P. (2006). Abreaction-catharsis: Stirring dull roots with spring rain. *Journal of Clinical Hypnosis, 7* (1): 26–36.

Hay, H. (1972).*The amateur magician's handbook.* Signet: Penguin.

Health and Welfare Canada. (1987). Suicide in Canada: Report of the national task force on suicide in Canada (Catalogue No. H39-107/1987E). Ottawa, ON: Statistics Canada.

Jenkins,J., Pious, C., &Jewell, M., (990). Special education and the regular education initiative.*Exceptional Children, 56*: 479–491.

Karg Academy Lifelines. *Grieving the loss of the perfect child.* Retrieved from http://www.kargacademy.com/lee-s-thoughts/ grieving-the-loss-of-the-perfect-child

Kedar, I. (2012). *Ido in autismland: Climbing out of autism's silent prison.* Ido Kedar.

Kahane, A. (2004, 2007).*Solving tough problems: An open way of talking, listening, and creating new realities.*San Francisco, CA: Berrett-Kohler Publishers.

Kelley, L. (2019), Doctoral dissertation, in press.

King, M.L. (2006). In Rucker, W.C. Jr. & Upton, J.N. (Eds.). *Encyclopedia of American race riots: Greenwood milestones in African American history* (p. 107): Greenwood.

Kim, C. (2015). *Nerdy, shy and socially inappropriate: A user guide to an Asperger life.* London, UK: Jessica Kingsley Publishers.

Kubler-Ross, E. (1969). *On death and dying.* New York, NY: McMillan.

Kunc, N. (1987). *Beyond acceptance: A value-based framework of family health for familes of children with disabilities.* Master's Thesis: University of Guelph.

Kunc, N. (1992). The need to belong: Rediscovering Maslow's hierarchy of needs. In R. Villa, J. Thousand, S. Stainback, & W. Stainback (Eds.), *Restructuring for caring and effective education* (pp. 25–39)Baltimore, MA: Paul H. Brookes.

Lindeman Nelson, H. (2001). *Damaged identities: Narrative repair.* Ithaca, NY: Cornell University Press.

Lipsky, D.K., & Gartner. A. (Eds.). (1989). *Beyond separate education: Quality education for all.* Baltimore, MD: Paul H. Brookes Publishing Co.

Lovett, H. (1996). *Learning to listen: Positive approaches and people with difficult behavior.* Baltimore, MD: Paul H. Brookes.

Madigan, S. (2011). *Narrative therapy.* Washington: DC:American Psychological Association.

March of Dimes. (1948). *The crippler.* Retrieved fromhttps://www.youtube.com/watch?v=RgJjmrkKlm4

Maslow, A. (1970).*Motivation and personality* (2nd ed.). New York, NY: Harper & Row.

Mate, G. (1999). *Scattered minds: A new look at the origins and healing of attention deficit disorder.* Toronto, ON: Alfred A. Knopf.

Marcus, N. https://www.facebook.com/ABILITYMagazine/photos/
disability-is-not-a-brave-struggle-or-courage-in-the-face-of-
adversity-disabilit/10153762004411482/

McArthur, S. (1979) http://odtmaps.com/detail.
asp?product_id=McA-23x35&Contents=TAB5

McKnight, J. (1995). *The careless society: Community and its
counterfeits.* New York, NY: Basic Books.

Mencken, H.L. Quotes. https://www.brainyquote.com/
quotes/h_l_mencken_141512

Miserando, C. (2003).The spoon theory. *But You Don't Look Sick.
com.* Retrieved from https://butyoudontlooksick.com/articles/
written-by-christine/the-spoon-theory/

Morgan, A. (2000). *What is narrative therapy? An easy to read
introduction.* Adelaide, Australia: Dulwich Centre Publications.

Nietzsche, F. (1977). *A Nietzsche Reader.* R. Hollingdale (Ed.).
London: Penguin Books.

NPR. (2012).*Teller talks: The science behind magic tricks.*
Retrieved from https://www.npr.org/2012/03/05/147980272/
teller-talks-magicians-use-science-to-trick-you

Olshansky, S. (1962). Chronic sorrow: A response to having a
mentally defective child. *Social Casework, 43*: 190–194)

Page, B. (2006). *At-risk students: Feeling their pain, understanding
their plight, accepting their defensive ploys.* Nashville, TN:
Educational Dynamics Publications.

Stainback, S., Stainback, W., & Forest, M.(Eds.). (1989).*Educating
all students in the mainstream of regular education.* Baltimore,
MD: Paul H. Brookes Publishing Co.

Patterson, J., Purkey, S., & Parker. J. (1986). *Productive school systems for a nonrational world*. Alexandria, VA: Association for Supervision and Curriculum Development.

Pearse, M. (1977). The child with cancer:Impact on the family. *Journal of School Health, 14*, 174.

Peters, T., & Waterman, R. (1982). *In search of excellence: Lessons from America's best run companies.* New York, NY: Harper & Row.

Pimentel, R. (n.d.).*Windmills: Overcoming fear and misperception.* Retrieved from http://www.miltwright.com/articles/windmills-overcomingfear.pdf

Reynolds, V. (2010).*Doing justice as a path to sustainable community work.* Dissertation, Tilburg University:Taos Institute.

Sacks, O. (1984). *A leg to stand on.*New York, NY: Touchstone.

Saxton, M. (1985).The something that happened before I was born. *Ordinary Moments: The Disabled Experience.* Syracuse, NY: Human Policy Press.

Shafir, E., Simonson, A.,&Tversky, I.(1993). Reason-based choice. *Cognition, 49* (1–2): 11–36.

Shalev, A.Y. (2009). Further Lessons from 911: Does stress equal trauma? *Psychiatry, 67*, 174.

Sobsey, D. (1994). *Violence and abuse in the lives of people with disabilities: The end of silent acceptance?* Baltimore:MA: Brookes Publishing.

Sobsey, D. (2004). Marital stability and marital satisfaction in families of children with disabilities: Chicken or egg? *Developmental Disabilities Bulletin, 32* (1):62–83.

Tavris, C. (1982). *Anger: The misunderstood emotion.*New York, NY: Simon & Schuster.

Van der Klift, E.,& Kunc, N. (1994). Beyond benevolence:Friendship and the politics of help. Previously published in part inThousand, J., Villa, R., &Nevin, A. (1994). *Creativity and collaborativelearning:A practical guide to empowering students andteachers.* Baltimore, MC: Paul Brookes. Reprinted in 2017.

Van der Klift, E., & Kunc. N. (1995). In spite of my disability. In Thousand, J., Villa, R., Eds., *The inclusion puzzle: Fitting the pieces together.* Washington, DC: Association for Supervision and Curriculum Development.

Van der Klift, E.,& Kunc, N. (2018).Ability and opportunity in the rearview mirror.In D. Sobsey&K. Scorgie,Eds., *Working with families for inclusive education: Navigating identity, opportunity and belonging.* Emerald Publications

Van der Klift, E. (In press). *Talk to me: What educators can learn about de-escalation from hostage negotiators.*

Van der Klift, E.,& Kunc, N. (2019). *Segregation versus solidarity: Rethinking the uncritical commitment to inclusion. International Perspectives on Inclusive Education, 13,* 17–24. Emerald Publishing Limited.

Villa, R.,Thousand, J., & Nevin, A. (2010). *Collaborating with students in instruction and decision-making: The untapped resource.* Thousand Oaks, CA: Corwin Press.

Wagner, M. (1989). Youth with disabilities during transition: An overview and description of findings from the national longitudinal transition study. In J. Chadsey-Rusch (Ed.), *Transition institute at Illinois: Project director's fourth annual meeting* (pp. 24–52). Champaign, IL: University of lllinois.

Walker, A. (1992). *Possessing the secret of joy.* New York, NY: Simon & Schuster.

Wendell, S. (1996). *The rejected body: Feminist philosophical reflections on disability.* New York: NY: Rutledge.

Winslade, J., & Monk, G. (2007). *Narrative counseling in schools: Powerful and brief.* 2nded. Thousand Oaks, CA: Corwin Press.

Winslade, J., & Monk, G. (2008). *Narrative mediation: Loosening the grip of conflict.* San Francisco, CA: Jossey-Bass.

White, M. (1995). *Re-authoring lives: Interviews and essays.* Adelaide, Australia: Dulwich Centre.

White, M. (2007). *Maps of narrative practice.* New York, NY: WW Norton.

White, M. (2011). *Narrative Practice: Continuing the Conversations.* NY: W.W. Norton & Company.

Young, S. (2012). Retrieved from https://www.ted.com/talks/stella_young_i_m_not_your_inspiration_thank_you_very_much?language=en

CPSIA information can be obtained
at www.ICGtesting.com
Printed in the USA
FSHW011320050122
87420FS